CW00376159

THE
PC
COMPANION

Robin Nixon

SIGMA PRESS – Wilmslow, United Kingdom

Copyright ©, Robin Nixon, 1993

All Rights Reserved. No part of this publication may be reproduced, stored in a retrieval system, or transmitted in any form or by any means, electronic, mechanical, photocopying, recording or otherwise, without prior written permission.

First published in 1993 by
Sigma Press, 1 South Oak Lane, Wilmslow, Cheshire SK9 6AR, England.

British Library Cataloguing in Publication Data
A CIP catalogue record for this book is available from the British Library.

ISBN: 1-85058-513-X

Typesetting and design by
Sigma Press, Wilmslow

Printed in Malta by
Interprint Ltd.

Distributed by
John Wiley & Sons Ltd., Baffins Lane, Chichester, West Sussex, England.

Acknowledgement of copyright names
Within this book, various proprietary trade names and names protected by copyright are mentioned for descriptive purposes. Almac is a trademark of Almac BBS Ltd. Ami Pro is a registered trademark of Lotus Development Corporation. Amstrad is a registered trademark of Amstrad PLC. BT is a registered trademark of British Telecom. CIX is a trademark of Compulink Information Exchange. Compaq is a registered trademark of Compaq Computer Corporation. CompuServe is a registered trademark of H&R Block. DESQview is a registered trademark of Quarterdeck Office Systems. DR-DOS is a registered trademark of Digital Research. Epson is a registered trademark of Epson America. Hayes and the AT commands are registered trademarks of Hayes Microcomputer Products. Hewlett-Packard is a registered trademark of Hewlett-Packard Corporation. IBM is a registered trademark of Business Machines Corporation. Intel is a registered trademark of Intel Corporation. Excel, GW-Basic, Microsoft, MS-DOS Windows and Windows NT are registered trademarks of Microsoft Corporation. Macintosh is a registered trademark of Apple Computer. MNP is a registered trademark of Microcom Systems. Norton Desktop is a trademark of Peter Norton Computing. Procomm Plus is a registered trademark of Datastorm Technologies. Protext is a trademark of Arnor Ltd. Superkey, Turbo C and Turbo Pascal are registered trademarks of Borland International. Virusguard is a trademark of S & S International.

Full acknowledgment is hereby made of all such protection.

Thanks to Chris and Dennis Nixon for their invaluable input.

PREFACE

Welcome to the first edition of *The PC Companion*. This book has been written to provide a one-stop reference to as wide a variety of PC-related subjects as possible.

From a number of years experience on national computing magazines, I have assembled a comprehensive collection of hints, tips and ideas offering solutions to some of the commonest (and often trickiest) problems that PC users come across. In addition, there are dozens of suggestions and short programs which will enhance your PC use by speeding up certain applications or routines, adding new commands or by making use of little-known, undocumented features.

For example, there is a DOS primer which takes a radical viewpoint on certain DOS commands and even gives them a rating out of five for Usefulness and Safety. In fact it tells you which DOS commands you should NOT use.

There's also a complete explanation of the Batch file programming language and, assuming no prior understanding, it takes you from first steps right up to creating sophisticated file and disk management applications.

In Chapter 3 there's the definitive guide to using Code Pages, which change your display's characters and remap your keyboard. There has never before been as complete an explanation as this that works with all versions of DOS and the techniques described will be particularly useful for people using non-UK or US setups.

If you're fan of GUIs (Graphical User Interfaces) the chapter on Windows contains advice on getting the most out of Windows and Windows applications, much of which has been suggested by the program developers themselves. Plus, the secret key sequences you need to display the 'Gang' screens showing the authors of some of the top Windows applications are revealed.

Programmers will find the chapter on programming contains several useful C, Basic and Pascal programs, including: Mouse handling, creating fractal displays, structured text input, data compression, floating point calculations, autodialling with a modem, and much more.

Chapter 10 explains everything you need to know about communications, from basics to the advanced. It also reveals what's going to be happening in the comms world in years to come, demystifies the obscure 'V DOT' terms, explains the Hayes command set and lists over 250 electronic bulletin boards you can dial up.

Along with the other topics covered such as making money, using Debug, configuring your PC, data security, hardware explanations and printing solutions, you'll find that no matter what you use your PC for there's something for you in this book.

Naturally, with a reference of this nature you may already know of some better or more interesting techniques, or perhaps you have discovered an undocumented feature of a program or a neat way of doing something. If so, please write to the author at the Publisher's address and the senders of all suggestions included in the next edition of this book will receive a complimentary copy.

Robin Nixon

To Julie and Naomi

CONTENTS

1. DABBLING WITH DOS..................................1

A DOS PRIMER 1

TEMPORARY FILES.....................................17

FASTER "MORE" AND "SORT".........................18

UNDOCUMENTED DOS COMMAND 19

MANIPULATING FILENAMES WITH "HIDDEN" CHARACTERS 19

SORTED DIRECTORY LISTINGS 21

DIRECTORY SHORT CUTS 21

TIME STAMPING......................................22

ATTRIB DIRECTORY SEARCH 22

DEBUG EXPLAINED 23

SIXTEEN COLOUR BACKGROUNDS....................26

CHANGING BORDER COLOUR 27

PRINTSCREEN COMMAND 28

DEACTIVATING PRINTSCREEN 28

NUM LOCK UTILITY..................................29

CAPS LOCK UTILITY...................................30

DOUBLING THE DISPLAY LINES 31

2. STOP PRESS! MS-DOS 6 Primer! 33

3. BUILDING BETTER BATCH FILES 50

AN INTRODUCTION TO BATCH FILES.................50

CUSTOMISING THE "PAUSE" MESSAGE...........................54
FINDING SUBDIRECTORIES 54
MORE ON FINDING SUBDIRECTORIES........................55
BLANK ECHO LINES.......................................55
DELETING WITH EXCEPTIONS..............................56
TYPING MULTIPLE FILES TO SCREEN........................57
USING WILDCARDS WITH ANY PROGRAM......................57
SINGLE-LETTER DIRECTORY PATHNAMES.....................58
FOOLING PROGRAMS INTO USING ANOTHER DRIVE.............58
UNPROMPTED DELETION....................................59
BATCH FILE SUBROUTINES 59
MORE BATCH FILE SUBROUTINES 60
PROMPTLESS DATE/TIME DISPLAY...........................61
FILE MOVER 61
FAST FORMATTER 62
CHKDSK FILE FINDER 62
FAST LOADER..63
LISTING OUT BATCH FILES 63
FASTER TYPE COMMAND 64
PROTECTING IMPORTANT FILES.............................64
READING VOLUME LABELS FROM BATCH FILES.................65
UNRAVELLING FILES 66

4. CONFIGURING YOUR PC............................ 68
FIGURING OUT CONFIG.SYS................................68
ALL THE CONFIG.SYS COMMANDS...........................72
THE COUNTRY CONFIGURATIONS 73
MULTIPLE BOOTUPS......................................73
UNDOCUMENTED SWITCH..................................76
AT YOUR COMMAND 76
LOCKED OUT OF DOS....................................77
DODGY DISK DRIVES....................................77
A CLEANER ENVIRONMENT 78
ANSI – A PROMPT EXPLANATION 79
A SWEDISH DATE.......................................82

CONFIGURING KEYBUK. 82
DUMMY DRIVES – A SMART SOLUTION 83
MEMORY EXPANDING 83
CREATING CODE PAGES 84

5. WORKING WITH WINDOWS. **88**

COMPAQ DOS 5 BUG WITH WINDOWS 3.0. 88
FORMATTING DISKS ON DISKLESS WORKSTATIONS. 88
IMPROVING WINDOWS ON AN IBM PS/1 89
MINIMAL WINDOWS SETUP. 89
MOUSING AROUND 90
BIGGER BORDERS WITH WINDOWS 90
ADDING ICONS TO BATCH FILES. 90
USING A PS/2 WITH EXPANDED MEMORY 91
MANAGING THE FILE MANAGER. 91
EASY DRIVER SWAPPING. 92
WINDOWS 3.1 AND 386/486 PCS 92
MS-DOS EXECUTIVE. 93
COMMON EXCEL QUERIES EXPLAINED 94
MAXIMISING MEMORY USE. 96
BACKGROUND PRINTING. 96
TRACKING DOWN ENHANCED-MODE COMMS ERRORS. 97
TRACKING DOWN COMMS PROBLEMS 98
ANOTHER COM3 AND COM4 SOLUTION 99
COMMON WINDOWS 3.1 SMARTDRIVE QUESTIONS AND ANSWERS. . . 100
COMMON WINDOWS 3.1 UPGRADE QUESTIONS AND ANSWERS. 102
WINDOWS NT – THE FUTURE. 108
A BIT OF UNDOCUMENTED FUN 110

6. LOOKING AFTER YOUR DATA **113**

FILE VERIFICATION 113
FORMATTING 5.25'' DISKS IN HIGH DENSITY DRIVES 114
DATA SECURITY. 115
WHAT IS A COMPUTER VIRUS? 116
HOW SERIOUS ARE VIRUSES? 116

DECREASING THE RISK OF VIRAL INFECTION .117
DETECTING VIRAL INFECTIONS 117
RECOVERING FROM VIRAL INFECTIONS 118
QUESTIONS AND ANSWERS ABOUT THE MICHELANGELO VIRUS 118
JUST WHAT IS A STEALTH VIRUS? 119
PC FILE/VIRUSGUARD CLASH WORK-AROUND 120
UPGRADING DISK DRIVES 120
RECOVERING FROM RECOVER 121
USING RESTORE ACROSS DOS VERSIONS 123
USING DEVICE NAMES AS FILE NAMES 124
SIMPLE COPY PROTECTION 125
HIDDEN FILES 126

7. HARDWARE PROBLEMS **128**
IBM COMPATIBILITY 128
PC BUSES – ISA, EISA and MCA EXPLAINED 129
PROCESSORS EXPLAINED 131
MEMORY MANAGEMENT 132
EXTENDED MEMORY AND DOS 5.00 134
WAIT-STATES EXPLAINED 135
MULTITASKING IN DOS 137
AMSTRAD MOUSE PROBLEMS 138
OPTICAL MOUSE IMPROVER 139
CAREFUL CACHEING 139
DIRTY KEYBOARDS 139
XT versus AT KEYBOARDS 139
INTERLACED versus NON-INTERLACED MONITORS 140
ADDING MEMORY 140
KEYBOARD TIPS FOR DISABLED PEOPLE 142
TIPS FOR MONOCHROME MONITORS 143
BOOT PROBLEMS 144
VIDEO CARDS 144

8. PROGRAMMING PROBLEMS SOLVED **147**
GW BASIC MOUSE HANDLING 147

GW BASIC BREAK KEY DISABLING. 148
GW BASIC FRACTAL GENERATOR. 149
GW BASIC IMPROVED INPUT COMMAND 150
TURBO C MOUSE HANDLING. 152
TURBO C FILE FINDER 155
TURBO C DATA COMPRESSION 156
TURBO C IN-LINE ASSEMBLER 160
TURBO C SAFE HEAP MANAGER. 161
TURBO C FLOATING-POINT CALCULATOR 165
TURBO C BREAK HANDLER. 170
TURBO C AUTODIALLER 171
TURBO C AUTOMATIC KEYSTROKES 175
TURBO C SUPER CHANGE DIRECTORY 176
TURBO C LCD DISPLAY FIXER. 178
TURBO PASCAL RANDOM FILE ACCESSING 182
TURBO PASCAL CURSOR CONTROL 183
NON LANGUAGE-SPECIFIC DATE FORMULAE MANIPULATION. 184

9 MAKING MONEY 185
MARKETING YOUR PROGRAMS. 185
SOFTWARE PROTECTION 187
EFFECTIVE ADVERTISING 188
WHICH HARDWARE? 189
GETTING FREE PUBLICITY. 191

10. PRINTING PROBLEMS. 194
CHECKING FOR FINISHED PRINTOUTS 194
LINING UP PRINTER LABELS 195
PROTEXT LINE DRAWING ON DMP3000 PRINTERS. 195
COLOUR SEPARATIONS 195
PRINTSCREEN FIX. 196
MISSING POUND SIGNS 196
PRINTER DIP SWITCHES. 197
USING THE IBM CHARACTER SET IN PRINTOUTS 198
EPSON CONTROL CODES 202

THE EPSON CONTROL CODES 203

THE ASCII CONTROL CODES 205

EMULATING IBM LINE CHARACTERS 206

11. COMMUNICATIONS 210

BULLETIN BOARDS 210

MAKING THE MOST OF MERCURY 216

THE HAYES COMMAND SET 216

THE 'V DOT' TERMS EXPLAINED. 218

OTHER COMMS TERMS 220

ELIMINATING LINE NOISE 220

MAJOR MODEM MANUFACTURERS. 221

CALL WAITING PROBLEMS 222

USING EMOTICONS. 222

The PC Companion

Reader Disk Offer

To save you typing them in, all the examples listed in this book are also available on a floppy disk for just £10 inclusive and, because there was some free space left on the disk, also included are a few fully-working examples of some of the best DOS and Windows Shareware utilities available for getting the most out of your PC.

So why not save the wear and tear on your fingers and make sure you eliminate the possibility of typing errors by ordering the disk of the book?

— —

The PC Companion Reader Disk Order Form

Please send me the **PC Companion Disk** on:

❑ 3.5" format

❑ 5.25" format

❑ I enclose a Cheque/Eurocheque/Postal Order(s) for £10, made payable to **ABS**

❑ Please charge my **Access/Visa** card:

Card Number: ☐☐☐☐ ☐☐☐☐ ☐☐☐☐ ☐☐☐☐

Expiry Date: _____

Signature: _____

Name: _____

Address: _____

_____

Post Code: _____

Telephone: _____

Send to: PC Companion Disk Offer, ABS, 85 Monks Orchard Road, Beckenham, Kent, BR3 3BJ. **Telephone:** (081) 777 9764; **Fax:** (081) 777 6328

CHAPTER 1

DABBLING WITH DOS

DOS is the unseen software behind your favourite programs. An unsung hero, often criticised and dismissed as antiquated, underpowered or both, it is nevertheless the mainstay of many millions of personal computers worldwide.

And for a very good reason; MS-DOS and PC-DOS – usually shortened simply to DOS – provide stability and compatibility to software the world over, which isn't something to be sniffed at by users of the more visually appealing operating systems. Even Windows, with several million sales already under its belt, has yet to make serious inroads on the DOS market for just these reasons.

But of course DOS has its faults too, ranging from obscure pitfalls just waiting to claim the unwary DOS experimenter to downright, honest-to-goodness bugs. In this chapter you'll find some of the more unknown aspects of DOS, all of them useful, including some totally undocumented (by Microsoft) commands and command switches.

But first there's a DOS Primer covering all the standard DOS commands and gives you the real low-down on each one. In it you'll find the truth, the whole truth and nothing but – in fact you'll learn when NOT to take the advice of your DOS manual.

A DOS PRIMER

The following DOS commands are common to all versions of MS-DOS from 3.30 to 5.00. Amendments to MS-DOS involving the removal or addition of commands were considered too involved for this section; utilities like LOADHIGH and MIRROR from MS-DOS 5.00 really need more space to do them justice. And besides, not so much is known about these new commands yet, at least in terms of potential problems and bugs, to guarantee them a fair crack of the whip in an honest-but-fair appraisal.

A word of explanation about the two types of command available under MS-DOS; A command marked as being ''internal'' is actually built into the operating system's command processor, and is always available no matter what you are doing. Commands marked "external" are actually just other programs in the DOS directory, which are nevertheless regarded as being part of the DOS command set.

External commands are only guaranteed to be as available as any other program on your hard or floppy disk. Having got that out of the way, read onward for the inside story on the world's favourite operating system where each command is marked according to its actual usefulness, as well as its potential for wreaking havoc with your system.

These two scores, Usefulness and Safety factor, are graded from 0 to 5, where a score of 0 is extremely bad, and 5 represents the best score possible. Again, these marks are nothing if not subjective, but they do give a good overview of each command, reflecting the relative usefulness and dangers of each. Perhaps users would benefit from this sort of approach in the standard DOS guides. Incidentally, it's interesting to note that very few commands score a 5 in both categories!

ASSIGN

Command type:	External
Official purpose:	Assigns a drive letter to a different drive, for applications that insist on looking for data on drives you might not have.
Usefulness:	5
Safety factor:	3
Correct usage:	ASSIGN [x[:]=y[:][...]] Where x is the drive to reassign, and y is the drive to be used instead.
General comments:	A useful command for fixing badly-behaved applications programmed to look for their data on a particular drive and no other. Installation utilities are the worst culprits, often refusing to look in any other drive except A:, which differs in disk size from one machine to another. Very dangerous to leave A: assigned to C: on some early versions of DOS, because dangerous disk operations intended for drive A: worked on C: instead.

ATTRIB

Command type:	External
Official purpose:	Displays or changes the attributes of selected files in a directory.
Usefulness:	4
Safety factor:	4
Correct usage:	ATTRIB [+r or -r] [+a or -a] [drive:]pathname [/s] Where r is Read-only and a is Archive.
General comments:	Use this command for protecting files you don't want deleted or modified (AUTOEXEC.BAT and CONFIG.SYS, for example) by other programs. Also use it do make other peoples' protected files easier to handle.

BACKUP

Command type:	External
Official purpose:	Backs up one or more files from one disk to another.
Usefulness:	3
Safety factor:	3
Correct usage:	BACKUP　[drive1:][path][filename]　[drive2:][/s][/m][/a] [/f][/d:date][/t:time][/L:[[drive][path]filename]]

Where drive1 is the source drive, drive2 is the target drive, and:

/s Backs up subdirectories.
/m Only backs up files which have changed.
/a Adds files to any already on the target disk.
/f Formats the target disk if necessary.
/d: Only backs up files modified after this date.
/t: Only backs up files modified after this time.
/L: Saves a backup log under this filename.

General comments: Not much used nowadays, with superior programs around. And backups made under one DOS version aren't guaranteed to be recoverable under another – a fatal, unforgivable flaw.

BREAK

Command type:	Internal
Official purpose:	Sets or clears extended [Ctrl][C] checking.
Usefulness:	1
Safety factor:	4
Correct usage:	BREAK [on] or [off]
General comments:	Setting BREAK ON forces MS-DOS to respond to [Ctrl][C] during disk reads and writes. This is rarely, if ever, needed and it's not a good idea anyway. The last thing you want is for a file to be left half-updated when all you wanted to do was quit a program. Use only if you really need this ability. Set BREAK OFF to restore [Ctrl][C] checking to screen, keyboard and printer operations only.

CHCP

Command type:	Internal
Official purpose:	Displays or sets the active Code Page number.
Usefulness:	0
Safety factor:	5
Correct usage:	CHCP [nnn]

Where nnn is the Code Page to set.

General comments: A little-used command, and quite difficult to get to grips with, CHCP selects one of two prepared system Code Pages. A Code Page is the table of shapes that is used to display characters on the monitor or printer, and hardly ever needs to be changed from the default. Don't bother with it unless you want a hard time.

CHDIR (CD)

Command type: Internal
Official purpose: Displays the name of or changes the current directory.
Usefulness: 5
Safety factor: 5
Correct usage: CHDIR [path]
General comments: One of the six most-used DOS commands. Essential.

CHKDSK

Command type: External, will not work over a network
Official purpose: Scans a disk and displays a status report.
Usefulness: 3
Safety factor: 3
Correct usage: CHKDSK [drive:][pathname] [/f] [/v]
General comments: Useful for finding and fixing lost clusters on your hard
                           disk, but not much else. Run it with the /f switch after a
                           crash or power cut, and press N in response to the
                           question "Convert lost clusters to files?" which you may
                           be asked. This regains valuable chunks of your hard disk
                           which are sometimes lost if the disk was active during a
                           crash.

CLS

Command type: Internal
Official purpose: Clears the screen.
Usefulness: 2
Safety factor: 5
Correct usage: CLS
General comments: Well, there's not a lot more to say about this one really,
                           apart from – it clears the screen.

COMMAND

Command type: External
Official purpose: Starts the command processor.
Usefulness: 1
Safety factor: 4
Correct usage: COMMAND [[drive:]path] [device] [/e:nnnnn] [/p] [/c
                           string]
                           Where drive:path is the directory containing COM-
                           MAND.COM, device specifies the device to be used for
                           command I/O, and e:nnnnn sets the environment size.
General comments: Not usually required. Typing COMMAND from the DOS
                           prompt is to be avoided, as all it does is load a new DOS
                           core over the old one, taking up between 40-70k each
                           time you try it – and there's nothing to stop you doing it
                           repeatedly, until you've got no Ram left!

COMP

Command type: External

Official purpose:	Compares the contents of two sets of files.
Usefulness:	4
Safety factor:	5
Correct usage:	COMP
General comments:	Useful for checking important files against their backups, as COMP can reveal if a virus has been at work by comparing the current file size with the original. Don't panic if they don't match, though; some programs modify themselves quite legally, and the only way to be sure you've got a virus it to buy a good anti-virus utility.

COPY

Command type:	Internal
Official purpose:	Copies one or more files to another location, under the same or different name(s).
Usefulness:	5
Safety factor:	3
Correct usage:	COPY [drive:]pathname1[drive:][pathname2][/v][/a][/b]
General comments:	One of the six most-used DOS commands. Essential, but disastrous consequences can arise when trying to copy one entire directory to another; if you mistype the name of the target directory or it doesn't exist, you'll get one huge file instead, as COPY decides you wanted to append everything together! Not a big problem, unless you've deleted the originals in a burst of misguided confidence...

CTTY

Command type:	Internal
Official purpose:	Changes the terminal device used to control your system.
Usefulness:	2
Safety factor:	4
Correct usage:	CTTY device
	Where device is one of:
	CON (the keyboard and display)
	AUX (auxiliary device, such as a terminal)
	COMn (one of the serial ports)
	LPTn (one of the printer ports)
	PRN (the default printer)
	NUL (the null device – data is discarded)
General comments:	Useful for redirecting control of your system to a different device, but it's rarely needed. Be careful not to use the command CTTY NUL or you won't be able to use the system until it's been reset!

DATE

Command type:	Internal
Official purpose:	Displays or sets the date.
Usefulness:	5
Safety factor:	5

Correct usage: DATE [mm-dd-yy]
General comments: Pretty essential, this, and not a great deal to say about it.

DEL

Command type: Internal
Official purpose: Deletes one or more files.
Usefulness: 5
Safety factor: 2
Correct usage: DEL [drive:]pathname
General comments: Needless to say, use with caution. These days it's fairly
                            safe to use the *.* wildcard, but prior to MS-DOS 4.00
                            you were only asked ''Are you sure'' in response to this.
                            Also beware using the directory short cuts ''.'' , ''..'' and
                            ''\'' unless you are completely sure of yourself.

DIR

Command type: Internal
Official purpose: Lists the files in a directory.
Usefulness: 5
Safety factor: 5
Correct usage: DIR [drive:][path][filename] [/p] [/w]
                            Where /p makes the computer wait for a key press after
                            filling the screen, and /w selects wide listing mode.
General comments: One of the six most-used DOS commands. Essential.

DISKCOMP

Command type: External, will not work over a network
Official purpose: Compares the contents of two disks for differences.
Usefulness: 2
Safety factor: 5
Correct usage: DISKCOMP [drive1:] [drive2:] [/i] [/8]
General comments: Little-used these days, with far more powerful utilities
                            available as part of cheap DOS toolkits. DISKCOMP can
                            possibly help to check a disk for virus infestation, but as
                            with COMP this sort of thing is best left to specialist
                            programs.

DISKCOPY

Command type: External, will not work over a network
Official purpose: Copies the contents of one floppy disk to another.
Usefulness: 4
Safety factor: 1
Correct usage: DISKCOPY [drive1:] [drive2:] [/1]

General comments: Quite useful for cloning floppy disks, but be careful not to overwrite data you meant to keep. DISKCOPY copies the complete binary image, warts and all, so if the source disk is fragmented, the target disk will be, too. Do not attempt to specify your hard disk as either the source or destination – if you're lucky, you'll get a warning. If not – well, you have been warned!

EXE2BIN

Command type: External
Official purpose: Converts .EXE (executable) files to binary format.
Usefulness: 1
Safety factor: 2
Correct usage: EXE2BIN [drive:]pathname1 [drive:]pathname2
General comments: Well. Very useful, this – no, honestly! If you've ever questioned the necessity of retaining this seemingly pointless file in your DOS directory, then wonder no more. People use this rather esoteric command to do weird and wonderful things to their EXE files, including turning them into (so I'm told) non-relocating COM files which apparently load faster from disk. Definitely only for the egg-heads among us.

EXIT

Command type: Internal
Official purpose: Exits the COMMAND.COM program (command processor).
Usefulness: 5
Safety factor: 5
Correct usage: EXIT
General comments: This command is used to get back into applications which have "shelled out" to DOS (usually by loading another copy of COMMAND.COM), and it's also a way to rescue yourself from typing COMMAND until you run out of memory. Unlike COMMAND, EXIT is totally harmless and can be used as often as you like.

FASTOPEN

Command type: External, will not work over a network
Official purpose: Decreases the amount of time needed to open frequently-used files and directories.
Usefulness: 4
Safety factor: 5
Correct usage: FASTOPEN [drive:[=nnn][...]]

General comments: FASTOPEN is a free disk-cacheing program, and so it's not fair to knock it too much. Most people won't know the difference between this and SMARTDRV.SYS, also free with most versions of DOS. The quick answer is that FASTOPEN is a true DOS command, unlike SMART-DRIVE.SYS which must be included in your CON-FIG.SYS file.

FC

Command type: External
Official purpose: Compares two files or two sets of files and displays the differences between them.
Usefulness: 4
Safety factor: 5
Correct usage: FC [/a] [/c] [/L] [/Lbn] [/n] [/t] [/w] [/nnnn]
                       [drive:]pathname1 [drive:]pathname2
                       or:
                       FC [/b] [/nnnn] [drive:]pathname1 [drive:]pathname2
                       Where:
                       /a Abbreviates the output of an ASCII comparison.
                       /b Forces a binary comparison – similar to COMP.
                       /c Turns case-sensitivity off.
                       /L Compares the files in ASCII mode.
                       /Lb Sets the minimum number of lines to compare – the default is 100 lines.
                       /n Displays line numbers during ASCII comparison.
                       /t Disables TAB character expansion to spaces.
                       /w Forces FC to treat consecutive white space characters (tabs and spaces) as one character.
                       /nnnn Specify the number of lines that must match after FC finds a difference.
General comments: Useful for finding differences between documents, to help establish which is out-of-date. Can be used in binary mode, which is similar to the COMP command.

FDISK

Command type: External, will not work over a network
Official purpose: Configures a hard disk for use with MS-DOS.
Usefulness: 1
Safety factor: 0
Correct usage: FDISK
General comments: Steer well clear of this command unless you know EXACTLY what you are doing. The contents of your entire hard disk are at risk from this formatting program, which is never needed unless you need to fiddle with the DOS partition, or really do need to wipe the disk.

FIND

Command type: External

Official purpose:	Searches for a text string in a file or set of files.
Usefulness:	5
Safety factor:	5
Correct usage:	FIND [/v] [/c] [/n] ''string'' [[drive:][pathname]...]
	Where:
	/v Displays all lines not containing the specified string.
	/c Displays only the count of matching lines in each file.
	/n Displays the line number of each line shown.
General comments:	Very useful for tracking down which document contains the text you are looking for. Perfectly safe to experiment with.

FORMAT

Command type:	External, will not work over a network
Official purpose:	Formats the disk for use with MS-DOS.
Usefulness:	5
Safety factor:	1
Correct usage:	FORMAT drive: [/1] [/4] [/8] [/n:xx] [/t:yy] [/v] [/s]
	or:
	FORMAT drive: [/1] [/b] [/n:xx] [/t:yy]
	Where:
	/1 Formats only one side of the disk.
	/4 Formats a 5.25'' 360k disk in a 1.44Mb drive.
	/8 Formats to 8 sectors per track.
	/b Formats with space for an operating system.
	/s Formats and copies the operating system over to the disk.
	/n:xx Sets the number of sectors per track.
	/t:yy Sets the number of tracks per disk.
	/v Makes FORMAT ask you to enter a volume label after the disk is formatted.
General comments:	In general, don't use any of the switches unless you have to. If you have to use the /4 switch, bear in mind that the resulting disk will not be 100 percent reliable thereafter.

GRAFTABL

Command type:	External
Official purpose:	Enables MS-DOS to display an extended character set in graphics mode.
Usefulness:	1
Safety factor:	5
Correct usage:	GRAFTABL [xxx]
	Where xxx is a Code Page number.
General comments:	Most programs which use graphics mode these days take care of everything for you.

GRAPHICS

| Command type: | External |
| Official purpose: | Allows you to print graphics screens. |

Usefulness:	3
Safety factor:	5
Correct usage:	GRAPHICS [printer] [/b] [/p=port] [/r] [/lcd]

Where printer is:
COLOR1 (IBM Color Printer with black ribbon)
COLOR4 (IBM Color Printer with RGB ribbon)
COLOR8 (IBM Color Printer with CMY ribbon – cyan, magenta, yellow)
COMPACT (IBM Compact Printer)
GRAPHICS (IBM Printer or Proprinter)
THERMAL (IBM PC-convertible)
/b Prints the background in colour.
/p=port Sets the printer port to 1, 2 or 3.
/r Reverse black for white on the printout.
/lcd Print from IBM PC Portable.

General comments: Again, most packages worth their salt take care of printing for you – but GRAPHICS is still useful; the command GRAPHICS GRAPHICS often allows you to get decent results when PRINTSCREEN is pressed in graphics mode.

JOIN

Command type:	External, will not work over a network
Official purpose:	Joins a disk drive to a directory path.
Usefulness:	3
Safety factor:	3
Correct usage:	JOIN [drive1: [drive2:]path]
General comments:	Useful, but can cause problems when you try and access the original drive – you can't.

KEYB

Command type:	External
Official purpose:	Loads a keyboard driver for a specific language.
Usefulness:	5
Safety factor:	4
Correct usage:	KEYB [xx[,[yyy],[[drive:][path]filename]]]

Where xx is a two-letter country code, yyy is a Code Page and filename is the keyboard file itself.

General comments: You need this command in your AUTOEXEC.BAT file if you don't want to get an American keyboard layout. The usual format for the UK is simply: KEYB UK

LABEL

Command type:	External, will not work over a network
Official purpose:	Creates, changes or deletes the volume label of a disk.
Usefulness:	3
Safety factor:	5
Correct usage:	LABEL [drive:][label]

General comments: There's not a lot more to say about this command other
                        than that it's useful for keeping track of large collections
                        of floppy disks.

MKDIR (MD)

Command type: Internal
Official purpose: Makes a new directory.
Usefulness: 5
Safety factor: 5
Correct usage: MKDIR [drive:]path
General comments: One of the six most-used DOS commands. Essential.

MODE

Command type: External
Official purpose: Sets operational modes for devices.
Usefulness: 5
Safety factor: 2
Correct usage: Far too many to list here!
General comments: This command seems to be the dustbin for every extra
                        feature Microsoft couldn't justify a separate command for.
                        You'll really need to refer to your own DOS manual for
                        this one, but basically it is the only way to officially
                        change display modes, keyboard rates and many other
                        things (of course, later on you will learn how to go ahead
                        and do some of them without using MODE!).

MORE

Command type: External
Official purpose: Sends output to the console one screenful at a time
Usefulness: 5
Safety factor: 4
Correct usage: MORE < source
                        or:
                        source | MORE
                        Where source is a file or command.
General comments: There's a lot more about MORE later – it has its faults,
                        but if used properly it's one of the handiest DOS utilities.

NLSFUNC

Command type: External
Official purpose: Loads country-specific information.
Usefulness: 1
Safety factor: 4
Correct usage: NLSFUNC [[drive:][path]filename]
General comments: Don't bother – it's too complicated, and not much use
                        unless you're into Code Page switching and you'll know
                        if you are!

PATH

Command type:	Internal
Official purpose:	Sets a command search path.
Usefulness:	5
Safety factor:	5
Correct usage:	PATH [drive:][path][;[drive:][path]...]
	or:
	PATH;
General comments:	Not usually used outside of AUTOEXEC.BAT, PATH is an essential command – put all of your little utilities together in one directory and include it in the PATH statement, and you'll be able to use them any time without having to type huge path names.

PRINT

Command type:	External
Official purpose:	Prints a text file in the background
Usefulness:	3
Safety factor:	4
Correct usage:	Too complex to detail here!
General comments:	PRINT can be useful, but do we really need it these days? It's a strange word processor that can't print its own files – even in the background.

PROMPT

Command type:	Internal
Official purpose:	Changes the MS-DOS command prompt.
Usefulness:	5
Safety factor:	5
Correct usage:	PROMPT [[text][$character]...]
General comments:	Everyone likes to customise their command line, and PROMPT is a thoughtful addition to MS-DOS. The most popular DOS prompt is: C:>\ Which can be set up with: PROMPT pg. If you have ANSI.SYS installed, PROMPT is also an excellent command for changing your screen's colours by sending special codes.

RECOVER

Command type:	External, will not work over a network
Official purpose:	Recovers a file or disk containing bad sectors.
Usefulness:	0
Safety factor:	0
Correct usage:	RECOVER [drive:][path]filename
	or:
	RECOVER [drive:]

General comments: Don't use this command! Ever! It's the fastest way there is to corrupt perfectly good disks. In fact, if you want to take the risk, there are people who use RECOVER as a quick formatter! But your best advice is to completely ignore any advice your manual might give you on the subject.

RENAME (REN)

Command type: Internal
Official purpose: Changes the name of a file
Usefulness: 5
Safety factor: 3
Correct usage: RENAME [drive:][path]filename1 filename2
General comments: One of the six most-used DOS commands. Essential, but beware of using wildcards with RENAME – you just might end up renaming more than you thought.

REPLACE

Command type: External
Official purpose: Updates previous versions of files.
Usefulness: 2
Safety factor: 1
Correct usage: Too involved to cover here!
General comments: You should rarely, if ever, use REPLACE. There are so many safer, better ways of doing things that it's hard to see why people use it at all. You see it's a very dangerous command because of its ability to overwrite read-only files without so much as a by-your-leave.

RESTORE

Command type: External
Official purpose: Restores files that were backed up with BACKUP
Usefulness: 3
Safety factor: 3
Correct usage: Too detailed to cover here!
General comments: This is, of course, the opposite command to BACKUP. There's not a lot more to say about it – if you use BACKUP you have to use RESTORE.

RMDIR (RD)

Command type: Internal
Official purpose: Removes (deletes) a directory
Usefulness: 5
Safety factor: 4
Correct usage: RMDIR [drive:]path
General comments: One of the six most-used DOS commands. Essential, and quite safe – you can't delete a directory unless it's empty.

SELECT

Command type:	External
Official purpose:	Installs MS-DOS on a new floppy disk with the desired country-specific information and keyboard layout.
Usefulness:	1
Safety factor:	4
Correct usage:	Too detailed to cover here!
General comments:	Little-used by man or beast.

SET

Command type:	Internal
Official purpose:	Sets up environment variables
Usefulness:	5
Safety factor:	5
Correct usage:	SET [string = [string]]
General comments:	Not a lot to say, really. Use it to set values which can be read by all programs that wish to.

SHARE

Command type:	External
Official purpose:	Installs file sharing and locking.
Usefulness:	1
Safety factor:	5
Correct usage:	Too detailed to cover here!
General comments:	SHARE is only for networked PCs and is responsible for ensuring that when two users try to access the same file on a network that file does not become corrupted in any way.

SORT

Command type:	External
Official purpose:	Produces sorted output from any file or command
Usefulness:	4
Safety factor:	4
Correct usage:	SORT [/r] [/+n] < source
	or:
	[source] I SORT [/r] [/+n]
	Where /r reverses the sort, and /+n sets the column number at which the sort takes place.
General comments:	SORT is one of those programs that sits forgotten on your disk until you need it, and then you're so grateful for it, because there's nothing else that'll quite do the job. A good use for it is to type DIR I SORT to obtain a sorted directory listing. Neat huh? You could pay money for programs to do that.

SUBST

Command type:	External, will not work over a network
Official purpose:	Substitutes a path with a drive letter.

Usefulness:	4
Safety factor:	3
Correct usage:	SUBST [drive1: [drive2:]path]
General comments:	This is useful for referring to long pathnames by a single letter, but it has some hidden dangers. Some other DOS commands will be confused by the substitution and can cause problems which are hard to spot later.

(SYSTEM) SYS

Command type:	External, will not work over a network
Official purpose:	Transfers MS-DOS to another disk.
Usefulness:	5
Safety factor:	3
Correct usage:	SYS drive:
General comments:	This is useful for creating bootable floppy disks, but some versions won't work if there's any data at all on the disk.

TIME

Command type:	Internal
Official purpose:	Displays or sets the date
Usefulness:	5
Safety factor:	5
Correct usage:	TIME [hours:minutes[:seconds[.hundredths]]]
General comments:	Pretty essential, this, and not a great deal to day about it.

TREE

Command type:	External
Official purpose:	Displays the path (and, optionally, lists the contents) of each directory and subdirectory on the given drive.
Usefulness:	4
Safety factor:	5
Correct usage:	TREE [drive:] [/f]
	Where /f displays the names of the files in each directory.
General comments:	This used to be a very powerful command, but it's been left behind by many much more useful PD and Shareware versions, which often display your entire directory tree in a text-mode graphical representation – something which TREE has only recently been able to do.

TYPE

Command type:	Internal
Official purpose:	Displays the contents of a text file on the screen
Usefulness:	5
Safety factor:	5
Correct usage:	TYPE [drive:]filename
General comments:	In conjunction with the MORE and SORT filters, TYPE is one of the most useful MS-DOS utilities.

VER

Command type:	Internal
Official purpose:	Prints the MS-DOS version number
Usefulness:	2
Safety factor:	5
Correct usage:	VER
General comments:	This command is rarely used – most people know which version of DOS they are using, unless they're trying to do something on someone else's machine.

VERIFY

Command type:	Internal
Official purpose:	Tells MS-DOS whether to verify that your files are written correctly to disk.
Usefulness:	3
Safety factor:	3
Correct usage:	VERIFY [on] or [off]
General comments:	Turning VERIFY OFF can marginally speed up some disk operations, but is it really worth the peace of mind that having all your disk save operations checked for you brings?

(VOLUME) VOL

Command type:	Internal
Official purpose:	Displays the disk volume label and serial number, if they exist.
Usefulness:	2
Safety factor:	5
Correct usage:	VOL [drive:]
General comments:	There's not a lot to add, except to say that some versions of DOS below 4.00 don't display the serial number – but then, so what?

XCOPY

Command type:	External
Official purpose:	Copies files (except hidden and system files) and directory trees.
Usefulness:	5
Safety factor:	1
Correct usage:	Too detailed to cover here!
General comments:	XCOPY is an invaluable tool once you understand how to use it safely. It's the only facility MS-DOS provides for copying entire directory structures, and even entire disks (including your hard disk, if you are so minded!). But be warned – a command this powerful can do a lot of damage if used incautiously.

TEMPORARY FILES

From time to time everyone finds strange, unwanted files appearing on their hard disks, usually with names less meaningful than a supermarket bar-code. These often puzzle newcomers to the world of computing.

Some programs create temporary files while they work, but not all are well-behaved and clean up after themselves. dBase IV version 1.0 was a notorious example, although Ashton-Tate says that version 1.1 now removes all temporary files when it closes down. But there is another, much more common explanation for these "phantom" files which most of us have experienced at one time or another.

Turning your PC off while an application is running often leaves temporary files floating around on the hard disk, and this is undoubtedly the root cause behind most of this unwanted clutter. Another way to get them is by pressing [Ctrl][C] (on DOS 3.3 or earlier) while TYPEing a file to screen using the |MORE filter. |MORE causes screen output to be sent to a temporary file (for some reason a second is also created) which is then sent to the display a screen at a time, pausing until a key is pressed to scroll the next screenful into view.

As it happens, the temporary files created by MORE will always be created in the root directory, and are easy to find and remove – but other DOS commands or filters may have this effect, so watch out for these too.

Temporary files often have the extension .TMP, and even when scattered all over the disk can be quickly found with a utility like WHEREIS. Others commonly take the following form:

```
0E211021      498688    7-03-92    2:33p
```

If this is translated into hexadecimal, it can be seen that the filename is not chosen at random; it actually represents the exact time the file was created.

```
Hexadecimal -> 0E 21 10 21
Decimal     -> 14 33 16 33
```

Making a time of 14:33, 16 seconds and 33 hundredths of a second.

The best way to remove this type of temporary file in one fell swoop is to type:

```
CD \
DEL 0*
```

assuming, that is, that you don't have any files you want to keep beginning with the number 0.

Of course, prevention is always better than a cure – so remember never to turn your PC off while an application is running.

FASTER "MORE" AND "SORT"

The traditional way to stop text from scrolling off the screen when you use commands like TYPE is to use the MORE filter. This usually takes the form:

```
TYPE filename | MORE
```

When MORE is used in this way it's actually much slower than necessary, and in fact it doesn't always work. This is because all of the screen output which is normally generated by the TYPE command is piped into a temporary file instead, for later screen-by-screen viewing. This causes a delay – sometimes quite a substantial one, if the quantity of output is large – before anything appears on screen.

Worse than that, if an error occurs during piping you'll get a DOS error message – again before anything else has appeared – and as a result some of the information might be lost. And to cap it all, the temporary file will almost certainly remain on the disk afterwards, leaving you to clear up the mess.

If this seems an unlikely occurrence, think what might happen if the default drive (the one on which MORE creates its temporary files) is either A: or B:, and is empty, or contains a disk without enough free space for the file, or is write-protected...

But all these problems can be avoided by using the command:

```
MORE < filename
```

This is because MORE is forced to run immediately; all input comes directly from the file, rather than from the output of the TYPE command, and no temporary file is created. This technique works equally well with the other well-known filter, SORT. Instead of typing:

```
TYPE filename | SORT
```

you can use this instead:

```
SORT < filename
```

But note that you can't do this with DOS commands like DIR, because filters need a file to work on; this command is illegal and will generate an error:

```
MORE < DIR
```

UNDOCUMENTED DOS COMMAND

There is a little-known, entirely undocumented command available in DOS versions 4.x through to 5.00, called TRUENAME. What it does is display the "true" path of any filename you give it, regardless of any logical drive or directory assignments you might have made with SUBST or JOIN.

For example, if you assign the directory C:\VEHICLES\CARS\BLUE to the logical drive Z: with SUBST, and in this directory you have a file called UNLEADED, then typing:

`DIR UNLEADED`

will display, as expected, just the filename itself. However, if you type:

`TRUENAME UNLEADED`

then you will get the following message on your display:

`C:\VEHICLES\CARS\BLUE\UNLEADED`

Interestingly, wildcards are allowed with TRUENAME – but they won't be expanded. All you'll get will be the same result but with question marks padding out any sections containing wildcards. For example, typing:

`TRUENAME *.*`

will display:

`C:\VEHICLES\CARS\BLUE\????????.???`

If you know a machine has at least DOS 4.00, TRUENAME is a good way of making sense out of a complex hard disk structure which has been masked with heavy use of the SUBST command.

MANIPULATING FILENAMES WITH "HIDDEN" CHARACTERS

A common ploy of software manufacturers is to embed a SPACE character in the filenames of certain files, to prevent them from being accidentally deleted, or listed to the screen with TYPE.

The reason that SPACE is used so often is that although it is perfectly "legal" to use this character from within custom-written applications (which use low-level file handling routines), DOS's command processor COMMAND.COM – which deals with commands entered from the DOS prompt – treats spaces as command separators, producing error messages if you include one in any filename.

The result is that a filename which has a space in it, like this:

`ZIP CODE.ASC`

will be displayed as part of a general DIR command, but when you try and copy, rename, delete or DIR the file by name, DOS reports syntax errors in the command.

Whilst you can't actually refer to these files individually, you can still manipulate them by indirect reference – in other words, by using wildcards.

The trick is to substitute the ? character for the SPACE or other ''illegal'' characters which may be in the filenames you want, and DOS will suddenly become much more obliging. For example, if all you wanted to do was delete the file, just type:

`DEL ZIP?CODE.ASC`

If you wanted to do anything else with the file (for example copy or rename it), the process is a bit more tricky. You have to think carefully about what you want the result of the operation to be; if the file is being copied, but is to keep the same names, use:

`COPY ZIP?CODE.ASC destination directory`

But you might want to remove the source of the trouble at the same time. In which case, use:

`COPY ZIP?CODE.ASC destination directory\ZIPCODE.ASC`

And, of course, you can just rename the file to something more sensible in the first place with:

`RENAME ZIP?CODE.ASC ZIPCODE.ASC`

Finally, you might be interested to know that you can actually create these filenames yourself, using ordinary DOS commands. This can be extremely useful, for exactly the same reasons mentioned earlier. Here's what you do. Copy the file using the inverse of the above RENAME example, like this:

`RENAME ZIPCODE.ASC ZIP?CODE.ASC`

One further point: Files protected in this way are sometimes set to be read-only. You'll know this is true if you get the message ''Access denied'', or similar, when you try and delete or rename the file. Simply type:

`ATTRIB *.* -r`

just beforehand and all will be well.

SORTED DIRECTORY LISTINGS

Here are some commands you can use to display different types of sorted directory listings:

Command:	Sort by:
DIR | SORT	(Name)
DIR | SORT /+10	(Extension)
DIR | SORT /+14	(Size)
DIR | SORT /+24	(Day)
DIR | SORT /+27	(Month)
DIR | SORT /+30	(Year)
DIR | SORT /+34	(Time)

Don't type in the words in brackets. They are there to show what type of sort each line performs.

These commands all work by taking the output from the DIR command and passing then to SORT, which is set to start its matching from the column given after the /. After sorting, the result is then displayed.

A useful hint might be to include these commands in small, single-line batch files which take a filename as a replaceable parameter (the chapter later in this book on batch files will tell you how to do this). The batch files could be given short, easy to remember names, saving the effort of typing in the same lengthy command each time you want a sorted disk catalogue displayed.

DIRECTORY SHORT CUTS

It's often necessary to specify long and complex pathnames when copying, renaming or deleting files from different drives and/or directories, and even a command-line history utility like DOSKEY or DOSEDIT can't eliminate all of the typing required when you come face to face with a directory like this:

`C:\PROGS\BASIC\UTILS\SCREEN`

But did you know that once you are in it, you can manipulate this entire directory with any one of the following commands?

COPY . A:	(Copy all files in current directory to A:)
COPY . ..	(Copy all files in current directory to parent directory)
COPY . \	(Copy all files in current directory to root directory)
COPY A:.	(Copy all files in A: root directory to current directory)
COPY \	(Copy all files in root directory to current directory)
DEL .	(Delete all files in current directory)

TIME STAMPING

Changing a file's date and time details usually requires a utility such as TOUCH.EXE, but there is a way you can update a file's details to show the current date and time – useful if you have several files which make up an application you are writing, and you want them all to show the same date of issue.

You need to copy the files to another drive or directory one by one, using a little-used option of the copy command for appending files together during the copy process. If you use the following command:

```
COPY source+,, destination
```

then each destination file will have the date and time of copying stored with its details. If there are more than a couple of files, you may find that not all of the times match – but they will be the same to within a minute or so of each other.

Note that wildcards are not allowed with this usage of the copy command, as the ''+,,'' syntax is a direct alternative to wild-carded appending.

ATTRIB DIRECTORY SEARCH

If you have ever misplaced a file on your hard disk and don't happen to have a file finding utility handy, you may be surprised to hear that DOS already offers a file find utility – only it goes under a rather unexpected name.

Suppose you wanted to find a file called TEXT, but you can't remember which directory it's in, or if the extension was .DOC, .TXT or even something else entirely. No problem – simply switch to the root directory of your hard disk and type:

```
ATTRIB TEXT.* /S
```

The ATTRIB command tells DOS to report on the file attributes (Hidden, System, Archive, Read-only) of all the files specified. In doing so it very kindly gives you each file's full path name as well.

This is because the /S parameter tells ATTRIB to search all subdirectories of the current directory and down, and as we started the search in the root directory, all files on the disk will be checked.

Incidentally, /S is commonly used by many DOS applications to signify that subdirectories are to be included in the search, but the only official DOS commands that use it below version 5.00 are ATTRIB, BACKUP, RESTORE and XCOPY. Only DOS 5.00 supports this option in other commands, and its presence is most welcome (finally) in DIR.

DEBUG EXPLAINED

Many of the tips in this chapter are in the form of DEBUG scripts. But just what are they? Well, DEBUG is a program distributed with every version of MS-DOS, billed by Microsoft as "a program testing and editing tool". But that's only part of the story; it also comes complete with a full machine-code assembler, and it's this aspect of DEBUG we are most interested in, as it allows a knowledgeable user to create stand-alone MS-DOS utilities of the sort to be found in your DOS directory.

That's where the DEBUG scripts come in; they're just program listings which anyone can type into a text editor and pass to DEBUG, which in turn translates them into machine code and saves the result as COM (COMmand) files. If you're sure of yourself you can even enter scripts directly into DEBUG, which has its own prompt and command processor – just like DOS.

DEBUG is definitely a no-frills utility, but even if you don't understand machine code it's easy to feed DEBUG listings into it and have useful programs come out the other end. As there are many of them in this book you might like to become familiar with this very useful tool before moving on to the scripts themselves.

At its simplest, to use any utility which is featured in this book in the form of a DEBUG script, simply type it into a text editor, save it, and then type a command from DOS to tell DEBUG that you want it to assembly the listing and produce an executable COM file.

The command to do this looks like this:

```
DEBUG < filename
```

Where FILENAME is the name of the script file to assemble. That's all you really need to know about DEBUG, but if you want to go further and learn how to better use its many powerful features – or perhaps you want to learn how to write your own DEBUG scripts – then the rest of this section may be of interest to you.

To run DEBUG in editing mode, type the following at the DOS prompt:

```
DEBUG
```

The DEBUG prompt (a minus sign) will then appear, and you are ready to give it some commands.

There are 18 DEBUG commands available, but as there isn't space in this book to cover an introduction to assembly language programming, you will need to refer to a good book on the subject before you can make full use of DEBUG's advanced programming and editing facilities.

Here is a brief run-down of what DEBUG offers and how it works. Hopefully you will begin to see how some of the scripts in this book work, and perhaps even have an idea of how to modify them:

A   Assemble code at the current address or at the address given if one is specified. All standard assembler commands and mnemonics are allowed but, as it is not a two-pass assembler, you cannot define labels to jump to.

C   Compares the area of memory specified in the first parameter with an area of the same size starting at the address in the second parameter. If the areas are the same there is no display, otherwise all the differences are reported.

D   Displays the contents of the current or specified address in hexadecimal and ASCII format.

E   Entry mode. Allows you to Enter byte values at a specified address. While using Entry mode, press [Space] to skip a byte and leave it unchanged – otherwise type in the new value and press [Space]. Type a hyphen to return to the previous byte or [Return] to exit Entry mode.

F   Fills the address in a specified range with the values in the list.

G   Goes to the current or specified address and begins execution. If you type GCS:5442 it will continue execution until it reaches location 5442. Or you can type G=1234 to begin execution at location 1234.

H   Hex calculator. Displays both the sum and difference of two Hexadecimal values.

I   Inputs and displays a single byte from the specified port.

L   Loads a file into memory at the current or a specified address.

M   Moves a block of memory specified by range to the location specified. Overlapping moves are handled intelligently without losing any data.

N   This assigns a Name to be used by later L or W (Read or Write) commands.

O   Outputs a single byte to the specified port.

Q   Quit. Terminates DEBUG and returns to the calling program (usually DOS).

R   Register display. Displays the contents of one or more Registers. Without a parameter it displays the values of all the registers. If a register name parameter is given, the value of that register is shown and you are given an opportunity to change it. Type F as a register name to see the flags.

S   Searches the specified range for the given sequence of bytes and reports on any matches.

T   Trace mode. Executes the next instruction (or the instruction at the given location) and then returns for you to check out the registers and memory and decide what to do next. To Trace from an address enter a command such as T=0123. To Trace through the next 10 instructions type T 10.

U   Unassembles code to the screen. Beware that it cannot distinguish between code and data so unassembled data will be so much gibberish.

W   Writes the file being DEBUGged back to disk. If you do not give Write any parameters you should set BX:CX to the number of bytes to be written, starting at CS:100. If you have used Go or Trace you will need to reset BX:CX first.

THE DEBUG COMMAND SET

A [address]	Assemble
C range address	Compare
D [range]	Dump
E address [list]	Enter
F range list	Fill
G [=address [address...]]	Go
H value value	Hex
I value	Input
L [address[drive:record record]]	Load
M range address	Move
N filename [filename]	Name
O value byte	Output
Q	Quit
R [register]	Register
S range list	Search
T [=address] [value]	Trace
U [range]	Unassemble
W [address [drive:record record]]	Write

DEBUG ERROR MESSAGES

BF   Bad Flag. You have tried to change a flag but you did not enter a recognisable two-character flag name.

BP   Too many Breakpoints. You passed more than 10 breakpoints to the Go command. 10 is the maximum allowed.

BR   Bad Register. An invalid register name was entered while using the Register command.

DF   Double Flag. Two values were entered for one flag. Flag values may only be set once per RF command.

ꓩ COLOUR BACKGROUNDS

There is a popular DEBUG script floating around which allows you to have sixteen-coloured backgrounds, so long as you are prepared to sacrifice the BLINKING bit, which isn't often used – but it only works on machines with EGA or VGA adaptors, which leaves out people who only have CGA displays.

Both the EGA and VGA BIOSes contain a routine to change the BLINKING bit (in the attribute byte for each screen position) into a BACKGROUND INTENSITY bit. The DEBUG script in question executes that routine by calling an interrupt that simply doesn't exist in the CGA adaptor. However, it's possible to create the same effect using CGA – but it must be done directly, by changing a value on one of the adaptor's registers (on port 3D9H).

The following new DEBUG script will do the job for all three types of graphics adaptor. It creates two little programs (one to turn off blinking and provide sixteen background colours, the other to reset things to normal).

Run DEBUG and type in the following lines exactly as shown and the two programs BLINKOFF.COM and BLINKON.COM will be automatically created. Remember that you must include the blank line where indicated, but you may leave out the comments (starting with semicolons) on each line if you wish.

```
A
MOV AL,10        ;intensive background
MOV DX,03D9      ;colour selection register
OUT DX,AL        ;adjust for CGA
MOV AX,1003      ;EGA BIOS service 03
MOV BL,0         ;intensive background
INT 10           ;adjust for EGA/VGA
RET              ;back to MS DOS

RCX
E
NBLINKOFF.COM
W
E101 0
E10A 1
NBLINKON.COM
W
Q
```

BLINKOFF will turn off blinking and permit bright backgrounds in its place, while BLINKON will restore things to normal. If you use either of these programs on a PC with CGA, you will lose your border colour, but since the border isn't generally used this probably won't bother you.

Note that changing mode will reset the intense background colours to blinking, so always call BLINKON after a mode change (such as typing MODE 80).

CHANGING BORDER COLOUR

The old CGA standard (IBM Colour/Graphics Adaptor) displays an empty border around the working screen area when in the standard 25 lines by 80 columns mode. You can set all of this area, right up to the bezel (the casing at the edge of the glass) to any one of sixteen colours with a simple program called BORDER.COM.

The more powerful EGA and VGA adaptors also display a border. It's only a small frame around the text area, but it can be coloured in the same way, and the colour change is instantaneous.

To create BORDER.COM, call up DEBUG and type in the following lines exactly as shown. Remember that you must include the blank line where indicated, but you can leave out the comments.

```
A
MOV AH,0B        ;BIOS set palette
MOV BX,0F        ;only four bits required
AND BL,[5D]      ;pick up parameter
INT 10           ;BIOS interrupt
RET              ;back to MS DOS

RCX
C
NBORDER.COM
W
Q
```

You use BORDER by typing its name at the DOS prompt (or from within a batch file) followed by a space, and then one letter from the table below representing the colour you want the border to be.

A	BLUE
B	GREEN
C	CYAN
D	RED
E	MAGENTA
F	BROWN
G	WHITE
H	GREY
I	BRIGHT BLUE
J	BRIGHT GREEN
K	BRIGHT CYAN
L	BRIGHT RED
M	PINK
N	YELLOW
O	BRIGHT WHITE
P	BLACK

PRINTSCREEN COMMAND

The following DEBUG script creates a DOS utility called PRTSCR.COM which you can run from the command line (or in batch files) to activate the Print Screen function, in the same way as if you had actually pressed [Shift][PrtScr].

Run DEBUG and enter each line exactly as it appears, including the blank line – just press [Return]. To use the utility at any time, type (or include in a batch file) PRTSCR.

```
A
INT 05
INT 20

R CX
4
NPRTSCR.COM
W
Q
```

DEACTIVATING PRINTSCREEN

Hitting the PRINTSCREEN key by accident can be a real pain, especially if you don't have a printer in the first place. You're forced to wait an eternity while the none-too-bright BIOS makes up its mind as to whether you were just pulling its leg, before returning control to your itchy fingers.

This is because the PRINTSCREEN key invokes an interrupt routine in the BIOS, which then has to wait a respectable time for the printer to come to life. It's only after this time limit that the routine decides that the printing of the screen must be abandoned.

There are two solutions that don't take up any extra memory. One is to stop the interrupt from doing anything, and the other is to reduce the waiting time to a bare minimum. Both of these are done with DEBUG script files, but neither produces a program as output.

The first takes no time at all, but cannot be guaranteed to work under future versions of MS DOS. It involves sending the Print Screen interrupt (number 05H) to another, unused interrupt, 2BH.

To use it, run DEBUG and enter the following lines. Remember you must leave out the blank line, but you can ignore the comments.

```
A
MOV AX,352B      ;find vector for interrupt 2B (no operation)
INT 21
MOV AX,2505      ;set vector for interrupt 05 (print screen)
MOV DX,ES        ;segment
MOV DS,DX
MOV DX,BX        ;displacement
INT 21
RET              ;return to MS DOS

G
Q
```

The other solution is not instantaneous, but means you only lose a second or so before the Print Screen interrupt gives up on your imaginary printer, and it doesn't cheat. This is to set the time-out constant for LPT1 in the BIOS information block to one second (the minimum possible).

As with the last example, enter the following two lines into DEBUG.

```
E0:0478 01
Q
```

You may wish to do this with a POKE instead. In GW-Basic it looks like this:

```
100 DEF SEG 0
110 POKE &H0478,1
```

NUM LOCK UTILITY

If you are one of those people who prefer using the numeric keypad as a second cursor key cluster, the first thing you probably do after your computer boots is to hit the NUM LOCK key, as there is no other way to disable the keypad (unless you have this option included in your CMOS Ram setup program).

Instead, here's a quick way of producing a COM file that you can add to your AUTOEXEC.BAT file to turn NUM LOCK off at boot up. Remember to type it exactly as shown, and save it as MAKENUM. Then type:

```
DEBUG < MAKENUM
```

And the program NUMOFF.COM will be written to your disk. Copy this program to a directory accessible during your boot up procedure and add this line:

```
NUMOFF
```

to your AUTOEXEC.BAT file.

```
A
XOR AX,AX
MOV DS,AX
AND BYTE [417],DF
RET

RCX
A
NNUMOFF.COM
W
Q
```

Where you see the blank line after the RET command, simply press [Return] without entering anything.

CAPS LOCK UTILITY

Perhaps even more useful than the DEBUG script which disables NUM LOCK at boot up (elsewhere in this section) is this script for forcing CAPS LOCK on in the same way.

In fact this is a slightly modified version of that other DEBUG script. Simply type the following file into a word processor and save it as ASCII using a file name such as MAKECAPS. Then type:

```
DEBUG < MAKECAPS
```

And the program CAPSON.COM will be written to your disk. Copy this program to a directory accessible during your boot up procedure and add this line:

```
CAPSON
```

to your AUTOEXEC.BAT file.

```
A
XOR AX,AX
MOV DS,AX
MOV BX,417
MOV WORD PTR [BX],40
RET

RCX
C
NCAPSON.COM
W
Q
```

Where you see the blank line after the RET command, simply press [Return] without entering anything.

DOUBLING THE DISPLAY LINES

The conventional way of switching between 25, 43 and 50 line display modes is to use the command:

```
MODE CON: LINES=n
```

Where n is one of the three possibilities mentioned above. But there is a problem with this method; you need to have ANSI.SYS installed to use it (see the chapter later in this book about configuring your PC for an explanation of ANSI.SYS).

There are sometimes very good reasons for not using ANSI, most notably the fact that it takes up valuable memory (unless you have DOS 5, in which case you can use the LOADHIGH directive to store it in extended memory) – and it even slows the display down under certain conditions.

Luckily help is at hand from the following DEBUG script, which creates two little programs that change the display mode to either 43 lines (for EGA or VGA) or 50 lines (VGA only).

Type the following listing into a word processor or editor, and save it as DOUBLE.SCR:

```
N43.COM
RCX
33
A
MOV AX,0500
INT 10
MOV BX,AX
MOV AX,1112
INT 10
MOV AH,12
MOV BL,20
INT 10
MOV AX,40
MOV DS,AX
MOV DL,[87]
OR BYTE PTR [87],1
MOV AH,1
MOV CX,0600
INT 10
MOV [87],DL
MOV DX,0384
MOV AX,0714
OUT DX,AX
RET

W
N50.COM
```

```
RCX
13
E12 90
W
Q
```

Next, type:

```
DEBUG < DOUBLE.SCR
```

and you will find two tiny programs in your current directory: 50.COM and 43.COM
– use them as you wish. When you want to switch back to the standard 25-line
display, simply type:

```
MODE CO80
```

CHAPTER 2

STOP PRESS! MS-DOS 6 Primer!

Just as this book was going to print (at the point of checking the proofs), MS-DOS version 6 was released. It is such an improvement on previous versions that we pulled out all the stops to update the book to include the features offered by this latest release.

You will find that all the examples in this book work on all versions of DOS from 3.2 up to DOS 6 (and some below version 3.2), although later versions of DOS do have in-built commands that obviate the need for some of the tricks revealed in this book.

But to keep you up-to-date, here's an extension of the DOS primer presented in Chapter 1 to include the major DOS 6 commands which are either new or have been improved from previous versions. Those commands which are not shown here are either listed in the Chapter 1 primer or are beyond the scope of this book.

Because DOS 6 is so new, if any readers come up with any tips specific to it they would like to share, please send them to the author at the publisher's address and the senders of any ideas used in the 2nd edition of *The PC Companion* will receive a complimentary copy.

APPEND

Command type:	External.
Official Purpose:	Allows programs to open data files in specified directories as if they were in the current directory.
Usefulness:	3
Safety factor:	3
Correct usage:	APPEND [[drive:]path[;. . .]] [/X[:ON or :OFF]]
	[/PATH:ON or /PATH:OFF] [/E]
	[drive:]path – Specifies a drive and directory to append.
	/X:ON – Applies appended directories to file searches and application execution.
	/X:OFF – Applies appended directories only to requests to open files.
	/X:OFF – is the default setting.

/PATH:ON – Applies appended directories to file requests that already specify a path. /PATH:ON is the default setting.

/PATH:OFF – Turns off the effect of /PATH:ON.

/E – Stores a copy of the appended directory list in an environment variable named APPEND. /E may be used only the first time you use APPEND after starting your system.

General comments: Type APPEND ; to clear the appended directory list. Type APPEND without parameters to display the appended directory list.

ATTRIB

Command type:	External.
Official purpose:	Displays or changes the attributes of selected files in a directory.
Usefulness:	4
Safety factor:	4
Correct usage:	ATTRIB [+R or –R] [+A or –A] [+S or –S] [+H or –H] [[drive:] [path]filename] [/S]

+ – Sets an attribute.

- – Clears an attribute.

R – Read-only file attribute.

A – Archive file attribute.

S – System file attribute.

H – Hidden file attribute.

/S – Processes files in all directories in the specified path.

General comments: Use this command for protecting files you don't want deleted or modified (AUTOEXEC.BAT and CONFIG.SYS, for example) by other programs. Also use it do make other peoples' protected files easier to handle.

CALL

Command type:	External.
Official purpose:	Calls one batch program from another.
Usefulness:	4
Safety factor:	4
Correct usage:	CALL [drive:] [path]filename [batch-parameters]

batch-parameters – Specifies any command-line information required by the batch program.

General comments: Use in place of COMMAND /p only if you are sure your users will have use of the CALL command in their version of DOS.

CHOICE

Command type: External.
Official purpose: Waits for the user to choose one of a set of choices.
Usefulness: 5
Safety factor: 5
Correct usage: CHOICE [/C[:]choices] [/N] [/S] [/T[:]c,nn] [text]
                        /C[:]choices – Specifies allowable keys. Default is YN
                        /N – Do not display choices and ? at end of prompt string.
                        /S – Treat choice keys as case sensitive.
                        /T[:]c,nn – Default choice to c after nn seconds
                        text – Prompt string to display
                        ERRORLEVEL is set to offset of key user presses in choices.
General comments: At last DOS offers a simple way of entering user input into batch files.

COMMAND

Command type: External.
Official purpose: Starts the command processor.
Usefulness: 1
Safety factor: 4
Correct usage: COMMAND [[drive:]path] [device] [/E:nnnnn] [/P] [/[C or K] command] [/MSG]
                        [drive:]path – Specifies the directory containing COMMAND.COM file.
                        device – Specifies the device to use for command input and output.
                        /E:nnnnn – Sets the initial environment size to nnnnn bytes.
                        /P – Makes the new Command Interpreter permanent (can't exit).
                        /C – command Executes the specified command and returns.
                        /K – command Executes the specified command and continues running.
                        /MSG – Stores all error messages in memory (requires /P as well).
General comments: Not usually required. Typing COMMAND from the DOS prompt is to be avoided, as all it does is load a new DOS core over the old one, taking up between 40-70k each time you try it – and there's nothing to stop you doing it repeatedly, until you've got no RAM left!

DBLSPACE

Command type: External.
Official purpose: Compresses and decompresses disk data on the fly to release extra space.
Usefulness: 5
Safety factor: 4

Correct usage(s):	DBLSPACE /CHKDSK [/F] [drive:] DBLSPACE /COMPRESS drive: [/F] [/NEW-DRIVE=drive2:] [/RESERVE=size] DBLSPACE /CREATE drive: [/NEWDRIVE=drive2:] [/SIZE=size or /RESERVE=size] DBLSPACE /DEFRAGMENT [/F] [drive:] DBLSPACE /DELETE drive: DBLSPACE /FORMAT drive: DBLSPACE [/INFO] drive: DBLSPACE /LIST DBLSPACE /MOUNT[=sss] [drive:] [/NEW-DRIVE=drive2:] DBLSPACE /RATIO[=r.r] [drive: or /ALL] DBLSPACE /SIZE[=size or /RESERVE=size] [drive:] DBLSPACE /UNMOUNT [drive:]
General comments:	To set up DoubleSpace or use the DoubleSpace program to manage compressed drives, type DBLSPACE at the command prompt. For more information about DoubleSpace command-line options, type HELP DBLSPACE or HELP DBLSPACE /switchname at the command prompt.

DEFRAG

Command type:	External.
Official purpose:	Reorganizes files on disks to optimize performance.
Usefulness:	3
Safety factor:	3
Correct usage(s):	DEFRAG [drive:] [/F] [/Sorder] [/B] [/SKIPHIGH] [/LCD or /BW or /G0] DEFRAG [drive:] [/U] [/B] [/SKIPHIGH] [/LCD or /BW or /G0] [drive:] – Drive letter of disk to be optimized. /F – Fully optimizes specified disk. /U – Unfragments files, leaving space between files. /S – Sort files by specified order. N – By Name (alphabetic) E – By extension (alphabetic) D – By date & time (earliest first) S – By size (smallest first) - – Suffix to reverse order /B – Restarts your computer after optimization. /SKIPHIGH – Loads Defrag into conventional memory. /LCD – Runs Defrag using an LCD color scheme. /BW – Runs Defrag using a black and white color scheme. /G0 – Disable the graphic mouse and graphic character set. /H – Moves hidden files.
General comments:	Defragmenting your hard disk (even if it has been doublespaced) will often improve your hard disk's speed. But note that defragmenting even a 30 megabyte disk could take a couple of hours.

DELOLDOS

Command type:	External.
Official purpose:	Deletes old DOS files after MS-DOS 6 installation.
Usefulness:	3
Safety factor:	3
Correct usage:	DELOLDOS [/B]

/B – Uses black-and-white instead of colour screen display.

General comments: Useful for removing unwanted 'clutter' from your hard disk, but after running the DELOLDOS command, you cannot use the 'UNINSTALL' disk (created by MS- DOS 6 Setup) to restore your previous DOS version.

DELTREE

Command type:	External.
Official purpose:	Deletes a directory and all the subdirectories and files in it.
Usefulness:	4
Safety factor:	1
Correct usage:	DELTREE [/Y] [drive:]path [[drive:]path[. . .]]

/Y – Suppresses prompting to confirm you want to delete the subdirectory.

[drive:]path Specifies the name of the directory you want to delete.

General comments: Use DELTREE cautiously. Every file and subdirectory within the specified directory will be deleted.

DIR

Command type:	Internal.
Official purpose:	Displays a list of files and subdirectories in a directory.
Usefulness:	5
Safety factor:	5
Correct usage(s):	DIR [drive:][path][filename] [/P] [/W] [/A[[:]attribs]]

[/O[[:]sortord]] [/S] [/B] [/L] [/C[H]]

[drive:][path][filename] – Specifies drive, directory, and/ or files to list.

/P – Pauses after each screenful of information.

/W – Uses wide list format.

/A – Displays files with specified attributes.

A – Files ready to archive

D – Directories

H – Hidden files

R – Read-only files

S – System files

- – Prefix meaning "not"

/O – List by files in sorted order.

C – By compression ratio (smallest first)

D – By date & time (earliest first)

E – By extension (alphabetic)

G – Group directories first
N – By name (alphabetic)
S – By size (smallest first)
- – Prefix for reverse order
/S – Displays files in specified directory and all subdirectories.
/B – Uses bare format (no heading information or summary).
/L – Uses lowercase.
/C[H] – Displays file compression ratio;
/CH – uses host allocation unit size.

General comments: The dinosaur of DOS commands has now been well overhauled (even if,perhaps, a bit too much now) and offers loads of bells and whistles. However, the switches may be preset in the DIRCMD environment variable. You can override preset switches by prefixing any switch with – (hyphen), like this for example: /-W.

DISKCOPY

Command type: External, will not work over a network.
Official purpose: Copies the contents of one floppy disk to another.
Usefulness: 4
Safety factor: 4
Correct usage: DISKCOPY [drive1: [drive2:]] [/1] [/V]
/1 – Copies only the first side of the disk.
/V – Verifies that the information is copied correctly.

General comments: Quite useful for cloning floppy disks, but be careful not to overwrite data you meant to keep. DISKCOPY copies the complete binary image, warts and all, so if the source disk is fragmented, the target disk will be, too. Do not attempt to specify your hard disk as either the source or destination – if you're lucky, you'll get a warning. If not – well, you've been warned here! The two floppy disks must be the same type. You may specify the same drive for drive1 and drive2.

DOSKEY

Command type: External.
Official purpose: Edits command lines, recalls MS-DOS commands, and creates macros.
Usefulness: 5
Safety factor: 5
Correct usage: DOSKEY [/REINSTALL] [/BUFSIZE=size] [/MACROS] [/HISTORY] [/INSERT or /OVERSTRIKE] [macroname=[text]]
/REINSTALL – Installs a new copy of Doskey.
/BUFSIZE=size – Sets size of command history buffer.
/MACROS – Displays all Doskey macros.
/HISTORY – Displays all commands stored in memory.

/INSERT – Specifies that new text you type is inserted in old text.

/OVERSTRIKE – Specifies that new text overwrites old text.

macroname – Specifies a name for a macro you create.

text – Specifies commands you want to record.

General comments: A useful addition this. The [Up] and [Down] curso keys recall commands, [Esc] clears command line, [F7] displays command history, [Alt][F7] clears the command history, [F8] searches the command history, [F9] selects a command by number, [Alt][F10] clears the macro definitions. Special macro definition codes include: $T: Command separator – Allows multiple commands in a macro. $1-$9: Batch parameters – equivalent to %1-%9 in batch programs. $*: Symbol replaced by everything following macro name on command line.

DOSSHELL

Command type: External.

Official purpose: Starts up a graphical shell front-end to DOS.

Usefulness: 2

Safety factor: 4

Correct usage: DOSSHELL [/T or /G[:res[n]]] [/B]

/T – Starts MS-DOS Shell in text mode.

:res[n] – A letter (L, M, H) and number indicating screen resolution.

/B – Starts MS-DOS Shell using black-and-white colour scheme.

/G – Starts MS-DOS Shell in graphics mode.

General comments: In the author's opinion it will take you longer to learn how to use this program than any time it may save you. Although at first sight it looks like a useful way of integrating your various DOS and applications programs you are probably better off using the DOS command line, DOSKEY and batch files, or running Windows.

EDIT

Command type: External.

Official purpose: Starts the MS-DOS Editor, which creates and changes ASCII files.

Usefulness: 3

Safety factor: 3

Correct usage: EDIT [[drive:][path]filename] [/B] [/G] [/H] [/NOHI]

[drive:][path]filename – Specifies the ASCII file to edit.

/B – Allows use of a monochrome monitor with a color graphics card.

/G – Provides the fastest update of a CGA screen.

/H – Displays the maximum number of lines possible for your hardware.

/NOHI – Allows the use of a monitor without high-intensity support.

General comments: Many newcomers to the PC are often unsure how to edit ASCII files (for example to modify a CONFIG.SYS or AUTOEXEC.BAT file). Well, if you have EDIT then this is your answer. With it you can quickly and easily edit any ASCII files, whether for configuring your PC or writing a letter to a friend.

EMM386

Command type: External.
Official purpose: Turns on or off EMM386 expanded memory support.
Usefulness: 5
Safety factor: 4
Correct usage: EMM386 [ON or OFF or AUTO] [W=ON or W=OFF]
ON or OFF or AUTO Activates or suspends EMM386.EXE device driver, or places it in auto mode.
W=ON or OFF Turns on or off Weitek coprocessor support.

General comments: Not much to say other than that if you have Expanded memory (and most people have these days) and your PC is a 386 or better then you will want to ensure that this program is activated in order to maximise your memory use.

EXPAND

Command type: External.
Official purpose: Expands one or more compressed files.
Usefulness: 3
Safety factor: 3
Correct usage: EXPAND [drive:] [path] filename [[drive:][path]filename [. . .]] destination
[drive:][path]filename – Specifies the location and/or name of a file or set of files to be expanded. You cannot use wildcards.
destination – Specifies the new location and/or name of an expanded file or set of files. Destination can be a drive letter and colon, directory name, filename, or combination.

General comments: The destination can only be a filename if you have specified a single filename for the source filename parameter. To expand a file or set of files to a different directory and keep the original filename(s), specify only a directory as the destination.

FASTHELP

Command type:	External.
Official purpose:	Provides help information for MS-DOS commands.
Usefulness:	5
Safety factor:	5
Correct usage:	FASTHELP [command]
	command – Displays help information on that command.
General comments:	A rough and ready, quick way to get the help you need without having to refer to the manual.

FASTOPEN

Command type:	External, will not work over a network.
Official purpose:	Decreases the amount of time needed to open frequently-used files and directories.
Usefulness:	4
Safety factor:	5
Correct usage:	FASTOPEN drive:[[=]n] [drive:[[=]n][. . .]] [/X]
	drive: – Specifies the hard disk drive you want Fastopen to work with.
	n – Specifies the maximum number of file locations Fastopen retains in its filename cache.
	/X – Creates the filename cache in expanded memory.
General comments:	FASTOPEN is a free disk-cacheing program, and so it's not fair to knock it too much.

FIND

Command type:	External.
Official purpose:	Searches for a text string in a file or set of files.
Usefulness:	5
Safety factor:	5
Correct usage:	FIND [/V] [/C] [/N] [/I] ''string'' [[drive:][path]filename[. . .]]
	/V – Displays all lines NOT containing the specified string.
	/C – Displays only the count of lines containing the string.
	/N – Displays line numbers with the displayed lines.
	/I – Ignores the case of characters when searching for the string.
	''string'' – Specifies the text string to find.
	[drive:][path]filename – Specifies a file or files to search.
General comments:	Very useful for tracking down which document contains the text you are looking for. Perfectly safe to experiment with. If a pathname is not specified, FIND searches the text typed at the prompt or piped from another command.

FORMAT

Command type:	External, will not work over a network.
Official purpose:	Formats the disk for use with MS-DOS.
Usefulness:	5
Safety factor:	1
Correct usage(s):	FORMAT drive: [/V[:label]] [/Q] [/U] [/F:size] [/B or /S]

FORMAT drive: [/V[:label]] [/Q] [/U] [/T:tracks / N:sectors] [/B or /S]

FORMAT drive: [/V[:label]] [/Q] [/U] [/1] [/4] [/B or /S]

FORMAT drive: [/Q] [/U] [/1] [/4] [/8] [/B or /S]

/V[:label] – Specifies the volume label.

/Q – Performs a quick format.

/U – Performs an unconditional format.

/F:size – Specifies the size of the floppy disk to format (such as 160, 180, 320, 360, 720, 1.2, 1.44, 2.88).

/B – Allocates space on the formatted disk for system files.

/S – Copies system files to the formatted disk.

/T:tracks – Specifies the number of tracks per disk side.

/N:sectors – Specifies the number of sectors per track.

/1 – Formats a single side of a floppy disk.

/4 – Formats a 5.25-inch 360K floppy disk in a high-density drive.

/8 – Formats eight sectors per track.

General comments: In general, don't use any of the switches unless you have to. If you have to use the /4 switch, bear in mind that the resulting disk will not be 100 percent reliable thereafter.

HELP

Command type:	External.
Official purpose:	Starts MS-DOS Help on MS-DOS commands.
Usefulness:	3
Safety factor:	5
Correct usage:	HELP [/B] [/G] [/H] [/NOHI] [topic]

/B – Allows use of a monochrome monitor with a color graphics card.

/G – Provides the fastest update of a CGA screen.

/H – Displays the maximum number of lines possible for your hardware.

/NOHI – Allows the use of a monitor without high-intensity support.

[topic] – Specifies the help topic to view.

LOADHIGH

Command type:	External.
Official purpose:	Loads a program into the upper memory area.
Usefulness:	5
Safety factor:	5

Correct usage:	LOADHIGH [drive:][path]filename [parameters]
	LOADHIGH [/L:region1[,minsize1] [;region2 [,minsize2]. . .] [/S]] [drive:][path]filename [parameters]
	/L:region1[,minsize1][;region2[,minsize2]]. . . – Specifies the region(s) of memory into which to load the program.
	region1 – Specifies the number of the first memory region.
	minsize1 – specifies the minimum size, if any, for region1.
	region2 and minsize2 – Specify the number and minimum size of the second region, if any. You can specify as many regions as you want.
	/S – Shrinks a UMB to its minimum size while the program is loading. /S is normally used only by MemMaker.
	[drive:][path]filename – Specifies the location and name of the program.
	parameters – Specifies any command-line information required by the program.
General comments:	A useful command for increasing the amount of DOS RAM below 640K available to your programs.

LOADFIX

Command type:	External.
Official purpose:	Loads a program above the first 64K of memory, and runs the program.
Usefulness:	5
Safety factor:	5
Correct usage:	LOADFIX [drive:][path]filename
General comments:	Use LOADFIX to load a program if you have received the message ''Packed file corrupt'' when trying to load it in low memory.

MEM

Command type:	External.
Official purpose:	Displays the amount of used and free memory in your system.
Usefulness:	5
Safety factor:	5
Correct usage:	MEM [/CLASSIFY or /DEBUG or /FREE or /MODULE modulename] [/PAGE]
	/CLASSIFY or /C – Classifies programs by memory usage. Lists the size of programs, provides a summary of memory in use, and lists largest memory block available.
	/DEBUG or /D – Displays status of all modules in memory, internal drivers, and other information.
	/FREE or /F – Displays information about the amount of free memory left in both conventional and upper memory.

/MODULE or /M – Displays a detailed listing of a module's memory use. This option must be followed by the name of a module, optionally separated from /M by a colon.

/PAGE or /P – Pauses after each screenful of information.

General comments: Just what DOS needed ages ago. Now you can discover exactly how your PC is configured (and more to the point, how it's behaving) as soon as you install DOS, rather than by having to buy third party utilities.

MEMMAKER

Command type: External.
Official purpose: Runs the MemMaker memory-optimisation program.
Usefulness: 5
Safety factor: 3
Correct usage: MEMMAKER [/B] [/BATCH] [/SESSION] [/ SWAP:drive] [/T] [/UNDO] [/W:size1,size2]

/B – Displays MemMaker in black and white.

/BATCH – Runs MemMaker in batch (unattended) mode.

/BATCH2 – Runs MemMaker in batch (unattended) mode and exit.

/SESSION – Used by MemMaker during memory optimization.

/SWAP:drive – Specifies the drive that was originally your startup drive, if drive swapping is in effect.

/T – Disables detection of IBM token-ring networks.

/UNDO – Undoes MemMaker's most recent changes to your startup files.

/W:size1,size2 – Specifies how much upper memory to reserve for translation buffers. Windows uses this space when running MS-DOS-based applications.

General comments: This is invaluable for optimising your PC's memory usage.

MOVE

Command type: External.
Official purpose: Moves files and renames files and directories.
Usefulness: 5
Safety factor: 3
Correct usage(s):   MOVE [/Y] [drive:][path]filename1[,. . .] destination

/Y – Suppresses prompting to confirm creation of a directory.

[drive:][path]filename1 – Specifies the location and name of the file or files you want to move.

destination Specifies the new location of the file. Destination can consist of a drive letter and colon, a directory name, or a combination. If you are moving only one file, you can also include a filename if you want to rename the file when you move it.

MOVE [drive:][path]dirname1 dirname2
[drive:][path]dirname1 – Specifies the directory you want
to rename.
dirname2 – Specifies the new name of the directory.

General comments: A welcome addition to DOS, normally only provided
until now by batch files with insufficient error checking
for disk free space and so on. Note that If the destination
you specify is an existing file, MOVE replaces that file
with the file you are moving.

MSD

Command type: External.

Official purpose: MSD (Microsoft System Diagnostics) provides detailed
technical information about your computer.

Usefulness: 4

Safety factor: 5

Correct usage: MSD [/I] [/F[drive:][path]filename] [/
P[drive:][path]filename] [/S[drive:][path][filename]]
MSD [/B][/I]
/B – Runs MSD using a black and white color scheme.
/I – Bypasses initial hardware detection.
/F[drive:][path]filename – Requests input and writes an
MSD report to the specified file.
/P[drive:][path]filename – Writes an MSD report to the
specified file without first requesting input.
/S[drive:][path][filename] – Writes a summary MSD
report to the specified file. If no filename is specified,
output is to the screen.

General comments: Yet another useful addition to DOS. Use MSD [/B] [/I] to
examine technical information through the MSD interface.

POWER

Command type: External.

Official purpose: Reduces power used by a laptop computer.

Usefulness: 5

Safety factor: 5

Correct usage: POWER [ADV[:MAX or REG or MIN] or STD or OFF]
ADV[:MAX or REG or MIN] – Reduces power by
monitoring applications and hardware devices. MAX
provides the most power conservation, REG provides
average power conservation, and MIN provides the least
conservation.
STD – Reduces power by monitoring hardware devices.
OFF – Turns off power management.

QBASIC

Command type:	External.
Official purpose:	Starts the MS-DOS QBasic programming environment.
Usefulness:	4
Safety factor:	4
Correct usage:	QBASIC [/B] [/EDITOR] [/G] [/H] [/MBF] [/NOHI] [[/RUN] [drive:][path]filename]

/B – Allows use of a monochrome monitor with a color graphics card.

/EDITOR – Starts the MS-DOS Editor.

/G – Provides the fastest update of a CGA screen.

/H – Displays the maximum number of lines possible for your hardware.

/MBF – Converts the built-in functions MKS$, MKD$, CVS, and CVD to MKSMBF$, MKDMBF$, CVSMBF, and CVDMBF, respectively.

/NOHI – Allows the use of a monitor without high-intensity support.

/RUN – Runs the specified Basic program before displaying it.

[[drive:][path]filename] – Specifies the program file to load or run.

SETVER

Command type:	External.
Official purpose:	Sets the version number that MS-DOS reports to a program.
Usefulness:	5
Safety factor:	3
Correct usage(s):	SETVER [drive:path]

(Displays the current version table)

SETVER [drive:path] filename n.nn

(Adds an entry)

SETVER [drive:path] filename /DELETE [/QUIET]

(Deletes an entry)

[drive:path] – Specifies location of the SETVER.EXE file.

filename – Specifies the filename of the program.

n.nn – Specifies the MS-DOS version to be reported to the program.

/DELETE or /D – Deletes the version-table entry for the specified program.

/QUIET – Hides the message typically displayed during deletion of version-table entry.

General comments:	This is essential for fooling programs that INSIST on working only with earlier versions of DOS that, in fact, the DOS you are running IS a version the program is prepared to work with.

SMARTDRV

Command type:	External.
Official purpose:	Installs and configures the SMARTDrive disk-caching utility.
Usefulness:	3
Safety factor:	3
Correct usage:	SMARTDRV [[drive[+or-]]. . .] [/E:ElementSize] [InitCacheSize][WinCacheSize]] [/B:BufferSize] [/C] [/R] [/L] [/Q] [/S] [/V]

drive – Specifies the drive for which to control caching. You can specify multiple drives.

+ – Enables write-behind caching for the specified drive.

- – Disables all caching for the specified drive.

/E:ElementSize – Specifies how many bytes of information to move at one time.

InitCacheSize – Specifies how many KB of XMS memory to use for the cache.

WinCacheSize – Specifies how many KB of XMS memory to use for the cache when running Windows.

/B:BufferSize – Specifies the size of the read- ahead buffer.

/C – Writes all write-behind information to the hard disk.

/R – Clears the contents of the cache and restarts SMARTDrive.

/L – Loads SMARTDrive into conventional memory.

/Q – Prevents SMARTDrive from displaying status messages when it starts.

/S – Displays additional information about SMARTDrive's status.

/V – Displays SMARTDrive status messages when starting.

General comments:	If you don't notice any major improvement in disk speed with SMARTDRV installed then you may prefer not to use it as it can be disconcerting having your PC reading from and writing to your hard disk at unexpected times. Also any program that reboots your PC just might lose you some data by rebooting before any outgoing data has been written to your disk.

UNDELETE

Command type:	External
Official purpose:	Restores files previously deleted with the DEL command.
Usefulness:	5
Safety factor:	3
Correct usage(s):	UNDELETE [[drive:][path]filename] [/DT or /DS or /DOS]
	UNDELETE [/LIST or /ALL or /PURGE[DRIVE] or /STATUS or /LOAD or /UNLOAD /UNLOAD or /S[DRIVE] or /T[DRIVE]-entrys]]

/LIST – Lists the deleted files available to be recovered.

/ALL – Recovers files without prompting for confirmation.

/DOS – Recovers files listed as deleted by MS-DOS.

/DT – Recovers files protected by Delete Tracker.

/DS – Recovers files protected by Delete Sentry.

/LOAD – Loads Undelete into memory for delete protection.

/UNLOAD – Unloads Undelete from memory.

/PURGE[drive] – Purges all files in the Delete Sentry directory.

/STATUS – Display the protection method in effect for each drive.

/S[drive] – Enables Delete Sentry method of protection.

/T[drive][-entrys] – Enables Delete Tracking method of protection.

General comments: A pretty handy tool this. But remember you can only use it if no new data or program has overwritten the old one(s) since you deleted it/them. You should therefore only treat this command as an emergency operation that can only usually be performed immediately after mistakenly issueing a delete command.

UNFORMAT

Command type: External.

Official purpose: Restores a disk erased by the FORMAT command or restructured by the RECOVER command.

Usefulness: 4

Safety factor: 3

Correct usage(s):   UNFORMAT drive: [/J]

UNFORMAT drive: [/U] [/L] [/TEST] [/P]

UNFORMAT /PARTN [/L]

drive: – Specifies the drive to unformat.

/J – Verifies that the mirror files agree with the system information on the disk.

/U – Unformats without using MIRROR files.

/L – Lists all file and directory names found, or, when used with the

/PARTN – switch, displays current partition tables.

/TEST – Displays information but does not write changes to disk.

/P – Sends output messages to printer connected to LPT1.

/PARTN – Restores disk partition tables.

General comments: This may well get you out of some tricky spots. But don't expect it to work every time!

VSAFE

Command type:	External
Official purpose:	Monitors your computer for viruses and displays a warning when it finds one (or a potential virus- like action).
Usefulness:	5
Safety factor:	5
Correct usage(s):	VSAFE [/option[+ or –] . . .] [/NE] [/NX] [/Ax or /Cx] [/N] [/D] [/U]

option One of the following:

1 – HD low level format warning

2 – Resident warning

3 – General write protect

4 – Check infected files

5 – Boot sector infection warning

6 – Protect hard disk BOOT area

7 – Protect floppy disk BOOT area

8 – Write Protect executable files

/NE – Prevents VSafe from loading in expanded memory.

/NX – Prevents VSafe from loading in extended memory.

/Ax – Defines the VSafe hotkey to be Alt plus the key defined by x.

/Cx – Defines the VSafe hotkey to be Ctrl plus the key defined by x.

/N – Allows VSafe to monitor network drives for possible viruses.

/D – Disables checksum creation.

/U – Unloads VSafe from memory.

CHAPTER 3

BUILDING BETTER BATCH FILES

Batch files are small control files you can write to automate certain procedures. For example, a common use is to set up a batch file to change to a particular directory containing an application you wish to run, and then to load and run that application, possibly passing it any relevant data file names to also be loaded.

You don't need any extra programs to run them as DOS (the Disk Operating System supplied with your PC) will do this for you. In this chapter you will discover the main elements of batch files as well as some very handy tricks.

AN INTRODUCTION TO BATCH FILES

All you need to create a batch file is a word processor or text editor that can read and write ASCII (plain text) files. If you don't have a wordprocessor you could try to get to grips with the text editor EDLIN, as long as you were also given the manuals for your PC. Anyway, once you've found a way of writing text files and saving them to disk, try creating a batch file looking like this:

```
ECHO OFF
CLS
ECHO Hello World
```

Save it to disk with the name TEST.BAT, and then run it by typing:

```
TEST
```

As long as the screen clears and you see the words "Hello World" appear on the screen, then you know everything's working fine.

Next, all you need to know are some of the more common batch file commands and what they do. Then you can start using them in your own batch files. So here are a few to get you started.

The first is ECHO, which is the command that, among other things, places text on the screen. You will frequently see it at the start of batch files, followed by the word OFF, like this:

```
ECHO OFF
```

This tells your PC not to display any text on screen unless you tell it to. If ECHO were left on you would see all the commands as they executed. Entering ECHO followed by some text will cause that text to be displayed on the screen, at the current text location (or cursor position). After being displayed, the cursor then moves to the start of the next line or, if it is already on the bottom line, the screen is scrolled up leaving a blank line at the bottom, where the cursor is then placed.

To get a blank line on your display (the same as moving the cursor down a line without displaying anything) you can use the command:

```
ECHO"
```

Make sure there is no gap between the O and the double quote. This means "Print a blank string and then go to the next line".

To help keep your batch files themselves clear and easy to read, you may enter as many blank lines as you wish. They help to separate various parts of the file and are ignored during execution. On versions 3.XX of DOS and above you can also use the command:

```
@ECHO OFF
```

This means that not even the ECHO OFF command itself is to be displayed (which it will be if the @ isn't used).

Another important command is CLS. For tidy screen displays, you should insert a CLS command before displaying more than a few lines of text. The CLS commands will then clear the screen to black and reset your text cursor to the top-left of the screen.

When you wish to temporarily arrest a batch file's execution, insert a PAUSE command. A string of text similar to "Hit any Key..." will then be displayed and the computer will wait for a key press. You will normally need to use this in places where you ask the user to swap disks or some other task.

To help remind you what a batch file is for and how it works (which you may forget if you don't use it for several months), you can use the REM command. Standing for REMark it tells your PC to ignore all the following text until it gets to the end of the line. An example of a REM statement might be:

```
REM The installation routine starts here.
```

To allow you greater control of batch files you are allowed to pass up to 9 parameters to them, each of which most be prefaced by a % (percent) sign. This means that to load a wordprocessor and accompanying document (for example) you could use a file like this:

```
ECHO OFF
ECHO Running the Wordprocessor

C:\WP\WORDPROC.EXE C:\LETTERS\%1
```

Then, assuming you save this file as WP.BAT, you need only type:

```
WP ARTICLE.DOC
```

And the wordprocessor will load itself from the directory WP, along with the document file ARTICLE.DOC, which is loaded by WORDPROC.EXE from the LETTERS directory.

Just think of the %1 to %9 parameters as equating to the (up to) 9 parameters you can enter, following the name of a program, at the DOS command prompt.

Getting on to more technical details (but essential to know if you are to make the most of batch files), all programs return what is called an error level when they return to DOS or a batch file. Typically it has a value of zero, if the program terminated correctly. Otherwise it could be another value (depending on the program) according to any errors the program encountered. You can quite easily detect the error level like this:

```
ECHO OFF
PROGNAME

IF ERRORLEVEL 3 GOTO ERROR3
IF ERRORLEVEL 2 GOTO ERROR2
IF ERRORLEVEL 1 GOTO ERROR1

ECHO Successful
GOTO END

:ERROR3
ECHO Unsuccessful: Error 3
GOTO END

:ERROR2
ECHO Unsuccessful: Error 2
GOTO END

:ERROR1
ECHO Unsuccessful: Error 1

:END
```

Remember that you should always check for the highest errorlevel first, simply because that's the way DOS likes it.

To allow for branching in batch files you also use the IF command. One example is when you want to check whether any parameters have been passed to a batch file. So, in the case of WP.BAT (mentioned earlier), you could adapt it to check whether a file name has been specified and, if not, remind the user to enter one.

```
ECHO OFF

IF "%1" == "" GOTO ERROR

ECHO Running the Wordprocessor

C:\WP\WORDPROC.EXE C:\LETTERS\%1
GOTO END

:ERROR
ECHO Error in running the Wordprocessor
ECHO No file name was specified.
ECHO"
ECHO Type: WP FILENAME.EXT

:END
```

The double equals '==' should be taken to read like this:

```
IF "%1" is equal to ""
```

because the single equals '=' is used to make assignments such as:

```
SET TMP=C:\WINDOWS\TEMP
```

Any IF statements can be turned completely on their head by placing the NOT key word at the start. So, say you wanted to check that a parameter passed to your batch file was NOT the text string FRED, you could use the following:

```
ECHO OFF

IF NOT "%1" == "FRED" GOTO OK

ECHO Sorry, FRED not accepted.
GOTO END

:OK
ECHO The parameter you passed was %1

:END
```

A particular use of NOT is during installation batch files when it is often used in conjunction with the command EXIST, to check for a previous installation, like this:

```
....
....
IF NOT EXIST "PROGNAME.EXE" GOTO MORE
ECHO Already installed....
GOTO END

:MORE
REM Installation procedure goes here
....
....

:END
```

I know there's quite a bit of information here, but if you try out each of the commands as explained, one at a time, you should quickly get to grips with them all and soon find yourself writing batch files for all manner of purposes, as and when you need them.

CUSTOMISING THE "PAUSE" MESSAGE

Do you ever get annoyed with the DOS prompts "Hit a key" or "Strike a key"?. Well you can change this message from inside batch files like this:

```
....
....
ECHO Press [Space] to continue
ECHO or [CTRL][C] to finish...
PAUSE >NUL
....
....
```

It works by redirecting the output from PAUSE to the Null device, allowing the ECHO lines to be displayed while still making use of PAUSE's keyboard wait.

FINDING SUBDIRECTORIES

Here is a relatively simple batch file which allows you to check for the existence of subdirectories. It relies on the fact that DOS makes use of special "logical" files – known as devices – such as PRN, NUL and CON. For example, by using the batch file command:

```
IF EXIST \TESTDIR\PRN
```

you can determine whether a given directory already exists. As a further example, the following batch file can avoid the "Unable to create directory" message that appears when you try to create a directory that already exists:

```
ECHO OFF
REM MDPLUS.BAT

IF "%1" == "" GOTO INVALID

IF EXIST %1\PRN GOTO END

REM If we got here the directory doesn't exist
REM So we create it.

MD %1
GOTO END

:INVALID

ECHO USE: MDPLUS dirname
ECHO"

:END
```

MORE ON FINDING SUBDIRECTORIES

This short method is similar to using ATTRIB with the /S switch for finding files, except that it uses TREE to find subdirectories. The output from TREE is passed to FIND, which then list the full path names of any matching directories:

```
ECHO OFF
TREE |FIND "%1"
```

To use the command, first save it as DIRFIND.BAT (or DF.BAT, to save typing) and then type:

```
DF WORD
```

to find all directories called WORD anywhere on your disk.

BLANK ECHO LINES

Blank lines in batch files are easy when you know how, but it might surprise you that no command exists within the batch language to do this small but important task.

How many times have you designed an effective batch file front-end to your favourite application or utility, only to find that each ECHO line has to be pushed up against the previous one, with no spaces in between? Installation routines especially suffer from this problem, and as a result software authors usually resort, quite unnecessarily, to writing a program in some other language just to get the on-screen presentation acceptable.

It's strange that the programmers at Microsoft didn't make it easy for people to add blank lines to their batch files, although many people have come up with solutions that work to some extent or other and until recently, one of the most popular ways of spacing out the ECHO lines in a batch file was with the line:

```
ECHO.
```

This works fine with most versions of DOS, but it isn't foolproof and the fullstop sometimes is displayed by some versions of DOS. However, the line:

```
ECHO"
```

seems to work with any version of DOS. Don't forget to place the double-quote immediately after the word ECHO, or it will drop down to the next line.

DELETING WITH EXCEPTIONS

This batch file deletes all the files in a directory other than those specified. It works by first setting the read-only attributes of all the specified filenames (which can include wildcards). It then deletes all those that remain, and finally resets the read-only files back to read-write.

The 'ECHO Y | DEL *.* >NUL'' is a sneaky way of passing the keystroke Y to the DEL command, and uses >NUL to ensure that output doesn't go to the screen.

```
ECHO OFF
IF NOT "%1"=="" GOTO LOOP
ECHO TYPE: DELBUT filename.ext filename.ext (etc...)
GOTO END
:LOOP
ATTRIB %1 +R
SHIFT
IF NOT "%1"=="" GOTO LOOP
ECHO Y | DEL *.* >NUL
ATTRIB *.* -r
:END
```

Save it as DELBUT.BAT to follow this example below, which deletes all non-DOC files from current directory.

```
DELBUT *.DOC
```

TYPING MULTIPLE FILES TO SCREEN

This short batch file allows TYPE to work with wildcards. It uses the FOR command to check the parameter %1, and if it contains wildcards it passes each matching file to the DO TYPE command phrase:

```
ECHO OFF
FOR %%a in (%1) DO TYPE %%a %2 %3 %4 %5 %6 %7 %8 %9
```

USING WILDCARDS WITH ANY PROGRAM

This extremely powerful and yet deceptively simple batch file utility allows wildcards to be used with any program or DOS command you like. You can apply wildcards to file-handling utilities which previously demanded that you repeat the entire command for each file to be processed.

It extends the FOR idea used in the multiple TYPE batch file utility (elsewhere in this chapter) a bit further, replacing the command phrase DO TYPE with DO %1.

This simple alteration allows the user to specify which command is to be multiply-executed, so long as the syntax of the original command is left unchanged. Here is the complete listing:

```
ECHO OFF
IF "%1" == "" GOTO HELP
IF "%2" == "" GOTO HELP
FOR %%a IN (%2) DO %1 %%a %3 %4 %5 %6 %7 %8 %9
GOTO END
:HELP
ECHO TYPE: MULTI DOSCOMMAND FILENAME.EXT
:END
ECHO
```

As an example, suppose you wanted to delete all directories from the root which had the extension .TMP. If you have saved this batch file as MULTI.BAT, the command would be:

```
MULTI RD \*.TMP
```

This is another example of how a simple trick can accomplish the same as an expensive third-party utility.

SINGLE-LETTER DIRECTORY PATHNAMES

If you insert the command LASTDRIVE=Z in your CONFIG.SYS file you can give many of your most frequently-used directory pathnames a single-letter drivename, using the SUBST command.

The following batch file shows you how you might like to add some similar lines to your AUTOEXEC.BAT file, once you've tested them out:

```
SUBST G: C:\GAMES
SUBST M: C:\MSDOS
SUBST S: C:\WORK\SPRDSHT
SUBST W: C:\WORKS\WORDPROC
```

Thereafter you can change to a specified directory such as C:\WORKS\WORDPROC just by typing:

```
W:
```

FOOLING PROGRAMS INTO USING ANOTHER DRIVE

As explained in the Single-letter Directory Pathnames tip (elsewhere in this chapter), SUBST is a powerful DOS command. Used another way it can fool disks that insist on being run from a particular drive to run from another.

The following batch file tells DOS that drives A: and B: are, to all intents and purposes, identical. This is invaluable for people who have Amstrad or Dell PCs – not to mention the growing army of clones – which have drive A: as the 3.5" drive and B: is 5.25".

A lot of software still comes on 5.25" disks, and for some unknown reason the installation programs are sometimes hard-wired to look on drive A: for the program files.

Type in this program, save it as FAKEB.BAT (or whatever), and run it whenever you need to pull the wool over some errant piece of software.

```
ECHO OFF
REM Sets drive A to drive B.
ECHO Insert a disk in drive B: then press Return...
PAUSE >NUL
B:
SUBST A: B:\
ECHO Drives A: and B: are now identical
```

The following batch file changes everything back to normal afterwards:

```
ECHO OFF
REM Sets drive A to normal.
ECHO Insert a disk in drive B: then press Return...
PAUSE >NUL
B:
SUBST A: /d
ECHO Drives A: and B: are restored to normal
```

UNPROMPTED DELETION

This handy little line is useful for quickly deleting large numbers of files, without having to sit at the keyboard waiting for the inevitable "Are you sure?" prompt. After all, the time could be much better spent putting the kettle on.

Type in the listing and save it as QD.BAT (for Quick Delete) or something that doesn't clash with another utility. Then type:

```
QD filename
```

to let it loose on your unwanted files. Here is the listing:

```
ECHO OFF
ECHO Y | DEL %1 >NUL
```

CAUTION: Wildcards are allowed, so be very careful not to wipe out your entire root directory – you have been warned.

BATCH FILE SUBROUTINES

Versions of MS-DOS from 3.3 upward allow the use of the command CALL in batch files to force the command processor to stop and save where it is, load and run another batch file, then re-load and continue running the original.

Earlier versions of DOS have this capability too – well, sort of; you can do it, but a new copy of COMMAND.COM has to be loaded along with the batch file you want to call – taking up around 40k or more. This is how to do it:

```
COMMAND filename /c
```

Where filename is the name of the batch file you want to load. It is possible to run out of memory quite quickly using this method, especially if you are calling batch files several levels deep – but in general there's no real need to call more than two files in a row.

MORE BATCH FILE SUBROUTINES

Here is another way to call one batch file from within another, and it doesn't need another copy of COMMAND.COM to be loaded as well. However, it is restricted to calling only one batch file "deep" at a time.

If you look at the following batch file you will see that the program begins by switching ECHO off and clearing the screen. The temporary variable TEMP is then created and initialised to contain the text string MAIN1 which is a return address or label, to which a called subroutine will jump on completion of execution. Next the subroutine DISPLAY1 is called, which clears the screen and displays some information.

```
ECHO OFF
CLS

SET TEMP=MAIN1
GOTO DISPLAY1

:MAIN1
PAUSE
SET TEMP=END
GOTO DISPLAY2

:DISPLAY1
CLS
ECHO Batch file subroutines
ECHO"
GOTO %TEMP%

:DISPLAY2
CLS
ECHO Press [Ctrl][C] to quit.
ECHO"
GOTO %TEMP%

:END
SET TEMP=
ECHO:
```

When program execution reaches one of the lines like this:

```
GOTO %TEMP%
```

at the end of each subroutine, execution will return to the label name stored in TEMP, ready to go onto the next line, just as if a subroutine had been called. In this example program execution will now jump to location MAIN1 where a PAUSE command is issued.

After the user has pressed a key to continue, the subroutine DISPLAY2 is then called, and execution jumps to END, where the batch file terminates.

PROMPTLESS DATE/TIME DISPLAY

The DATE and TIME commands sometimes seem rather crude, with their continual prompting. It would be nice just to be able to check the date or time occasionally...

This batch file utility does just that. Here, the file must be saved as DT.BAT, because it is "piped" back into itself when run.

The first line should be created by entering no text followed by pressing [Return], so that the blank line sends a carriage return to DATE and TIME; the remaining characters in the file are then ignored, which prevents them from being accepted as inputs to DATE and TIME.

```
(THIS LINE MUST BE LEFT BLANK)
ECHO OFF
REM There must be a blank line before the
REM first ECHO OFF.
REM Type in & save this file as DT.BAT.
DATE <DT.BAT
TIME <DT.BAT
```

FILE MOVER

Many other operating systems offer a command called MOVE or MV, the purpose of which is to move files around a disk from one place to another, deleting the original so that only the one copy is ever in existence at one time.

DOS isn't equipped to do this; there isn't even a switch on the COPY command which says "Delete original afterwards", which is a great pity. Instead you have to clean up after COPY, which is time-consuming and can leave unnoticed duplicated scattered around our disks.

The batch file utility MOVE.BAT gets around this by copying the specified file(s), and then deleting the originals using a built-in promptless delete utility (See Unprompted Deletion elsewhere in this chapter).

CAUTION: This routine can be dangerous as it doesn't check whether the files have been correctly copied before deleting the originals.

```
ECHO OFF
IF "%1" == "" GOTO HELP
COPY %1 %2
ECHO Y | DEL %1 >NUL
GOTO END
:HELP
ECHO TYPE: MOVE FILENAME.EXT FILENAME.EXT
:END
```

program type:

```
Move FILENAME.EXT FILENAME.EXT
```

FAST FORMATTER

RECOVER is supposed to help you recover data on corrupt disks. In fact, RECOVER is potentially extremely dangerous as it removes entire directory structures at a stroke, turning them into files with the extension REC. So a much better use of RECOVER is as a quick'n'dirty disk wiper, for use when you haven't got time to delete all the files by hand or re-format a disk. Use it with caution:

```
ECHO OFF
ECHO A | RECOVER %1 >NUL
DEL %1*.REC
```

To use the utility above, type it in and save it as QF.BAT. Then type the following command to quickly clean all information from used disks:

```
QF drive:
```

Note: This utility goes like lightening, but only on disks which already contain data. Unformatted disks still require the use of FORMAT.

CHKDSK FILE FINDER

Here is another file finding utility, this time making use of the CHKDSK command to do the dirty work as it searches the whole disk, highlighting any matching files it finds. It uses CHKDSK with the /v parameter to make a list of all the files on the disk specified in parameter %1. It then sorts through this list removing any entries which are just names of directories, and sorts through the resulting filenames to remove any entries which don't contain the search string, and then displays all the matching entries.

```
ECHO off
REM Save this as FF.BAT to a directory in your path
ECHO n | chkdsk %1 /v >looking3.$ff
FIND /v "Directory" looking3 >looking2.$ff
FIND /v "\%2\" looking2 >looking.$ff
FIND "\%2" looking.$ff
DEL looking*.$ff
```

Type it this listing and save it as FF.BAT. To use it, type:

```
FF DRIVE: SEARCH
```

where DRIVE: is the drive in which to search, and SEARCH is the filename or part of filename to search for (remember that the search string must be typed in using upper case). The temporary "looking" files have the extension $FF because ⸍ highly unlikely that any other program would use that extension, and it also me⸍⸍⸗ that all three files can be removed using a single DEL *.$FF. It may be a little slow, but it works and you can pay money for programs that do the same thing.

FAST LOADER

How's this for a handy batch file – it lets you run any program stored in a subdirectory of the same name and is only two lines long, except for the REM and ECHO OFF:

```
ECHO OFF
REM RUN.BAT
CD \%1
%1 %2
```

So if you have any applications where the EXE file is the same name as the directory in which it lives – like Protext – and you haven't got around to putting them in your PATH, this mini-utility can save you some time. Type RUN PROTEXT and the batch file will change to the directory \PROTEXT and run the program PROTEXT.EXE – all in one fell swoop. The %2 parameter allows you to pass parameters to the program you are running, like this:

```
RUN PROTEXT \AUTOEXEC.BAT
```

which will start Protext with AUTOEXEC.BAT ready-loaded.

LISTING OUT BATCH FILES

If you, like many of us, share the habit of creating lots of little batch files to do every job under the sun – and then forget what they're called – you might like to try these two batch files out, which display the contents of each one as a reminder. Type in the first listing and save it as DISP.BAT:

```
ECHO OFF
REM DISP.BAT
FOR %%F IN (*.BAT) DO COMMAND /C READ %%F
```

Note: For DOS 3.3 and above you can replace the last line with:

```
FOR %%F IN (*.BAT) DO CALL READ %%F
```

Now type in this listing and save it as READ.BAT:

```
ECHO OFF
REM READ.BAT
CLS
ECHO This is %1
TYPE %1 |MORE
```

```
PAUSE
```

To find out what batch files you have on your hard disk, go to your batch file directory and type:

```
DISP
```

Don't try to improve on DISP.BAT by replacing the call to the second batch file with simply:

```
DO TYPE %%F |MORE
```

You might think that this would save on the extra disk accessing and speed things up because you'd then only need to use the first batch file. But you can't then get each batch file's name to be displayed before the file itself is listed – the whole point of the exercise!

FASTER TYPE COMMAND

This short batch file utility allows you to list files to the screen by typing only part of their name:

```
ECHO OFF
CLS
COPY %1*.* CON
```

If you save the file as SHOW.BAT you can use it to display files to the screen more quickly and easily than you can with TYPE. For example, to see your AUTOEXEC.BAT file from another directory you would normally have to enter the following, or similar, TYPE command:

```
TYPE \AUTOEXEC.BAT
```

But with SHOW, all you need to do is type:

```
SHOW \AU
```

And all the files that start with the letters AU in your root directory will be displayed. To make it even faster you could save the file as S.BAT.

PROTECTING IMPORTANT FILES

If you've ever inadvertently deleted your AUTOEXEC.BAT or CONFIG.SYS files while editing them, you'll appreciate the following batch file utility, EDIT. It's a safety-buffer between you and your word processor, and if you get into the habit of using it to edit your important configuration files (and any other crucial text files) then you'll increase the integrity of your system without any of the usual inconvenience.

Type in the listing and save it as EDIT.BAT, but note that if you already have an editor with the same name – EXE or COM – you'll have to use something else like E.BAT.

```
ECHO OFF
IF "%1"=="" GOTO SYNTAX
ATTRIB -R %1
PROTEXT %1
ATTRIB +R %1
DEL *.BAK
GOTO DONE

:SYNTAX
ECHO"
ECHO SYNTAX: EDIT FILENAME

:DONE

ECHO"
```

What EDIT does is to take the first parameter, which is the file to be edited, and remove its read-only attribute, if set. Then a word processor (in this instance PROTEXT) is called up and passed the file's name.

When you exit from the word processor, control returns to the batch file where the file's read-only attribute is set, so that DOS will not allow it to be deleted. Finally, any .BAK files are deleted – but you could remove this line if it's not needed, or you simply don't want it. To use EDIT, just type the following:

```
EDIT CONFIG.SYS
```

READING VOLUME LABELS FROM BATCH FILES

Here is an easy way of reading volume labels from within a batch file without resorting to complicated and dangerous (if you don't know what you're doing) DEBUG scripts. The most obvious use for such a technique is during software installation, when you want to be sure that the user has in fact inserted the correct disc in the drive.

Type in this listing and save it as CHEKDISK.BAT:

```
ECHO | MORE | VOL A: >VOLLABEL.BAT
VOLLABEL
```

It works like this. If you redirect the text produced by VOL to a batch file, with this command:

```
OLLABEL.BAT
```

Then you end up with a file called VOLLABEL.BAT containing – depending on the DOS version – something like the following:

```
Volume in drive A is TESTVOL
Volume Serial Number is 302E-0FF1
```

If – on the face of it, rather stupidly – you now run this file, the first thing DOS does is take the first word of the file as a program name and try to run it. In this case it will try and run a program called VOLUME, passing the rest of the text to it as parameters.

This is in fact just what we want! All we need now is a batch file called VOLUME.BAT, looking like this:

```
:DISKLOOP
IF "%5" == "DISK_1" GOTO CORRECT_DISK
ECHO PLEASE INSERT DISK 1
PAUSE
GOTO DISKLOOP

:CORRECT_DISK

...
```

To prepare your disk you should give it the same volume label as in the batch file VOLUME.BAT – in this case DISK_1 – and once you've run CHEKDISK the batch program VOLUME will sit in a loop until you insert the correct disk. Simple!

Note that if you use more than one disk in your installation routine you'll also need lots of "VOLUME.BAT" files, each called different names – for example VOL1.BAT, VOL2.BAT and so on – and each containing a check for a different volume label – for example DISK_1, DISK_2 and so on. Just before you need to make the next disk check, rename the relevant VOLx.BAT file to VOLUME.BAT – but don't forget to rename it back afterwards!

As a bonus the drive name is passed to %3, which will probably come in handy. But note that you will have to use volume labels made up of a single word without spaces for this to work. If you want spaces, for example to have the name DISK 1, you should use and underline character instead of the space.

UNRAVELLING FILES

Have you ever managed to copy a set of files on top of another and spent ages unpicking the mess? You know the sort of thing; you craftily type something along the lines of:

```
COPY A:\
```

to re-install your DOS directory from the master disk. Except you were running windows just beforehand and forgot to change directories first – and now your windows directory is chock-full of strange and unwelcome EXE and COM files. So how do you separate the two again, when both directories have loads of those peculiar files with strange names, and you don't know for the life of you what came from where?

Well, here's a batch file that will do the job for you, called TAKEAWAY.BAT:

```
ECHO OFF
REM TAKEAWAY.BAT
FOR %%1 in (*.*) DO DEL C:%%I
```

So, in this example, you have copied all the files from a disk in drive A: into your Windows directory on drive C:. Make sure you are in the cluttered directory, and then log on to drive A:. Now type:

```
TAKEAWAY
```

Then all the files in your Windows directory that match those on the disk in drive A: will be deleted.

CHAPTER 4

CONFIGURING YOUR PC

In order to obtain the maximum performance from your PC it is necessary to understand a little about how your PC can be configured and exactly what options are open to you. To a new PC user this can appear somewhat daunting but it needn't be. Configuring usually just requires slightly modifying one or two text files using a text editor or word processor and can be done in a minute or two.

This chapter covers many of the more useful ways you can configure your PC and you should find a few tips in it that will help you get the maximum performance from your PC.

FIGURING OUT CONFIG.SYS

Many problems can be sorted out by correcting mistakes in a user's CONFIG.SYS files. The reason seems to be that many manuals do not explain this aspect of the PC's software thoroughly enough and often are misleading. So here is a comprehensive summary of all the CONFIG.SYS commands available to you and how to use them.

CONFIG.SYS is a text file which resides in the ROOT (startup) directory. When you turn your PC on it looks for this file and, if it finds it, follows the commands contained in it. There are only a few of them and it doesn't take long to discover what they are and what they can do.

Each command is entered into CONFIG.SYS on its own line and the commands are followed in the order they appear. Unlike a program, no branching to other parts of the file is allowed. A typical CONFIG.SYS file might look like this:

```
FILES=30
BUFFERS=20
DEVICE=c:\dos\ramdrive.sys 384 512 64 /e
COUNTRY=044,437,c:\dos\country.sys
```

Here it is telling the PC that up to 30 files should be allowed open at any one time (a pretty standard requirement), that 20 buffers of 512 character each should be available for temporary data storage during file accesses, that a ram drive of 384K should be created using extended memory above the PC's standard 640K area (a ram drive being an area of RAM that is treated just like a floppy disk by DOS, but is much, much faster to use), and that the country of use is the United Kingdom (area telephone dialling code 44), and where all the country dependant information, such as the currency symbol and so on is to be found.

So, here are the commands in detail:

BREAK   Sets [Ctrl][C] checking
Syntax   BREAK=on
                   or
                   BREAK=off

By default BREAK is on but, depending on the program you are running, you may wish to use [Ctrl][C] to stop an activity. Normally DOS checks whether you have pressed [Ctrl][C] only when reading from the keyboard or writing to the screen or printer. Setting BREAK to on extends this checking to other functions such as disk reading and writing.

BUFFERS   Sets the number of sector buffers
Syntax   BUFFERS=x

The parameter x is the number of disk buffers to allocate, between 2 and 255. The default is 2 for a Base system, 10 for a system with under 512K of RAM and 15 for a PC with more than 512K or RAM. A disk buffer is a block of memory that DOS uses to temporarily store data during disk reading and writing operations.

For Applications such as wordprocessors and spreadsheets a number of about 15-20 will be sufficient. If you will be using software that opens a lot of files like a DTP program you should consider setting BUFFERS to about 30. But remember, the more buffers allocated, the more system RAM they take up as each buffer requires 512 bytes. 30 buffers will therefore take up 15 Kbytes of RAM.

COUNTRY   Allows for international times, dates and currencies
Syntax   COUNTRY=xxx[,[yyy][,[drive:]filename]]

Here, xxx is the country code which is simply the international dialling code. In the case of the UK it should be 044. yyy is the code page (the character set required. The current selectable pages are 437 for the US and Canada, 850 for multi-lingual (this includes all the characters for most European, North and South American languages), 860 for Portugal, 863 for France and French Canada and 865 for Nordic. I actually use 437 without any problems, even though it is for the US and Canada.

drive: and filename refer to a file containing further country-specific information. Unless specified otherwise, US settings are assumed by default. The file is usually called COUNTRY.SYS and resides in your DOS directory. For your interest, here's what my COUNTRY line looks like:

```
COUNTRY=044,437,C:\DOS\COUNTRY.SYS
```

DEVICE   Installs a device driver in the system
Syntax   DEVICE=[drive:][path]filename[argument]

There are various installable devices supplied with DOS, including ANSI.SYS, and RAMDRIVE.SYS. Also items of hardware such as mice sometimes have to be installed using a device driver.

ANSI.SYS offers extensive control over the way your PC's screen and keyboard are handled, including controlling colours and defining keyboard macros. To install ANSI.SYS use the command:

```
DEVICE=C:\DOS\ANSI.SYS
```

Of course, change the path name if ANSI.SYS is stored somewhere else. RAMDRIVE.SYS is useful for single-disk PCs as you can copy COMMAND.COM into a RAM drive so that you don't have to keeps swapping disks every time the system wants to make use of COMMAND.COM. You can also get the (usually supplied) extra 384K of RAM on ATs and turn that into a RAM disk. To set up a RAM disk in normal memory, type:

```
DEVICE=C:\DOS\RAMDRIVE.SYS 384 512 64
```

The first number, 384, is the number of kilobytes of RAM to give to the RAM disk. If you simply want to make room for COMMAND.COM, then about 26k should be sufficient. The second number, 512, is the number of bytes in a sector. Acceptable values are 128, 256, 512 and 1024 bytes. The third number, 64, is the number of entries to be allowed in the root directory. The default is 64, the minimum, 4 and the maximum 1024.

If you have an AT and wish to convert your 384K of extended memory into a RAM disk simply add the switch /e to the end of the above line.

DRIVPARM   Defines the parameters for block devices
Syntax   DRIVPARM=/d:number [/c][/f:factor] [/h:heads]
                   [/n][/s:sectors][/t:tracks]

DRIVPARM allows you to define parameters for block devices such as floppy disks, overriding the original settings. This command is very useful for PCs with problems recognising the types of drives fitted, particularly likely after adding a new drive to the system.

If for any reason, when you enter the DRIVPARM command into your CONFIG.SYS file, it throws up a syntax error, it could be that you have one of the versions of DOS that require a slightly modified from of the command. Instead of just entering DRIVPARM, add ^A^A^A to the end of the command. (That is, hold down the [Ctrl] key and press [A] three times). If your word processor doesn't allow direct entry of control codes into files you will have to edit your CONFIG.SYS file using EDLIN or a similar editor.

The switches available are: /d: the physical drive number between 0 and 255, where 0 is A, 1 is B and so on. The /c sets drive door change-line checking, that means that if the door is not shut the PC will assume there is no disk in the drive.

The /f: switch can have one of several values out of the following, depending on the type of drive and its capacity:

0 = 160/180 or 320/260 Kbytes
1 = 1.2 Mbytes
2 = 720 Kbytes (3.5")
3 = 8" single density
4 = 8" double density
5 = Hard disk
6 = Tape drive
7 = 1.44 Mbytes (3.5")

If you don't specify the /f: switch a default of 720K, 3.5" disk is assumed. The remaining four switches are: /h: which is the maximum head number between 1 and 99. The default is 2. /n specifies a non-removable device, such as a hard disk. /s is the number of sectors per track between 1 and 99. The default is 9. /t is the number of tracks per side between 1 and 999.

FCBS   Specifies the number of File Control Blocks
Syntax   FCBS=x,y

Some older applications require you to use File Control Blocks instead of the more common File Handles. You should only need to use this command if an application requires you to do so. x is the number of files that File Control Blocks can open at any one time, and y is the number of files opened by FCBs that DOS cannot automatically close. The default is 4,0. To open up to four files and protect the first two from being closed you would use the following line:

FCBS=4,2

FILES   Sets the number of files that can be opened
Syntax   FILES=x

Here x is the number of files that can be opened at any one time by the system in the range 8 to 255. The default is 8.

LASTDRIVE   Sets the maximum number of drives you may have
Syntax   LASTDRIVE=x

The x represents the last drive that the system is allowed to access. At start up the system recognises up to five drives on your system. If you have more, either because you are on a network or intend to use the SUBST command to create single drive letter substitutions for longer path names, then you will have to tell the system the name of the last drive you will be using. Generally, to avoid having to change this command in the future, allowing access to all 26 possible drives, I would recommend keeping the following line in your CONFIG.SYS file:

`LASTDRIVE=Z`

SHELL   Begins execution of the shell from a specific file
Syntax   SHELL=[drive:][path]filename

This tells the system the name and whereabouts of the command processor to use. Generally it will be COMMAND.COM which, without this command, should be in your root directory in order for the system to find it. If you want your PC to use another command processor or you simply wish to move COMMAND.COM out of the root directory and have it load from elsewhere, the SHELL command is the way to do it. Incidentally, 4DOS, the powerful Shareware replacement for the standard command processor is called in exactly this manner.

STACKS   Supports the dynamic use of data stacks
Syntax   STACKS=n,s

n is the number of stacks to create and s is the size to allocate to each. When there is a hardware interrupt, DOS allocates one stack from the n specified. If STACKS is set to 0,0 DOS will not switch stacks at interrupt time. The default for IBM PC, XT and compatible machines is 0,0 while for ATs and all others it is 9,128. To allocate four stacks of 256 bytes each for hardware interrupt handling, you would use:

`STACKS=4,256`

ALL THE CONFIG.SYS COMMANDS

COMMAND	ACTION
BREAK	Sets [Ctrl][C] checking
BUFFERS	Sets the number of sector buffers
COUNTRY	Allows for international times, dates and currencies
DEVICE	Installs a device driver in the system
DRIVPARM	Defines the parameters for block devices
FCBS	Specifies the number of File Control Blocks
FILES	Sets the number of files that can be opened
LASTDRIVE	Sets the maximum number of drives you may have
SHELL	Begins execution of the shell from a specific file
STACKS	Supports the dynamic use of data stacks

THE COUNTRY CONFIGURATIONS

(The date and time used is the 1st of April 1994 at 3:42pm)

COUNTRY/LANGUAGE	CODE	DATE FORMAT	TIME FORMAT
United States	001	4-01-1994	15:42:00.00
French-Canadian	002	1994-04-01	15:42:00,00
Latin America	003	01/04/1994	15:42:00.00
Netherlands	031	01-04-1994	15:42:00,00
Belgium	032	01/04/1994	15:42:00,00
France	033	01/04/1994	15:42:00,00
Spain	034	01/04/1994	15:42:00,00
Italy	039	01/04/1994	15:42:00,00
Switzerland	041	01.04.1994	15.42.00.00
United Kingdom	044	01-04-1994	15:42:00.00
Denmark	045	01/04/1994	15.42.00.00
Sweden	046	1994-04-01	15.42.00,00
Norway	047	01/04/1994	15.42.00,00
Germany	049	01.04.1994	15.42.00,00
English (Int.)	061	01-04-1994	15:42:00.00
Portugal	351	01/04/1994	15:42:00,00
Finland	358	01.04.1994	15.42.00,00
Arabic	785	01/04/1994	15:42:00,00
Israel	972	01 04 1994	15:42:00.00

MULTIPLE BOOTUPS

Many people use their PCs with both DOS and Windows and some memory-hungry programs require you to boot up without any TSRs loaded and it can be quite annoying, not to say time consuming, to edit your CONFIG.SYS and AUTO-EXEC.BAT files each time you need to boot up a new configuration. There are programs you can get that allow you to store several types of configuration and simply select the one you want at boot up. But they're not at all necessary as it's really easy to create the same type of system using batch files and a simple DEBUG script (for rebooting your PC). So, assuming you use three main types of configuration, here's what you do. First of all, type in the following DEBUG script into a word processor and save it as ASCII using the file name RESET.

```
A
XOR AX,AX
MOV DS,AX
MOV BX,472
MOV WORD PTR [BX],1234
JMP FFFF:0000

RCX
10
NRESET.COM
W
Q
```

Remember to just press [Return] where you see the blank line following the JMP FFFF:0000 command.

```
DEBUG <RESET
```

And a file called RESET.COM will be created. Then, once created, you should copy RESET.COM to a directory mentioned in your path, such as UTILS. Having done that you will need to create three AUTOEXEC files and three CONFIG files, each one ending with the extension MB1, MB2 or MB3. Here's an AUTOEXEC.MB1 which you can use for DOS applications when memory is not too tight and it is alright to load in the FRIDAY pop-up program.

```
ECHO off
REM AUTOEXEC.MB1
\DOS\MOUSE /s52 >NUL
\DOS\KEYB UK,437,c:\DOS\KEYBOARD.SYS
\FRIDAY\FRIDAY x C4T S2400 T50
PATH C:\;C:\DOS;C:\BATCH;C:\UTILS;C:\TC\BIN;C:\NU;C:\GAMES;
PROMPT $p $t$h$h$h$h$h$h$g
SET TMP=C:\TEMP
```

For convenience you could store all of these files in a directory called BATCH which is mentioned in the PATH statements so that files in it can be easily accessed. Next is AUTOEXEC.MB2 which is also for DOS but uses up a bare minimum of system RAM:

```
ECHO OFF
REM AUTOEXEC.MB2
\DOS\KEYB UK,437,C:\DOS\KEYBOARD.SYS
PATH C:\;C:\DOS;C:\BATCH;C:\UTILS;C:\TC\BIN;C:\NU;
PROMPT $p $t$h$h$h$h$h$h$g
```

And finally, this is AUTOEXEC.MB3, especially configured for running WINDOWS:

```
ECHO OFF
\DOS\KEYB UK,437,c:\DOS\KEYBOARD.SYS
PATH C:\WINDOWS;C:\;C:\DOS;C:\BATCH;
PROMPT $P $T$H$H$H$H$H$H$G
SET TEMP=C:\TEMP
WIN
```

Next you need the three CONFIG files. Here is CONFIG.MB1:

```
LASTDRIVE=Z
FILES=30
BUFFERS=20
DEVICE=c:\DOS\RAMDRIVE.SYS 384 512 64 /E
COUNTRY=044,437,C:\DOS\COUNTRY.SYS
```

This is CONFIG.MB2:

```
FILES=20
BUFFERS=10
DEVICE=C:\DOS\RAMDRIVE.SYS 384 512 64 /E
COUNTRY=044,437,C:\DOS\COUNTRY.SYS
```

And here's CONFIG.MB3:

```
FILES=30
BUFFERS=20
DEVICE=C:\HIMEM.SYS
DEVICE=C:\WINDOWS\EGA.SYS
COUNTRY=044,437,C:\DOS\COUNTRY.SYS
```

Now all that remains is to write a batch file to process the rebooting process, like this:

```
ECHO OFF
REM REBOOT.BAT

IF "%1"=="" GOTO ERROR

IF "%1"=="MB1" GOTO MB1
IF "%1"=="mb1" GOTO MB1

IF "%1"=="MB2" GOTO MB2
IF "%1"=="mb2" GOTO MB2

IF "%1"=="MB3" GOTO MB3
IF "%1"=="mb3" GOTO MB3

GOTO ERROR

:MB1

COPY C:\BATCH\AUTOEXEC.MB1 C:\AUTOEXEC.BAT >NUL
COPY C:\BATCH\CONFIG.MB1 C:\CONFIG.SYS >NUL
GOTO DONE

:MB2

COPY C:\BATCH\AUTOEXEC.MB2 C:\AUTOEXEC.BAT >NUL
COPY C:\BATCH\CONFIG.MB2 C:\CONFIG.SYS >NUL
GOTO DONE

:MB3

COPY C:\BATCH\AUTOEXEC.MB3 C:\AUTOEXEC.BAT >NUL
COPY C:\BATCH\CONFIG.MB3 C:\CONFIG.SYS >NUL

:DONE

RESET

:ERROR

ECHO TYPE: REBOOT MB1, MB2 or MB3
```

Save this batch file as REBOOT.BAT and make sure that it is in a directory mentioned in your path, such as BATCH then, when you want to swap configurations, simply type one of the following lines:

```
REBOOT MB1
REBOOT MB2
REBOOT MB3
```

Be careful that you have saved all your data and that you don't call up REBOOT.BAT from inside a command shell of an application which has an unsaved file, or it will be lost during the boot process. For extra security you could add the following four lines before the RESET command in REBOOT.BAT to ask for a confirming key press:

```
ECHO WARNING - REBOOTING!
ECHO PRESS [Ctrl][C] to abort or
ECHO any other key to continue...
PAUSE >NUL
```

UNDOCUMENTED SWITCH

There is an undocumented switch (/F) you can use with the SHELL command in CONFIG.SYS using DOS 3.3. Try adding the line:

```
SHELL=\COMMAND.COM /P /F
```

to your CONFIG.SYS file, then "accidentally" log on to a floppy drive with no disk inserted and see what happens. At a guess the switch is there for testing purposes, but if you've ever had any "Drive not ready" type errors, and sat in front of the keyboard repeatedly bashing the [F] key to try to get back to what you were doing, then you might well find this very useful.

In tests it appears to keep issuing [F] keystrokes for you until it returns, and it does so quickly. However, it does appear to only work with DOS 3.3 but, still, it might be worth trying it out on your version of DOS. And, because it is undocumented, make sure you don't edit any valuable files while you test it, unless you've backed them up first.

AT YOUR COMMAND

If you use a single floppy PC then a handy way to stop DOS from continually requesting you to insert your disk with COMMAND.COM is to create a ram drive and copy COMMAND.COM into it. Here's what you should add to your CONFIG.SYS file:

```
DEVICE=RAMDRIVE.SYS 24 128 2
```

This creates a small, 24k ram drive, large enough for DOS 3.21 (28k is needed for DOS 3.3). And here are the changes you should make to your AUTOEXEC.BAT file:

```
COPY COMMAND.COM C:
SET COMSPEC=C:\COMMAND.COM
```

You should note, however, that when a ram disk is installed it may not appear as drive C: – it depends on how many other drives you have. If in doubt, watch the screen when you re-boot and you will see a message similar to this:

```
Microsoft RAMDrive version x.xx Virtual disk C:
```

Even non-Microsoft virtual disk device drivers should tell you the drive letter assigned to the new ram disk. If your screen clears during re-boot just after the ram disk is loaded, press the Pause button to catch the message before it disappears – any other key unfreezes the PC and resumes re-booting.

LOCKED OUT OF DOS

Whenever you change your AUTOEXEC.BAT or CONFIG.SYS files you risk getting into boot loading problems because, if they are present on the device from which the boot-up started, those two files are used to control how your PC sets itself up. To prevent this happening you should always have a system disk available (with no AUTOEXEC.BAT and no CONFIG.SYS) so that you can boot up from your A: drive.

This will give you a very primitive startup with a US keyboard rather than UK, no colours and no path. But you'll have enough to get up and running so that you can look at and repair AUTOEXEC.BAT and CONFIG.SYS with an editor.

A simple emergency disk can be created with FORMAT A: /S which tells DOS to place boot up system files on the disk after formatting. Another good reason to have an emergency system disk is so that you can start cleanup operations with a virus toolkit, safe in the knowledge that there is not a virus hidden in memory (which there might be, if you reboot from hard disk).

If you have no system disk, you can borrow one, or create one on another system. If the system disk was made using a different version of DOS, you must not change drive or directory while repairing AUTOEXEC.BAT or CONFIG.SYS. The safest thing to do is to rename them, then reboot from your hard disk. Then you can correct the two files using your own version of MS DOS.

DODGY DISK DRIVES

Occasionally you may experience unfathomable and unexpected problems with a floppy disk drive, such as issuing a DIR command only to be presented with a directory listing of the contents of the PREVIOUS disk in the drive.

Some causes could be a faulty disk drive, a buggy cache program or, perhaps, a disconnected lead (typically the one which carries the signal telling whether the drive door is open or not). To check whether it's a cache, you should copy your AUTOEXEC.BAT and CONFIG.SYS files to files with different names (so you can restore them later), then strip everything out of them you don't need. Your AUTOEXEC.BAT file should look something like this:

```
PATH C:\;C:\DOS;
KEYB UK
```

And your CONFIG.SYS file like this:

```
FILES=30
BUFFERS=20
COUNTRY=044
```

Next reboot your PC and see if the problem has gone. If so, contact the supplier of your cache program and ask for a bug-fixed version. If you are still having problems, try decreasing the number of buffers allocated in CONFIG.SYS to 1. DOS may decide this is too few and set it to some default, but you'll still have the smallest number of buffers you can select. Now reboot your PC.

You will probably find it runs a lot slower, but check whether your faulty drive is working. If it is now, then you may have a faulty BIOS, because you now only have a few buffers available and should be forcing DOS to mostly read data from disk, rather than from the buffers. However, if it still doesn't work, it's possible the drive door open/closed switch is not passing its signal back to your PC, so your drive needs checking. In either case I would suggest you consult your local dealer or repair centre.

A CLEANER ENVIRONMENT

When considering the space taken up by TSRs (Terminate and Stay Resident programs) such as KEYB, mouse drivers or utilities such as Sidekick, it may be worth pointing out that a new copy of the environment (the system variables you may have set, such as your PATH and PROMPT) is stored alongside each TSR you install. So, if memory is tight, it is best to install all your TSRs before setting your environment variables. That is, at the start if your AUTOEXEC.BAT file. This way only the smallest necessary environment will be duplicated. Make sure, though, that if you had previously called up any TSRs by just their file names, knowing that DOS will find them in your PATH, then you'll have to refer to them by their absolute path and file names.

ANSI – A PROMPT EXPLANATION

The DOS command PROMPT is normally only thought to display the current drive, directory and date on the screen. But the command is actually very powerful as it can make use of the ANSI screen control codes to change screen colours and so on. Just as PROMPT recognises $d as representing the date, and the time as $t, it accepts $e as representing the Escape character. But, before you can use any of these characters, ANSI.SYS must be installed in your CONFIG.SYS file with a line like this:

```
DEVICE=C:\DOS\ANSI.SYS
```

Here are a few example programs that illustrate the power of ANSI over both your screen AND the keyboard. The first program lets you control the foreground and background screen colours and looks like this:

```
ECHO off
CLS
IF "%1" == "" GOTO ERROR
PROMPT $p$g$e[%1;%2m
CLS
GOTO END

:ERROR

ECHO To use this batch file type:
ECHO"
ECHO COLOUR col1 col2
ECHO"
ECHO Where these are the colours:
ECHO"
ECHO 30=Black Foreground
ECHO 31=Red Foreground
ECHO 32=Green Foreground
ECHO 33=Yellow Foreground
ECHO 34=Blue Foreground
ECHO 35=Magenta Foreground
ECHO 36=Cyan Foreground
ECHO 37=White Foreground
ECHO 40=Black Background
ECHO 41=Red Background
ECHO 42=Green Background
ECHO 43=Yellow Background
ECHO 44=Blue Background
ECHO 45=Magenta Background
ECHO 46=Cyan Background
ECHO 47=White Foreground

:END
```

Enter the code for the two colours as the 1st and 2nd parameters and the program will do the rest. The codes for the colours are displayed by the program for your

79

at the end of the above PROMPT command tells the system that the
s to be used to control the screen colours.

ᵤₛₒ allows you to redefine any character to any other character or string
ᵤᵣ characters. In the following batch PROMPT is used to allow you to create your
own macros.

```
ECHO off
CLS
IF "%2" == "" GOTO ERROR
PROMPT $e[%1;%2p$n$g
GOTO END

:ERROR

ECHO Type:
ECHO"
ECHO MACRO (character or code) ("string")

:END
```

This PROMPT command assigns the string %2 to the character %1 and the p defines
the redefinition. It should not be too difficult to modify the program to write the
macros to a file and to read them in again.

Next is a program which allows you to enter DOS commands without others prying
into your work. The program conceals all the text that is sent to the screen. Runs the
program and use [Ctrl][A] to activate it. When you've finished doing your secret bit
of work press [Ctrl][D] to deactivate it. The prompt command is used to define these
two keys and to switch the conceal on and off:

```
ECHO OFF
REM Save this file as VANISH.BAT

IF "%1" == "on" GOTO ON
IF "%1" == "off" GOTO OFF
PROMPT $p$g$e[1;"vanish on";13p$e[4;"vanish off";13p
GOTO END

:ON

CLS
PROMPT $p$g$e[0;8m
GOTO end

:OFF

PROMPT $p$g$e[1;1p$e[4;4p

:END
```

The following batch file is very useful for protecting your system from prying eyes. It is used to make the system unusable until the correct code is entered. It uses PROMPT to redefine particular keys.

The interesting bit is where [Return] (ASCII character 13) is redefined as character 255 followed by [Return]. As a result MSDOS will not understand commands when they are typed in.

```
ECHO off
CLS
IF "%1" == "off" goto OFF
PROMPT $g$e[13;255;13p$e[250;"halt off";13p$e[32;255p$e[77;"halt message";13p
GOTO END

:OFF

PROMPT $p$g$e[13;13p$e[250;250p$e[32;32p$e[77;77p

:END
```

In case you didn't spot it, the code to turn off HALT is 250. (Hold down ALT and press 250 on numeric keypad, then release ALT).

The final batch file displays the time or date at the touch of a button. The program acts like a TSR (Terminate and Stay Resident) program and only uses up the few bytes of memory used to hold the PROMPT format.

```
ECHO ~ off
CLS
IF ~ "%1" ~ == ~ "off" ~ goto ~ OFF
ECHO ~ TD ~ Installed
ECHO"

PROMPT $e[4;"        $d ";3p$e[20;"        $t ";3p$n$g
REM ^D displays date,^T displays time.
GOTO END

:OFF

PROMPT $e[4;4p$e[20;20p$n$g

:end
```

Here [Ctrl][D] is set to display the date, and [Ctrl][T] is used for the time.

A SWEDISH DATE

By making one small change to your CONFIG.SYS file, changing the country code to that of Sweden you can set the date format to YY:MM:DD (which is conveniently sortable having the most significant parts first), and it retains the same numeric punctuation we use in Britain.

The international dialling code for Sweden is 046, so your CONFIG.SYS file should read like this:

`COUNTRY=046`

Or, if you have DOS 3.3 or later:

`COUNTRY=046,437,C:\DOS\COUNTRY.SYS`

assuming that DOS is where you keep your SYS files.

One word of warning, though. A few programs may find the new date format confusing and refuse to cooperate. For example, some versions of XCOPY do not accept the /D switch unless the date is in the original format. And some programs such as the Norton Utilities 4.50 FD command will not accept data at all with this configuration.

You may be interested to know that some companies (Philips being one example) use full international date format as part of their house style, in all business correspondence.

CONFIGURING KEYBUK

Because Amstrad supplied the 1512/1640 range of machines with MSDOS 3.2 and it uses a non-standard version of the keyboard command KEYBUK.EXE, users of these machines may find it hard to upgrade to MSDOS 5. But it is possible to use the keyboard correctly by taking the following steps: Firstly install MSDOS 5 in the normal way then, using the SETVER command, re-version the KEYBUK.EXE program by typing:

`SETVER KEYBUK.EXE 3.2`

Finally replace the line

`KEYB UK`

in your AUTOEXEC.BAT file with

`KEYBUK`

and re-boot the system.

DUMMY DRIVES – A SMART SOLUTION

To copy files from a disk in one drive to another disk in the *same* drive you can either use DISKCOPY (but then you can only copy the entire disk, not a part of it), or copy the files to another disk first, swap disks in the drive and then copy the files on to the target disk.

If you do this a lot it can be very time consuming and annoying, but there is a better way. You can install TWO device drivers for the two floppy drives using DRIVER.SYS, giving three physical drives (A, B and C) and two logical ones (D and E).

Unlike DRIVPARM, DRIVER.SYS does not change the drive settings but installs another driver with new drive letters. So you can now COPY or XCOPY files on the same drive, like this:

```
COPY B:*.TXT E:
```

DOS then responds with the prompts normally only associated with single drive computers because drive B and E are both referring to the same physical drive, but the system has to assume there is a different disk in each of the logical drives and asks for the correct disk to be inserted whenever you swap between either of these drives.

Here are the lines to insert into CONFIG.SYS:

```
DRIVPARM=/D:1 /F:2
DEVICE = C:\DOS\DRIVER.SYS /D:0 /F:0
DEVICE = C:\DOS\DRIVER.SYS /D:1 /F:0
```

The first line sets up drive B as a 3.5", 720 K drive, while the next two lines install drives D and E using 0 for drive A and 1 for drive B.

MEMORY EXPANDING

Extended memory (called XMS) – beyond the 1Mb mark – can be used only by certain programs. DOS itself cannot make use of it directly. By employing a little addressing trick, MS-DOS 5.0 can manage to address the first 64K region in the second megabyte (well, all but sixteen bytes of it).

If you have a 286, 386 or 486 and MORE than one megabyte of memory, this trick can be exploited by the HIMEM.SYS driver, which can be installed in your CONFIG.SYS. Much of DOS and all of your BUFFERS can be kept there, giving you at least 42k for other programs. To do this, start your CONFIG.SYS with:

```
DEVICE=[path]HIMEM.SYS
DOS=HIGH
```

The first 64K (of the second megabyte) is called High Memory Area (HMA).

To use the memory between the 640K mark and the end of the first megabyte, your processor must be at least a 386. Then you can use the driver EMM386.SYS. This driver has two purposes: it converts extended memory into expanded memory (EMS) – which can be used by quite a number of programs (for example Lotus 1-2-3); its other purpose is to give you a way of addressing some of the extra 360k – by creating blocks of memory called Upper Memory Blocks (UMB).

HIMEM.SYS gives you a large region in which you can load most of DOS, but it doesn't use up all the space available. You can get at that extra memory by installing EMM386.SYS, and then changing the DOS directive in CONFIG.SYS to say:

```
DOS=HIGH,UMB
```

The command to install this driver is:

```
DEVICE=[path]EMM386.EXE NOEMS
```

and it should appear in CONFIG.SYS before the DOS command. You can then load drivers and TSR programs into this free region – up to about 100K extra – using DEVICEHIGH in CONFIG.SYS and LOADHIGH in BAT files and from the command line. There's one big drawback in this: you probably won't use the UMB scheme at the same time as converting XMS memory to EMS; you can, but you will only save about 35K instead of 100K. (This is for technical reasons: the EMS method requires a working area of 64k in this area, leaving less for UMBs).

If you have big TSRs (or a lot of little ones) you would be better to use NOEMS as the parameter on the:

```
DEVICE=[path]EMM386.EXE
```

to give you back that 100K memory they would normally gobble. If you need the EMS for Lotus 1-2-3, though, you would use RAM as the parameter instead of NOEMS.

CREATING CODE PAGES

Code pages are IBM's answer to the needs of non-American PC users. When the PC was first released only American symbols were included in the character set and it was only later that European and other symbols such as currency and accented letters were incorporated.

Even though it was a step forwards, many symbols were not easily available (often requiring you to hold down the [Alt] key and then press three keys on the keypad, just to get one character), while some characters were missed out all together.

Clearly this wasn't good enough if the PC was to become a global standard, so IBM came up with the idea of Code Pages. Simple in concept but, until now, almost incomprehensible in application, Code Pages allow you to load in a completely different character set for display on your monitor. But because they are difficult to install they are a largely under-used PC resource. In fact, to add to the confusion, many books and other manuals, INCORRECTLY detail how to use them – they probably quote the original documentation (which is not very clear) but the authors haven't actually tried it for themselves.

So here's a chance to put the record straight and show you how easy it is to use code pages – if you ever need to write documents in foreign languages or have a non UK or American keyboard, this is just what you've been looking for.

Please note that when reading the following it is assumed that you keep your DOS files in a directory called DOS on drive C. If it is elsewhere you should modify the paths shown accordingly.

So, to begin. Normally, in the UK, when you set up your PC you will have this line in your CONFIG.SYS file:

```
country=044,437,c:\dos\country.sys
```

And this one in your AUTOEXEC.BAT file:

```
keyb uk,437,c:\dos\keyboard.sys
```

However, you can actually support several more languages by altering these files like this. If you want a French layout, make sure these two lines appear in your CONFIG.SYS file:

```
country=033,437,c:\dos\country.sys
device=c:\dos\display.sys con=(ega,437)
```

And that these four are in your AUTOEXEC.BAT file:

```
nlsfunc c:\dos\country.sys
mode con cp prep=((437) c:\dos\ega.cpi)
mode con cp select=437
keyb fr,437,c:\dos\keyboard.sys
```

The first two tell your PC to use French (33 is the international dialling code for France and 437 is the default code page of characters (seeing as all the French accented characters are in the default character set).

The first of the other four lines sets up your PC for National Language Support FUNCtions, the first mode command prepares Code Page 437 ready for use and the second one selects it, while the final line maps your keyboard to the French (fr) AZERTY layout.

Similarly you could arrange to have a Norwegian PC by including these two lines in your CONFIG.SYS file:

```
country=047,865,c:\dos\country.sys
device=c:\dos\display.sys con=(ega,865)
```

And these lines in your AUTOEXEC.BAT file:

```
nlsfunc c:\dos\country.sys
mode con cp prep=((865) c:\dos\ega.cpi)
mode con cp select=865
keyb no,865,c:\dos\keyboard.sys
```

In this case 47 is the dialling code for Norway but we are now using Code Page 865 as we need some new characters which are not available in the default character set. Also the Norwegian keyboard (no) is chosen on the final line.

You will find that when you use the French keyboard you can press the left square bracket key '[' followed by any vowel in order to get a character with a circumflex. Other shorthand key presses are also available. And in Norwegian, you press the right square bracket ']' prior to any vowels.

The valid code pages are:

Value	Code Page
437	United States/Default
850	Multilingual
860	Portuguese
863	French-Canadian
865	Nordic

And the languages you can set your keyboard to using KEYB are:

Code	Keyboard Type
fr	France
gr	Germany
it	Italy
sp	Spain
uk	United Kingdom
po	Portugal
sg	Swiss-German
sf	Swiss-French
df	Denmark
be	Belgium
nl	Netherlands
no	Norway
la	Latin America
sv	Sweden
su	Finland

Here's a tip that very few PC users know, so make a note of it . . . If you mess up your PC's configuration by accident while trying to install a Code Page or simply wish to return to the American/default set up, at any time you can press [Ctrl][Alt][F1] and your keyboard will be restored.

On the other hand, once a Code Page has been set up you can return to its configuration from the American/default one by pressing [Ctrl][Alt][F2]. Remembering these two will get you out of most Code Page problems.

CHAPTER 5

WORKING WITH WINDOWS

Windows is the way of the future, at least, if you listen to Microsoft and whether you like Windows or believe them (or not), Microsoft have certainly sold several million copies, as opposed to estimates of less than a million for IBM's competing GUI (Graphical User Interface – often pronounced "gooey"), OS/2.

The only problem really with GUIs is that they require a lot of computing power and bags of memory (both internally and on your hard disk). And you really need a 386, an 80 Mb hard disk and 4 Mb of extra RAM before you can really start using Windows. However, GUIs are fun to use, a lot of people like them (let's face it, Windows is a lot brighter than a standard DOS screen) and multitasking environments can make for better productivity and efficiency. To that aim, here's an assortment of ideas you should find useful.

COMPAQ DOS 5 BUG WITH WINDOWS 3.0

It appears that Windows 3.0 sometimes doesn't install – nor will SWAPFILE.EXE run – under Compaq DOS 5 when DOS, device drivers and TSRs are all loaded into high memory. If you experience this problem try loading DOS, device drivers and TSRs into base memory before installing or configuring Windows, and load them high later. Better still, if you're upgrading to both Compaq DOS 5 and Windows 3.0 at the same time, make sure you install Windows first. Incidentally, [Ctrl][PrtScr] works as it always did in earlier versions of Compaq DOS, but now it puts a ^P on the screen at the same time. This could very well be a DOS 5 bug.

FORMATTING DISKS ON DISKLESS WORKSTATIONS

If you are running Windows from a network on a diskless workstation, you cannot format a floppy disk from the File Manager. You can, however, do so from the DOS Prompt by choosing the DOS Prompt icon from the Main Group in the Program Manager and typing:

`FORMAT n:`

where n is the letter for the drive containing the disk you want to format. See your DOS manual for further details on using the FORMAT command.

IMPROVING WINDOWS ON AN IBM PS/1

Here's a piece of advice for IBM PS/1 users running Windows 3.0. If you run Windows from the PS/1's graphical shell it loads in Real Mode, with about 330K free. Windows can, however run in Standard Mode with 560K free.

When installing itself, Windows also installs HIMEM.SYS, and expanded memory driver. To make use of the expanded memory on the PS/1, press [Alt][SysRq] on the opening menu screen of the graphical shell – but make sure the isn't a disk in the drive or the computer will try to boot off it. The DOS prompt will appear saying that the High Memory area is now available for use. Change to the Windows directory and type WIN to begin in Standard Mode.

MINIMAL WINDOWS SETUP

Many people find Windows 3 is just too greedy with their hard disks, and wonder if there are any non-essential bits they can strip out of their particular setup without damaging their working environment. For example, the Cardfile and Windows Write are seldom used by anyone other than outright Windows enthusiasts, so these look like a likely choice – but how do you go about removing them without making such a complete mess of things that a complete re-installation is needed?

The first thing to do is remove the icons which represent the programs' presence in the Windows environment. To do this, go to the Program Manager, click once on a program icon you don't want – such as Write, which should be in your Accessories group – and then select File at the top left of the screen. Now click on Delete, and reply Yes to the safety prompt.

When you've done this you'll see that the icon has been removed from the group. However, it is still on your hard disk, so shell to DOS and delete the files WRITE.EXE and WRITE.HLP – and you will have saved about 256 Kilobytes of disk space. Do the same thing for any other unwanted icons and program files (making sure you have correctly identified them first). Chapter 13 of your Windows manual will help you in this regard – it should contain all the information you need.

Incidentally, you should be aware that a lot of windows programs (particularly PD and Shareware ones) come supplied with a .WRI, Windows Write, formatted document file. If you delete Write, you won't be able to view these files in their original format and, if you load them into another word processor, they are likely to look a bit garbled.

MOUSING AROUND

Many people have asked how they can get a mouse attached to COM 3 or COM 4 to be recognised by Windows. Well the simple and unfortunate answer is that Windows only supports serial mice on COM 1 and COM 2. Apparently all you can do is swap whatever devices you have connected to the first two ports over to the last two and then connect your mouse to one of the first two.

BIGGER BORDERS WITH WINDOWS

Here's a quick tip for anyone who uses Windows and has difficulty in 'grabbing' the window border when resizing or moving a window. Launch the Control Panel and open the desktop dialog box (either by double clicking on the Desktop icon or using the command from the Settings menu).

Near to the bottom-right corner of the Desktop window you will see a Border Width text box. The value in that box determines the width of the border in pixels. By default this value is set to 3 but it can be changed to any value between 1 and 49. Try about 7 to be going with though. When you have finished, click on the Desktop dialog box's OK button to put it into effect.

ADDING ICONS TO BATCH FILES

If you have many DOS programs which behave well under Windows 3, you can launch them using batch files created in the program directory.

One source of irritation is the fact that when making a new entry for use with Windows 3 the only icons immediately available are the rather dull Program Manager offerings. To use a .ICO icon file it is necessary to modify the properties/change icon selection. If for any reason you have to edit the command, Windows will forget the icon and you must remember the name of the required icon to re-enter the details.

As Windows 3 EXE files contain one or more icons which are automatically recognised, it's natural to wonder if DOS programs could also be made to include icon information, so that the association could be permanent and no directory of .ICO files would need to be kept on the disk. In fact this can be achieved with batch files in the following way. First, create a directory to work in and then create and test your batch file. You must ensure that the file starts with at least one blank line, otherwise your first command will be lost when COMMAND.COM executes it.

Next, select or create a .ICO file and use the COPY command to combine the two files, the icon file first, followed by the batch file, like this:

```
COPY /b MY.ICO+MY.BAT COMBINED.BAT
```

The /b ensures that everything is copied in binary mode (that is, the files are copied in their entirety). Finally copy the resulting combined batch file to the directory where it will be run and rename it as required.

Now, when a new entry is made to launch the program from Windows 3, the icon image will be automatically recognised and will not get lost. When COM-MAND.COM executes the batch file, the icon image will be treated as an unrecognised command and a "Bad command or filename" message will be given. On faster machines this will hardly be seen and the remainder of the commands will be executed as normal.

USING A PS/2 WITH EXPANDED MEMORY

If you have a PS/2, if you ran Setup to install Windows and chose to let Windows modify your CONFIG.SYS file, a line was removed. If you want your 286-based PS/2 computer configured to use expanded memory, you must add the following line to your CONFIG.SYS file:

```
DEVICE=PCSX2EMS.SYS
```

MANAGING THE FILE MANAGER

If you often need to use the Windows File Manager on your A:, B: or D: drive you may have found yourself inconvenienced by the fact that its default startup drive is the drive on which Windows is installed – usually C:. As a result, File Manager must read all C: directories before it can be pointed to the required drive, which can be a time-consuming process, especially if you are using a large C: drive.

There is a simple solution though. First create a ram disk by inserting a line such as the following in CONFIG.SYS, using Notepad or Sysedit:

```
device=c:\dos\ramdrive.sys 350 128 64 /e
```

This configuration is really best suited to large applications like dBASE IV. To create a really small ram disk you could use a minimal configuration, like this:

```
device=c:\dos\ramdrive.sys 16 128 2 /e
```

For more information on RAMDRIVE.SYS you should refer to your DOS manual.

After rebooting, open File Manager and, after it has done its usual search of the default drive, click on the Ram Disk icon, followed by "Options" and "Save settings on Exit". Next click on "File", and select "Exit" to return to the Program Manager. Finally reopen the File Manager, switch off "Save settings on Exit" and exit again.

From now on, every time you open the File Manager it will display (very quickly) the directory tree of the ram disk and allow you to access other drives with minimum delay. This is a very useful hint for users of Windows 3.0. But bear in mind that the Windows 3.1 File Manager has been comprehensively overhauled, so this should not be necessary if you're using it.

EASY DRIVER SWAPPING

Many Windows users may have a printer attached to their system on LPT1, which is capable of being driven by more than one of the printer drivers provided with Windows. For example the Citizen 120-D falls into this category.

You may be using several different printers – for example the Proprinter, IBM Graphics, Generic/Text-only and Citizen drivers – all at various times and for various jobs because, for example, the Proprinter driver may produce better graphics and the IBM Graphics better text. But you would probably get tired of having to go into the Control Panel to set up each new active driver and then attach it to the LPT1 port. But it is possible to add fake ports to the WIN.INI file, by editing it using Notepad and adding two new ports to the end of the [ports] listing – for example LPT1.ADD and LPT1.AD2.

If, you then go to the Control Panel and, keeping the Proprinter allocated to LPT1, allocate the IBM Graphics driver to LPT1.ADD and the Citizen driver to LPT1.AD2 – and then make ALL these printers active, you'll find that Windows won't complain at all. When you want to swap from one driver to another, simply select Printer Setup from an application's File menu and the application obligingly displays all the available printers.

The technical reason behind this is that Windows "thinks" it's printing to a port, but DOS refers to LPT1 as a reserved device name. So anything printed to something called LPT1.??? is automatically sent to the printer. This technique is also useful for Windows users who have more than one printer attached to their PC via a printer sharer switch box, or laser printers – like the Ricoh 6000 – that accept different emulation cards.

WINDOWS 3.1 AND 386/486 PCS

Windows 3.1 running in enhanced mode includes what could almost be described as a "hidden option" that enables the use of a 32-bit disk access path. (But it is not offered if you are using a SCSI drive controller – which is a shame, as it can dramatically speed up disk accesses by bypassing the system BIOS).

You can find out if your machine can take advantage of 32-bit access by selecting the Control Panel followed by "386 Enhanced", "Virtual Memory" and finally "Change". If 32-bit access is possible you will see an empty check box near the bottom of the window. Simply click on it to select it.

While you are in this area you can choose to set up a permanent swap file on your hard disk which will also help to speed Windows up. It will display the available space and offer a suitable size for the swap file, unless you want to change it – simply follow the prompts and then re-start Windows.

Windows 3.1 uses a new version of Smartdrive which appears as an EXE file in your AUTOEXEC.BAT file, instead of a SYS file in your CONFIG.SYS file. This is fine unless you are using a SCSI drive controller and the NOEMS switch with EMM386.EXE – in which case Windows 3.1 puts Smartdrive in what it describes as "double buffering" mode, which seems to slow Windows down to a fast crawl. The problem is that EMM386 will not run without Smartdrive, and without EMM386 you cannot access the upper memory blocks to load device drivers and files into high memory.

Failing any better advice, the best solution is to use SMARTDRV.SYS from Windows 3.0 in the CONFIG.SYS file after HIMEM.SYS, and before EMM386.EXE NOEMS. Then remove SMARTDRV.EXE from your AUTOEXEC.BAT file. It is possible that these problems with SCSI drives also apply to ESDI and removable drives too.

MS-DOS EXECUTIVE

If you find the Windows 3.0 File Manager to be slow and often clumsy to use, you might be interested to know that there is an undocumented file in your Windows directory called MSDOS.EXE. Its full name is MSDOS Executive, and it appears to be a rough and ready, text-only file manager. You don't get all of the File Manager extras like directory expanding, but it's very fast to use.

To switch to another directory click on the directory name shown at the top of the window, or double click on it to return to the root directory. You can then double click on directories to move to them, or on programs to run them. One thing you can't do is pick up a program and drag it out of the window into a Program Manager program group. You'll have to resort to using the File Manager for that.

Overall it seems to do the job quite nicely. You will also find that the apparently, undocumented file SYSEDIT.EXE will load in all of your AUTOEXEC.BAT, CONFIG.SYS, WIN.INI and SYSTEM.INI files in one go, so that you can switch between them, editing your entire system configuration in one session. This would seem to be yet another one of the many undocumented features to be found in Windows 3.0 and 3.1.

COMMON EXCEL QUERIES EXPLAINED

Q.   Why does Excel Setup hang after I enter my User Name and Company name?

A.   According to Microsoft, PC Tools can cause this problem. It is apparently the fault of the virus checker included with earlier copies of PC Tools 7.0; when the virus checker sees the Setup program writing back to the disk after entering User Name and Company Name, it assumes that a virus is at work.

To eliminate this problem, run Windows and load the WIN.INI file using Notepad (from the File Open option). Now disable the line beginning with "load=" by placing a semicolon ";" in front of the word load:

```
;load=c:\pctools\wnschedl.exe c:\pctools\wnlaunch.exe
```

Save the WIN.INI file and reinstall Excel. Once installation is complete, take the semicolon out of the <i>Load=<i> line again.

Q.   Why, when I enter text into a cell, isn't there an automatic overflow into the adjacent cell?

A.   Excel allows you to view either values or formulas in a worksheet. While in Formula view, any text entered into a cell will not extend into an adjacent cell, regardless of the length of the text.

If this is happening to you then you should check whether or not the worksheet is in formula view; you can toggle the view by choosing Display from the options menu and then selecting the formulas option. Or you can use the keyboard short cut by pressing [Ctrl][`] (the left single quotation mark).

Q.   Why, when you print from Excel 3.0 with the Hewlett Packard (HP) Deskjet 500 scalable driver, is text either missing or it prints at 75 dpi resolution.

A.   The Work-around is to add prtresfac=0 to the [DJ500,<port>] section of the WIN.INI file, where <port> is the currently selected port. Note that this command is case sensitive. Here is an example:

```
[DJ500,LPT1]
prtresfac=0
```

Q.   Is there a way to modify Excel default chart types?

A.   These formats are built into Excel to give the most common chart types. The easiest way is to set the preferred format of the chart. To do this, create a new chart or load an existing chart that is formatted in the manner you use most frequently. Then choose Set Preferred from the Gallery menu. To make the preferred format permanent for all future sessions of Excel, you must choose Save Workspace from the File menu.

Q. How can I get Excel to automatically load into a default directory of my choice?

A. To change the default directory,click on the Excel icon. From the Program Manager go into File and then Properties. The command line will read:

`c:\excel\excel.exe`

To change this use the -p parameter as follows:

`c:\excel\excel.exe -p c:\data`

When Excel is next executed it will by default set the directory to c:\data.

Q. Why do I get the error message "Invalid Print Titles"?

A. The area selected for print titles must be an entire row, an entire column or a combination of both.

Q. How can I quickly hide the contents of a cell?

A. Select the cell range you want to hide the contents of. Select Number from the Format menu and set up a custom number format of three semicolons (;;;). Within your spreadsheet you will see that the range you highlighted is now blank.

Q. How do I delete the four most recently saved documents at the bottom of the File menu?

A. To permanently delete the list, use the Notepad to load the EXCEL.INI file, delete the whole section that says [Recent File List] and the four files below this section.

Q. How can I include graphics in a worksheet?

A. You can combine graphics with Excel's own drawing tools by Using Windows Paintbrush, open the file containing the graphic, or create one. Then choose Edit Copy to copy it to the Clipboard. Next start Excel 3.0 and open a worksheet you want to contain the graphic and finally choose Edit Paste. The graphic is then placed on your worksheet.

Q. How can I delete formulas in selected cells from my Excel spreadsheet, but maintain the values in those cells?

A. Select the cells and choose Copy from the main Edit menu. Then with the same cells selected, choose Paste Special from the Edit menu, select Values and click on OK.

MAXIMISING MEMORY USE

If you receive any messages about being out of memory. You can find out how much is available and of what type by choosing the About command from the Help menu in either the Program Manager or File Manager. The information includes:

Amount of memory free.   This number is the amount of conventional memory available for applications. When you run Windows in standard mode, this number includes extended memory. When you run Windows in 386 enhanced mode, it includes virtual memory and could actually be much larger than the physical amount of memory in your computer. If you need more memory or if the amount of free memory is less than about 30K or so, you should close one or more applications.

Amount of EMS free.   When you run Windows in real mode with an expanded memory driver installed, this number shows the amount of expanded memory currently available. Close one or more applications to free up some conventional memory.

Smartdrive Amount.   This number is the amount of expanded memory used by Smartdrive which is a utility designed to speed up Windows. For more information on how to use Smartdrive, see "Optimizing Windows," in your Windows User's Guide.

System Resources.   This is the percentage of system resources available. It never reaches 100% because the system itself takes up some system resources. If this number is less than about 15%, you will not be able to run any more applications, regardless of how much free memory you have. You should close one or more applications to free up some system resources.

BACKGROUND PRINTING

A common problem is the inability to get Windows to multitask during printing. For example, you may not be able to minimise Word for Windows once a print job is under way. The short answer to this problem is that Windows will not allow you to minimise a window during a print run, but having said that you can use the Print Manager instead; it still freezes you out until the job has been spooled to disk, but then you can get on with things while your printer chugs away happily.

TRACKING DOWN ENHANCED-MODE COMMS ERRORS

If you find Windows throws up messages like this one:

```
The COM port is currently assigned to a DOS application.
Do you want to reassign the port to Windows?
```

Then you might find the solution in this section, which provides two possible reasons for this error, and tells you things you can try to prevent it from happening.

IF THE PORT IN QUESTION IS COM3 OR COM4

COM3 or COM4 must never be used from Microsoft Windows 3.00 enhanced mode by ANY Windows or DOS application, without making a modification to the SYSTEM.INI file as follows. Insert the following two lines in the [386ENH] section:

```
COM3Base=3E8h
COM4Base=2E8h
```

This modification should eliminate the problem. If it persists, check that you have properly inserted the lines as shown above (case is unimportant). If they are correct, the hardware interrupt (IRQ) and/or base I/O addresses may be incorrect for one or more hardware COM ports in your system. The following are the IBM standard port settings for COM3 and COM4. For further information about this topic, and IBM standard settings for COM1 and COM2, see the next section.

COM3 – hardware interrupt (IRQ) 4, base I/O address 3E8
COM4 – hardware interrupt (IRQ) 3, base I/O address 2E8

IF THE PORT IN QUESTION IS COM1 OR COM2

Is COM3 or COM4 being used? COM1 and COM3, or COM2 and COM4, cannot be used simultaneously on any machine that does not have a micro channel architecture (MCA) bus – such as IBM PS/2 machines – or the new extended industry standard architecture (EISA) bus, such as the COMPAQ SystemPro. This is a hardware limitation; there is no work around. If neither COM3 or COM4 are being used, then the hardware interrupt (IRQ) channels and/or base I/O addresses for COM1 and COM2 may be set incorrectly. On a non-PS/2 machine, these settings are made by using hardware DIP switches or jumpers. Consult your hardware documentation for information on such settings. If you need further assistance in properly configuring your hardware, contact your hardware vendor or manufacturer. The correct IBM standard settings for COM1 and COM2 are as follows:

COM1 – hardware interrupt (IRQ) 4, base I/O address 3F8
COM2 – hardware interrupt (IRQ) 3, base I/O address 2F8

The following table depicts the standard settings for the four communications ports that Microsoft Windows 3.00 and DOS support. This information is useful for troubleshooting communications problems under Windows 3.00. A brief description for each column appears below the table.

Port	WIN3 COMM.DRV Procomm Plus I/O Range IRQ	WIN3 Default SYSTEM.INI Settings I/O Range [386ENH]	WIN3 Desired SYSTEM.INI Settings I/O Range [386ENH]
COM1	3F8h......4	COM1BASE=3F8h	COM1BASE=3F8h
COM2	2F8h......3	COM2BASE=2F8h	COM2BASE=2F8h
COM3	3E8h......4	COM3BASE=2E8h	COM3BASE=3E8h
COM4	2E8h......3	COM4BASE=2E0h	COM4BASE=2E8h

The first column lists the ports. The second column describes the settings for the ports that both the Windows COMM.DRV and most popular communications packages use by default. The third column shows what Windows 3.00 sets by default and the fourth column shows what should be set in the [386ENH] section of the SYSTEM.INI file for proper functioning of the ports under enhanced-mode Windows 3.00.

Note: You must make the changes shown in column 4 above if you want to share IRQs. These procedures are described in good detail in the file SYSINI2.TXT in your Windows directory, under the [386ENH] section.

The headings "I/O Range" specify the base port addresses for the respective ports. IRQ represents the normal interrupts used in IBM-AT compatible computers and should not be changed under normal conditions. Under enhanced-mode Windows 3.00, you can change the base port addresses, IRQ lines, communications protocol, and communications IRQ sharing.

TRACKING DOWN COMMS PROBLEMS

1. You can use two communication ports simultaneously that share the same interrupt (for example, COM1 and COM3, or COM2 and COM4) only if the hardware is capable of it. The ability to share communications port IRQs is hardware dependent. Currently, the only hardware that you can be assured that IRQ sharing is supported on is MicroChannel.

Although EISA (Extended Industry Standard Architecture) does have IRQ sharing as part of its specifications, implementation on current machines is spotty. If you are unable to successfully share an IRQ with the COMIrqSharing switch set to true, the hardware does not support IRQ sharing and Windows 3.00 is not able to overcome the lack of support for this feature using software.

2. COM3 and COM4 may not be reliable under Windows 3.00 (standard and real mode) unless both COM1 and COM2 are first activated. If you use only COM3

and/or COM4, you may experience problems (with printing, communications, your mouse).

If you use COM1 and COM3 without using COM2, you also may have problems. The easiest way to remember this is to not use a higher serial port (2, 3, or 4) unless all lower number ports (1, 2, and 3) are first activated (or in use).

3. Standard and real mode Windows 3.00 use the COMM.DRV directly whereas enhanced-mode Windows 3.00 virtualizes the ports using a device called the virtual communications driver (VCD). For this reason, serial communication can theoretically be considered more reliable under standard and real mode because there can be no mis-communication between the VCD and the COMM.DRV.

In cases where you are using multiple communications ports under Windows 3.00 enhanced mode, verify that the base port addresses are set as described in the table located earlier in this article.

IRQ sharing is possible under enhanced-mode Windows 3.00 only if you make the necessary changes to the [386ENH] section of the SYSTEM.INI file as outlined above.

ANOTHER COM3 AND COM4 SOLUTION

The following DEBUG instructions should persuade your BIOS that you have COM3 and COM4 serial ports. It's fairly simple, but you have to be careful when doing anything with the BIOS, for obvious reasons – it's no place for the uninformed to be poking around in.

First, find your manual and identify the port addresses that your modem, fax cards and other serial devices use and write them down (the default should be COM3 at 03E8 and COM4 at 02E8 – but yours may be different, so be certain to check).

Type DEBUG at the DOS prompt and you'll see a single dash. At this point, you'll need to tell DEBUG that you want to write COM3 and COM4 information to the area that keeps track of such things. COM3 information is stored at 0040:0004 and COM4 is stored at 0040:0006.

Assuming that your COM3 and COM4 addresses are the same as for the example above; 03E8 and 02E8. To enter these values you first take the last two numbers (or letter/number combination) and place them in front of the first two, and put a space between them. For example, 03E8 becomes E8 03 so, to tell BIOS that you have a COM3 serial port at 03E8, you would enter:

```
E 0040:0004 E8 03
```

If you want to set addresses for both COM3 and COM4, you can do it all at once by entering the command:

```
E 0040:0004 E8 03 E8 02
```

If you wanted to do just COM4, you would enter:

```
E 0040:0006 E8 02
```

To exit DEBUG and return to DOS, type:

```
Q
```

Note: Although this fix works perfectly well on most PCs, it is not guaranteed to work on yours. And if you have any hesitation about using DEBUG, don't.

COMMON WINDOWS 3.1 SMARTDRIVE QUESTIONS AND ANSWERS

Q.   Why is SmartDrive in both my CONFIG.SYS and AUTOEXEC.BAT files?

A.   This is because there are really two device drivers in a single file: a disk cache and a double buffer driver. See the next question for a description of double buffering. The cache component of SMARTDRV.EXE is installed in the AUTOEXEC.BAT file and the double buffer driver is installed in the CONFIG.SYS file.

Q.   What is double buffering?

A.   Certain disk controllers support something called bus mastering. This is where the disk controller takes over a computer's bus in order to directly transfer data to and from memory.

Sometimes a problem can occur when running a DOS-based application in the 386 Enhanced mode of Windows where DOS applications are running in a virtual machine which doesn't have any physical memory addresses. And the address that is passed to your bus mastering controller is not always a physical memory address. This can cause data to be read from the wrong location or, worse, can cause data to be written to the wrong place in memory. The result can be erratic system behaviour.

Microsoft created a standard called Virtual DMA Services which provides an interface that allows these bus master controllers to get correct addresses and avoid this problem. But some older bus master controller cards do not support this standard.

To provide a solution for this Microsoft have added a feature to SmartDrive so that it can provide a memory buffer that has physical and virtual addresses that are the same. This allows you to avoid the problem even with an older bus mastering controller.

You can used this feature by placing the following line in your CONFIG.SYS file:

`DEVICE=SMARTDRV.EXE /double_buffer`

This will only install the double-buffering capabilities of SmartDrive. You'll need to also add SmartDrive to your AUTOEXEC.BAT file in order to install the disk cache.

Q.   Do I need the double buffering that Smartdrive provides?

A.   Most disk controllers do not need double buffering. These include all MFM, RLL and IDE controllers as well as many ESDI and SCSI devices.

SmartDrive has a feature to help you determine if your system needs double buffering. Once your system is running with SmartDrive loaded for double buffering, type SMARTDRV at the DOS prompt and you will see a table with some information. Notice the column labelled buffering. For each drive that is being cached, it can have one of three values: 'YES', 'NO' or '-'.

'YES' indicates that double buffering is needed, 'NO' indicates that buffering is not needed and '-' indicates that SmartDrive has not yet determined the necessity of double buffering. If the buffering column has all Nos in it, the double buffer driver is not needed. If the double buffer driver is not loaded, you will see only 'NO's in the buffer column, whether or not your system needs double buffering.

Q.   Is it alright to load the double buffer driver into the Upper Memory Area or to load it high?

A.   The double buffer driver must be loaded into conventional memory, or, in other words, it must be loaded low. In order for the double buffer driver to work, it needs to operate in memory that has real, physical addresses.

Memory that is provided by software memory managers, like EMM386, QEMM386 or 386MAX, should not be used. Loading the double buffer driver into the Upper Memory Area will result in the same problem that you are trying to avoid. You will not lose much conventional memory as the double buffer driver only takes about 2.5K.

Q.   Can the disk cache portion of SmartDrive be loaded high?

A.   Yes, it will automatically load itself high under MS-DOS 5.0 if EMM386 is loaded and configured to provide Upper Memory support. If you are unsure how to configure EMM386, check your MS-DOS 5.0 Upgrade documentation or you Windows User's Guide for version 3.1.

SmartDrive can also be loaded high with third party memory managers such as 386MAX or QEMM386. Check your memory manager documentation for more information on loading programs into Upper Memory.

Q.   Does SmartDrive work with Stacker?

A.   Yes, SmartDrive is aware of Stacker and will automatically cache the underlying drive that Stacker uses. This provides significantly better cache performance due to the fact that SmartDrive will be caching compressed code. For the same amount of memory, you can cache twice as much code because of Stacker's compression ratio.

Q.   Why doesn't my Stacker Volume show up in the SmartDrive status screen?

A.   This is because SmartDrive is caching underneath Stacker. You should see the underlying drive letter listed in the SmartDrive status screen.

COMMON WINDOWS 3.1 UPGRADE QUESTIONS AND ANSWERS

Users who have hit problems trying to upgrade from Windows 3.0 to version 3.1 will find the following hints and tips invaluable.

Q.   Why are there print problems in Windows 3.1 which didn't happen under Windows 3.0?

A.   Some of your printer drivers may not have been updated properly to the latest version. To ensure this happens properly, try out the following procedure:

1. Remove the printer driver that you are using from your system by running Control Panel and choosing Printers. Select the printer driver in question and click on the Remove button.

2. Now use File Manager to change to the WINDOWS\SYSTEM directory, and then click on the printer driver's filename. Press the [Del] key to delete that file.

3. Reinstall the printer driver by running Control Panel and selecting Printers. Click on the Add button, select your printer, and then click on the Install button.

Nearly all printing problems will be solved by reinstalling your printer drivers.

Q.   Can I use TrueType fonts with my Hewlett-Packard (HP) DeskJet printer?

A.   The printer drivers supplied by Hewlett-Packard don't support TrueType fonts. You can use the DeskJet printer driver that comes with Windows 3.1, but it doesn't support Hewlett-Packard scalable fonts.

Q.   Using my Hewlett-Packard DeskJet 500c printer, can I print in colour?

A.   You can print in colour using this printer by using the printer driver supplied by Hewlett-Packard. But printer drivers supplied by Hewlett-Packard don't support TrueType fonts, so if you need them you can use the printer driver that comes with Windows 3.1 – however, you won't be able to print in colour.

Q. What is the most common reason for an unsuccessful Windows installation?

A. The number-one cause of Windows 3.1 installation problems are TSR programs loaded from the CONFIG.SYS and AUTOEXEC.BAT files. If you are having such problems, you need to boot from a disk containing only skeletal versions of these files, with all TSRs and device drivers removed – but note that you do need to make sure that any hard disk managers are included.

Q. Why does Setup hang just after changing from the initial text mode part of the program to the full graphics mode Windows part, throwing me back into MS-DOS or even crashing the system?

A. You may still have earlier or corrupted versions of SETUP.INF or SETUP.EXE in your WINDOWS or WINDOWS\SYSTEM directory. Rename them with a .OLD extension, and repeat the installation from the disk set. If you're successful, delete the files altogether.

Q. Why can't I use the OLE features in Excel or Word for Windows since I upgraded to Windows 3.1?

A. Windows 3.1 may not recognize the OLE database if you upgrade from Windows 3.0 to Windows 3.1, and you had installed in Windows 3.0 an application that supports object linking and embedding (OLE). You need to update the database, which is a file named REG.DAT. To update the REG.DAT file, choose the Run command from the File menu in Program Manager, type REGEDIT in the Command Line box, and the Registration Information Editor appears.

Then choose the Merge Registration File from the File menu, select the registration file that corresponds to the OLE server application you are using. For example, if you are using Microsoft Publisher, choose MSPUB.REG. Finally click on the OK button.

Q. Why did I receive the following error message when I tried to upgrade to Windows 3.1 using DR-DOS 6.0?

`Standard Mode: Fault in MS-DOS Extender`

A. Microsoft can only ensure the stability of Windows 3.1 running on MS-DOS or PC-DOS versions 3.1 or later. Digital Research has announced the availability of a software update for running Windows with DR-DOS. Microsoft neither endorses nor ensures the stability of Windows 3.1 running on DR-DOS either with or without the Digital Research software update.

Q. Does SmartDrive make my system run more slowly in Windows 3.1?

A. If SmartDrive is set up to use double buffering, it is going to run more slowly than without double buffering. To make SmartDrive faster when it is using double buffering, try adding the /L switch to the SmartDrive command line in your AUTOEXEC.BAT file. This switch forces SmartDrive to load its buffer "low," into conventional memory.

Note: When your hard disk requires the use of double buffering, Windows places a SmartDrive command in your CONFIG.SYS file as well as in your AUTO-EXEC.BAT file. You should place the /L switch on the command line in your AUTOEXEC.BAT file.

Q.   When running Windows, why do I get the following error message:

`"Call to Undefined Dynalink"`?

A.   This error is usually caused by an old .DLL file located in the WINDOWS directory. The most common one is TOOLHELP.DLL. Locate this file and rename it. Then, restart Windows. The correct version of this file is located in the WINDOWS\SYSTEM directory and has a date of 3/10/92 and a size of 14128. This problem can also occur with an earlier version of SHELL.DLL, OLECLI.DLL, OLESVR.DLL, and COMMDLG.DLL. All of these file should be located in the WINDOWS\SYSTEM directory and have a date of 3/10/92.

Q.   I have a sound card that plays the Windows file CANYON.MID, but when I choose the Sound icon from Control Panel, all of the dialog box selections are unavailable (dimmed). Why?

A.   You are using a sound card that is a MIDI synthesizer. You must use a card that supports the playing of audio files (files with the .WAV filename extension). For example, if you are using the original Adlib Music Synthesizer Card, it must be upgraded to the Adlib 2000 or Gold card.

Q.   In my CONFIG.SYS file, I have the line:

DEVICE=C:\WINDOWS\SmartDRV.EXE /DOUBLE_BUFFER

Why is it there? And why can't I run Windows in 386 enhanced mode even through I have a 386 computer with 4 megabytes of memory?

A.   When Windows is set up, it tests to see if it can understand the hard drive. If the hard drive uses a SCSI controller or a caching controller, then Windows adds the line:

`DEVICE=C:\WINDOWS\SmartDRV.EXE /DOUBLE_BUFFER`

to CONFIG.SYS.

Sometimes, double buffering may not be activated even though you have the line in CONFIG.SYS. If you have a SCSI controller and double buffering is not active, then you may not be able to run Windows in 386 enhanced mode. To force double buffering, add a + to the end of the SmartDrive (SmartDRV.EXE line):

`DEVICE=C:\SmartDRV.EXE /DOUBLE_BUFFER+`

Q.   Why doesn't my Novell NWPOPUP.EXE messaging utility initialize properly? When I exit Windows I get all my messages.

A.   If you are running Windows in 386 enhanced mode and a version of Novell NetWare's NWPOPUP.EXE with a file date earlier than 3/10/92 is in your WINDOWS directory, or if NWPOPUP.EXE is located in a directory prior to the Windows directory entry in the PATH= statement, then NWPOPUP.EXE will get loaded and will not initialize properly under Windows 3.1. It may also be necessary to try placing the following line in the [386Enh] section of your SYSTEM.INI file:

```
TimerCriticalSection=10000
```

This increases the amount of time (specified in milliseconds) before the critical section is timed out.

Q.   When I choose the Ports icon in Control Panel, the Advanced button in the Ports dialog box is unavailable (dimmed). Why is this?

A.   If the Windows 3.1 COMM.DRV file is not installed correctly, the Advanced button in the Ports dialog box will be unavailable. If you upgrade from Windows 3.0 to 3.1 and you were using a third-party communications driver in 3.0, the Windows 3.1 Setup program will not update the communications driver. To make sure your COMM.DRV file is installed correctly, try the following:

1. Make sure you have the following setting in the [boot] section of your SYSTEM.INI file:

```
COMM.DRV=COMM.DRV
```

2. Using the MS-DOS expand command (installed in the WINDOWS directory of your hard drive during Windows setup), reinstall the COMM.DRV from the Windows Setup disks (Disk 1 for 3.5-inch disks; Disk 2 for 5.25-inch disks) into the SYSTEM subdirectory of your WINDOWS directory by typing the following:

```
expand a:\comm.dr_ c:\windows\system\comm.drv
```

Q.   Most of my network workstations run with no problem, but two of them only run in standard mode and not in 386 enhanced mode. If I do not log onto the network, then I can run in 386 enhanced mode.

A.   There are four possible causes of the problem you are experiencing:

1) Incorrect network software drivers; 2) IRQ conflict; 3) RAM address conflict; or 4) Base address conflict:

1. Read the NETWORKS.WRI file for the steps necessary to upgrade your current versions of IPX and NETX. If necessary contact your network card manufacturer if you need new low-level drivers.

2. Most machines do not support having two devices using the same IRQ at the same time. This means that if you are using your network card on IRQ3 or IRQ4, then you will have to either disable COM2 or COM1, which use the same respective IRQ, or reconfigure the network card for a free IRQ. On most machines, IRQ5 and IRQ2 are free, meaning no other hardware device is attempting to use them.

3. Many network cards use a RAM address in the Upper Memory area between 640K and 1024K. If your card is using this range, then exclude use of this range with EMM386.EXE or an EMMEXCLUDE statement in the SYSTEM.INI file's [386Enh] section. Some cards will not function properly at D000 and need to be reconfigured for D800.

4. Many hardware devices have Base memory addresses (for example, COM ports). There may be a conflict with an existing device. Try reconfiguring the network card for an address of 300h or greater.

Q.   When I start File Manager, I see the following error message. What causes this?

`Cannot read from drive I.`

A.   An MS-DOS version 4.x file named GRAPHICS.COM might be the cause. Try removing from your AUTOEXEC.BAT file the command line that specifies GRAPHICS.COM. If you choose the OK button when you receive this error message, File Manager displays all of your drives; however, it cannot access any of your files. The MS-DOS version 5.0 GRAPHICS.COM file does not cause this problem.

Q.   When I print in landscape mode on a Linotronic printer, the Encapsulated PostScript (EPS) graphic portions of the document are rotated. Why?

A.   If you are using the Linotronic or another PostScript printer driver, try adding the following line to the [ModelName,Port] section of the WIN.INI file. This is the section that says:

`[Linotronic 200/230,LPT1]`

and not the section that says

```
[PostScript,LPT1]:
LandScapeOrient=270
```

Q.   What should I do when I receive the "Inadequate DPMI server" error message?

A.   This error message appears when the files KRNL386.EXE and WIN386.EXE are from different versions of Windows (when one is from 3.0 and the other from 3.1). To see if this is the problem, check the dates on the these files. They are located in the SYSTEM subdirectory of your WINDOWS directory.

It is possible that an older version of these files may be in the path or the WINDOWS directory; search the entire path for these files. If necessary, use the MS-DOS expand command to reinstall the files from the Windows Setup program. (The expand command is installed in the WINDOWS directory of your hard drive during Windows setup).

This error message can also appear when your system memory-configuration settings (sometimes referred to as CMOS settings) don't match the amount of memory the system actually has. The way you change the settings depends on the type of hardware you have. For more information about changing these settings, see your hardware documentation.

Q.   When switching to the MS-DOS Prompt from Windows, I receive the following error message:

```
Incorrect system version. Please install the 386 Enhanced section and run
Setup again.
```

What does this mean and what should I do?

A.   There are two possible solutions to this problem:

1. An old WINOA386.MOD may be located in the WINDOWS directory or the path. Delete the old file and use the MS-DOS expand command to expand an updated version from the Windows 3.1 disks by typing:

```
expand a:\winoa386.mo_ c:\windows\system\winoa386.mod
```

The expand command is installed in the WINDOWS directory of your hard drive during Windows setup.

2. In the SYSTEM.INI file, there are three lines that specify what kind of video driver Windows uses when running in 386 enhanced mode. These are 386Grabber= and display.drv= (located in the [boot] section) and display= (located in the [386Enh] section). The "Incorrect system version" error message usually occurs when one of these entries is not consistent with the others. To reset these drivers exit Windows and change to the WINDOWS directory, then type SETUP and press [Return]. Next select the current Display option and press enter then, from the Display list box, select VGA (version 3.0) and press [Return]. Finally, if you are asked to use an existing driver, press the [Esc] key to load new drivers.

Q.   Can I set up a permanent or temporary swap file on a "stacked" disk drive?

A.   Windows 3.1 does not support the use of a permanent or temporary swap file on a "stacked" drive. A stacked drive is one on which you are running the Stac Electronics' Stacker utility.

WINDOWS NT – THE FUTURE

When Microsoft first released Windows, it wasn't taken very seriously by software manufacturers. When you understand its origins, this is hardly surprising. The first version of Windows didn't appear until three years after its announcement by Microsoft, and when it finally hit the streets Windows 1 was slow and unattractive. GUIs were far from new in 1986, and so were PCs, and at that point there was no way Windows was going to encroach on the new Colour Macintosh II's ground-breaking WIMP environment. This wasn't entirely Microsoft's fault as advances in PC hardware had not been as rapid as expected, and even in its fledgeling first version Windows required just too much power for the average PC to cope with it.

Software companies started to lose interest, and Windows started to go through a bad patch. It fought back by releasing Windows 2, which was a considerable improvement over its predecessor, but it was still only designed for the 286 processor, and by now the 386 had made its appearance, and software companies were looking for something else. Not only were they finding it more and more expensive writing programs for Windows that didn't sell, but they had discovered that it was rather lucrative to produce programs for the Mac's more powerful hardware and software platform. Microsoft, meanwhile, were releasing versions of Windows left, right and centre out of sheer desperation; Windows/286 was followed by Windows/386, both in an attempt to take advantage of each chip to the fullest. And then, of course, there was OS/2...

A joint venture between Microsoft and IBM, OS/2 was supposed to ultimately replace the symbiotic relationship between Windows and DOS. It was a stand-alone operating system with a Windows-like front end (known as Presentation Manager) but with the advantage that it was complete unto itself and therefore theoretically more solid.

Because of IBM's apparent failure to sell OS/2, Microsoft saw their chance and decided to push the team currently working on the next Windows version even harder, and when Windows 3.0 was released in 1990, it started the split between Microsoft (who swore blind that it wasn't in direct competition with the forthcoming OS/2.2) and IBM (who swore blind that it was). And the rest is history, as they say. But now that we have Windows 3.1, does this mean that Microsoft will just keep pushing better and better versions of the same old software at us?

The main problem with Windows 3 – both 3.0 and 3.1, and any other potential 3.x version that Microsoft might have up their sleeves – is that it isn't a true operating system. It sits between DOS and Windows applications, translating calls from each program into plain old DOS and BIOS calls. It's really nothing more than an attractive insulator, with the one advantage (admittedly a gigantic one) that all programs written for Windows use the same user interface, thus shortening the learning curve for otherwise dauntingly-powerful applications.

It is this fact, aside from the visual appeal of Windows 3, that is single-handedly responsible for sales of over a million copies a month, and Microsoft know it. But they also know it could sell even better if it was one single operating system with DOS – and that's exactly what Windows NT is. A full 32-bit, object-oriented operating system, Windows NT (for New Technology) is set to take on all-comers – specifically OS/2.2, which this time has turned the tables and beaten it into the shops.

OS/2.2 has already won a lot of respect for its solid, fast environment (and its pre-emptive multitasking is undoubtedly better suited to running a network) but it's even more greedy of system resources than Windows NT is reputed to be, and that won't sell machines to the public.

Which will be the best (or even the ultimate winner) remains to be seen. But one thing is undeniable, windows has millions more users than OS/2, and when IBM lose the right to build the latest Windows compatibility into new version of OS/2, they will no longer be able to make the claim: "Better Windows than Windows"

HALFWAY HOUSE

Already there is available a way of writing Windows 3.1 software which will run under Windows NT when it arrives. It is called Win32s and is Microsoft's first step towards providing a Windows NT environment on MS-DOS based operating systems. With Win32s, programs written for tomorrow's 32-bit operating systems will run on Windows version 3.1.

32-bit development means that applications no longer have to deal with the segmented memory addressing of 16-bit systems. This will facilitate memory allocation in most applications because 64K memory boundaries no longer apply.

32-bit applications are faster and more efficient because they take advantage of the 32-bit specific instructions and register sets available in 80386 and 80486 computers. Moreover, Intel is optimizing the 80486 and future processors for 32-bit operation instead of 16-bit operation.

Applications developed for UNIX or other 32-bit environments are often difficult to port to 16-bit systems because of memory constraints. Win32s removes the 64K memory barrier so these 32-bit applications are easier to port. According to Microsoft, Win32s is an "integral part" of their system strategy and represents the first step in the evolutionary process towards 32-bit processing in Windows. Although Windows for MS-DOS will continue to run 16-bit applications, Microsoft plans to convert the Windows operating system code to 32 bits.

A BIT OF UNDOCUMENTED FUN

Most program developers like to 'hide' their names (and often photos) inside their applications, viewable only if you know (or can discover) the devious combination of key presses and mouse clicks. Here are some of the more interesting of them:

WINDOWS 3.0 GANG SCREEN

There is a 'Gang Screen' in Windows three which lists all the people involved in its development. To see it, reduce the size of program manager or drag it down so that only the very top is visible, at the bottom of the screen. The press and hold [F3]. type the four characters WIN3, release [F3] and press the back space key. You can clear the display by clicking on it with the left mouse button.

WINDOWS 3.1 GANG SCREEN

A similar (but better) hidden feature also exists in Windows 3.1 To get it hold down [Control] and [Shift] simultaneously and keep holding them down for all of the following steps.

Next select the Help Menu of one of the applications supplied with Windows 3.1, such as the Program Manager), and select "About Program Manager". When the box pops up, double-click inside one of the four panes in the Windows 3.1 logo and click on OK.

Now repeat the steps in the previous paragraph to see a flag waving. Repeat them one more time to see the credits – the display terminates immediately when the OK button is pressed.

The character appearing in the graphic with the name scroll changes each time you see it. There are four distinct figures, a bald man (Steve Ballmer), a man with a beard and dark hair (Brad Silverberg), a man with glasses and fair hair (Bill Gates), and a Teddy bear.

WORD FOR WINDOWS 1.1 GANG SCREEN

To see the authors' names and some fireworks, turn CAPS LOCK on, choose Format, Define Styles, Options. Then, in the Based On field, select Normal and you will get an error message. Ignore it and select OK. Now select Cancel, Help and About. Then make sure your mouse cursor is inside the help box and hold down the keys OPUS, all at the same time.

WORD FOR WINDOWS 2.0 GANG SCREEN

To see some cute animation, a not-so-subtle jab at WordPerfect, and a list of those responsible for "wizardry", "quality", and so on, on the Word for Windows 2.0

project, start Word for Windows 2.0. In the Tools menu, click on Macro and for the Macro Name, type

`spiff`

Then click on Edit and delete the following two lines

```
Sub MAIN
End Sub
```

Now, in the File menu, choose Close and you will be asked if you want to save the changes so click on Yes. Then, in the Help menu, click on About and then click on the Word icon in the upper left.

If you have high resolution drivers, you might not see that awful green WordPerfect monster or the little people jumping up and down in glee after they make it go away. If all you see is the fireworks with the credits rolling in the foreground, then this is the case. Change to a lower resolution (800x600 or 640x480) driver to also see the first part.

NORTON DESKTOP FOR WINDOWS 2.0 GANG SCREEN

With NDW 2.0 in the foreground, hold down the N, D, and W keys, then click on HELP and ABOUT, then double-click on the Symantec icon in the upper left corner. You will then see a window pop up which contains 15 black and white pictures of people with a status bar entitled NDW Development Team.

The title scrolls to the left and is replaced with a list of names followed by quotations from famous people.

PROCOMM PLUS FOR WINDOWS GANG SCREEN

To get at this gang screen, from the Window menu, select Monitor and make sure monitor is active (not the Procomm Plus terminal window). Then type GO DATASTORM! (the exclamation mark is necessary), and choose Help, About and Credits. Now, instead of the usual list of names, you will see a nice colour picture of the primary developers.

AMI PRO GANG SCREEN

For this screen go to the About box under the Help menu and hold down the [Shift], [Control], and [Alt] keys. Then press [F7] and then type the letters SPAM followed by the last and third-to-last numbers in the Available Memory display. Then release the [Shift], [Control, and [Alt] keys. Tiny photo images of the Ami Pro developers will then appear.

COREL DRAW! V3.0 GANG SCREEN

This is quite an interesting gang screen. To get to it hold down [Control][Shift] and select Help followed by About]. Then, while still holding down [Control][Shift], double click on the balloon on the left side of the help box. The box will now expand and the text disappear as the balloon moves to the bottom of the box.

Hold down the left, then the right mouse button to light the burner on the balloon. If you hold it down you'll see the balloon move up, pulling a text banner listing authors and beta testers.

WINDOWS SOLITAIRE CHEAT

If you're playing "Draw Three" where you only get to see every third card, you can hold down [Ctrl][Alt][Shift] (all together) and click on the deck to draw single cards.

MINESWEEPER CHEAT

Start Minesweeper normally and, when it has loaded, type "xyzzy [Enter]" followed by "[Shift][Enter]"; the upper left-hand pixel on your screen will light up whenever your mouse is over a safe square.

CHAPTER 6

LOOKING AFTER YOUR DATA

Data is a valuable commodity and as more and more of it is stored on magnetic media, the chances of losing it become greater. There are many potential causes of data or program loss, ranging from hard disk crashes caused by a faulty or damaged drive, floppy disk failure possibly due to being exposed to magnetic fields or condensation (or even finger prints), or the current scourge, computer viruses.

But if you take the right precautions you won't need to worry so much because it is possible to prevent virtually all types of data loss by make frequent backups, having regular hardware checks and installing a virus detector and eradicator. Here are some suggestions in detail.

FILE VERIFICATION

Using ordinary DOS it is not possible to perform a true read-after-write check when copying files. But the VERIFY command can be of some use in this respect as it turns on (or off) a flag that tells DOS to do extra checking when writing to disk or diskette.

When the verify flag is ON, the Cyclic Redundancy Check (CRC) characters written to the disk with each cluster of information are compared with the same calculation done in memory beforehand. This is very fast, so the speed reduction is slight. Though CRC-checking is not 100% effective, it should catch most errors when data is written to disk, and these errors should be few and far between anyway.

A bad problem sometimes can occur when data is written to a defective disk where it can be written, but not always read back again. Unless the error occurs in the CRC bytes themselves, even VERIFY will not warn you. To get over that problem you can always do a short test of the files on a disk before storing or sending someone files using the COPY command, like this:

```
COPY *.* NUL
```

This reads all the files in the directory, copying them into thin air. If there is a problem reading part of a file, it is the last one whose name is displayed that has the problem.

If you want to verify an entire disk, and there are no subdirectories on it, type:

`DISKCOMP A: A:`

This checks the entire disk against itself, reporting any errors in the process.

FORMATTING 5.25" DISKS IN HIGH DENSITY DRIVES

If you ever get this message when trying to format 5.25" disks in a high-density (1.2Mbyte) drive:

```
Invalid media or track 0 bad - disk unusable
Format failure
```

Then don't immediately blame the computer – you might very well be doing something wrong.

FORMAT is one of those programs that requires a wide variety of parameters to cover all format types. If in doubt you should check your manual carefully before using it. For example the command:

`FORMAT A: /N:9`

is intended to format 720K disks in a high-density 1.44 Mbyte 3.5" drive, not 360K 5.25" disks in a 1.2 Mbyte drive. So if this is what you are trying to do, the command line you need is this:

`FORMAT A: /4`

But it's not infallible. Check your DOS manual and you'll see that while this is a perfectly acceptable command, there is no guarantee that disks formatted in this way will be readable in another machine which uses true 360K drives. And if you get a message like the one above just by typing a simple command like:

`FORMAT A:`

Then there are two possibilities – firstly, a failed attempt at using the N:/9 switch may well have rendered the disk unusable, even for subsequent normal formatting. And secondly – obvious though it sounds – make absolutely sure that the disks you are using are true 1.2 Mbyte disks. The disk box label should state explicitly that the disks are double-sided, high-density – don't attempt to format ordinary 5.25" disks as high density or you will definitely get this error every time.

DATA SECURITY

Data security is a common theme amongst business users, who often ask what they can do to prevent unauthorised people seeing sensitive data which is kept on a publicly-accessible PC.

Those who know something about DOS soon realise that some office programs designed to keep staff locked firmly within their environment actually include the facility to "shell out" to DOS – thus providing access to the entire hard disk, and defeating the object of a "secure" program.

This whole question of security is quite a tricky one. Automenu is a good program to try, and offers a fair amount of protection – but, unfortunately, it's one of those systems that allow users to shell to DOS.

Alternatively you could use one of the many file encryption programs to scramble your data. The only problem is you have to descramble it before you can use it, and it would be unwise to forget the password!

Or, of course, you could copy your sensitive files onto a floppy disk and delete the originals using a file wiper (which writes zeros over a file before deleting it, to ensure it can't be un-deleted), and then just lock the floppies in a safe.

Another program you could try is called MENUGEN from Microft Technology which will prevent unwanted shelling to DOS. With its numerous other features like different security levels and restricted time slots, at £48 plus VAT it is excellent value for money.

You can even modify the batch file used to launch an application (or the menu definition file in the case of Automenu) to disable DOS shelling completely. Try adding these lines:

```
Set comtemp=%comspec%
set comspec=
<run application>
set comspec=%comtemp%
```

As there will no longer be a COMSPEC in the environment while the application is running, the shell facility is fully disabled. However, it is still not a complete solution as many applications actually need the COMSPEC environment variable to be set correctly to fully function.

This is because a lot of programs often need to perform DOS-type functions such as copying files and running other applications in a suite. It is possible to write code to perform these type of functions, but a quick and easy method is to call up a second instance of COMMAND.COM and pass it the COPY command, or the name of a program to run.

WHAT IS A COMPUTER VIRUS?

Computer viruses have acquired a popular mystique over the last few years, mainly as a direct result of tabloid press sensationalism. The net result is widespread confusion and alarm, over what is a fairly rare and completely avoidable occurrence. So what exactly is a computer virus? What can they do? And how dangerous and widely-spread are they really?

Computer viruses only became possible because of the way in which modern computers themselves work. Operating systems which load themselves from the same location on your hard or floppy disk at the start of each session are immediately susceptible to "infection" from a program which has deliberately been put in its place, or even incorporated into its structure.

The ultimate source of all infections is always from an ordinary program, which has either been deliberately infected by the virus writer, or is in fact a full-blown virus going under the guise of a useful application or utility. Such programs are known as "Trojan horses", because they serve no purpose other than to infect a machine under cover of a legitimate job.

You can establish the presence of a virus, and even destroy it with the appropriate virus killer, but how can you be sure that your system has been fully "sterilised" after an attack? This is where modern memory-resident virus protectors come into play. Like viruses, they are TSR programs which sit in memory, watching all disk accesses carefully.

The difference is that they are on the watch for improper disk and memory writes. Any attempt to write to a PC's boot sector, for example, is of major concern as no program has any business in this area of a hard disk, unless it is a hard disk format utility like FDISK.

However, writes to normal areas of the disk are more difficult to spot, as are attempts to modify a program image held in memory but, even so, it's possible to thwart even these violations (although it would be incautious to explain exactly how).

HOW SERIOUS ARE VIRUSES?

Limiting the number of initial viral infections of an organization is important, but it is often not feasible to prevent them entirely. As a result, it's important to be able to deal with them when they occur.

Most viruses discovered to date have either been relatively benign, or have spread rather slowly. The actual damage that they have caused has been limited accordingly, but in some cases thousands of machines have been affected. Here are some steps you can follow to decrease the risks:

Keep good backups of critical data and programs, periodically review overall controls to determine weaknesses, consider limiting electronic mail communications to non-executable files, make security education a prerequisite to any computer use, develop a plan to deal with viruses before there is a problem, know how to recover from a viral infection, test the plan periodically, (as you would with fire drills) and DON'T use a real virus to test your security measures.

DECREASING THE RISK OF VIRAL INFECTION

Viruses can spread from one user to another on a single system, and from one system to another. A virus can enter a company either by being written within the company, or by being brought in from the outside. Although a virus cannot be written accidentally, a virus may be brought in either intentionally or unintentionally.

Because the sharing of programs between people is so commonplace, it is difficult to prevent an initial infection from "outside." An employee may take a program home to use it for business purposes on his or her home computer, where it then becomes infected. When the program is returned to the work place, the infection can spread to the work place. Similarly, an outside person can bring a set of programs into a company in order to perform work desired by the company. If these programs are infected, and they are executed on the company's systems, these systems may also become infected.

DETECTING VIRAL INFECTIONS

All of the methods outlined above for preventing viral infections are fairly reliable but viruses can still reach some systems despite the implementation of preventative measures. No perfect defence exists that still allows programming, and sharing of executable information and there is no instant cure.

The two most important resources available for the detection of viruses are watchful users and watchful programs. The best approaches to virus detection include both. The users should be aware of the possibility of viruses, just as they are aware of the need for backups, and to know what kinds of things to watch for. System programs and utilities should be available to help the users, and the computer centre staff, to take advantage of this awareness.

Computer viruses generally spread exponentially. If a virus has infected only one system in a network on Monday, and spread to four by Tuesday, sixteen systems could easily be infected by Wednesday, and over five hundred by Friday. Because viruses can spread so fast, it is very important to detect them as early as possible after the first infection. The surest way of doing this is to have every vulnerable user run the best available virus-detection software as often as feasible. This solution may be too expensive and time-consuming for most environments.

RECOVERING FROM VIRAL INFECTIONS

Once a virus has been detected and identified, and measures have been taken to stop it from spreading further, it is necessary to recover from the infection, and get back to business as usual. The main objective of this activity is to provide each affected user with a normal, uninfected computing environment.

For individual work stations, this means ensuring that no infected files remain on the work station. For more complex environments, it means ensuring that no infected files remain anywhere on the system where they might inadvertently be executed.

The basic recovery activities are replacing every infected object in the system with an uninfected version and restoring any other objects that the virus' actions may have damaged. It is of critical importance during these activities to avoid re-introducing the virus into the system. This could be done, for instance, by restoring an infected executable file from a backup tape.

COMMON QUESTIONS AND ANSWERS ABOUT THE MICHELANGELO VIRUS

The Michelangelo virus rears its head in the news media as each March 6th comes around, so here's a roundup of the most common questions asked about this virus, and their answers:

Q: What is the Michelangelo virus?

A: The Michelangelo is a computer virus that attaches to the boot sector of floppy disks and the partition table (sometimes referred to as the master boot record) of hard disks. In other words, the virus replaces the bootstrap code at the beginning of a disk. In this manner, the virus will be loaded from that disk the next time it is booted from.

Q: How does it spread itself?

A: When a floppy disk infected with the Michelangelo virus is booted from, the computer reads in the boot sector to find out where the operating system is on the disk. Instead of running the boot code that is normally there, the virus is loaded first. It then installs itself in memory like a device driver or TSR program. The virus proceeds to monitor the system for accesses to the first floppy and hard disk drives on the system. When a non-infected disk is inserted into the computer and accessed, the virus infects the disk.

Q: What type of damage can it do?

A: When it infects a floppy disk, it copies the original boot sector from the first sector of the disk into the last sector used to store directory information about the disk. This may cause the corruption or loss of files on floppies.

Because of this, the original floppy disk boot sector may become corrupted when directory entries overwrite it. This may make disks non-bootable. Also, conflicts with software that perform low-level accesses to the disk such as disk optimizers and sector editors may occur.

On March the 6th of any year, the Michelangelo virus will trigger if an infected disk is booted from. The virus will proceed to copy the contents of memory starting at address 5000:0000h across heads 0-3, tracks 0-255, sectors 1-9 of the hard disk.

This will overwrite about the first 9Mb of a hard disk. Information that was stored in this area of the hard disk will be lost and be unrecoverable. Since the erased area also includes the system area of the hard disk, the hard disk will no longer boot and will either need to be FDISKed and FORMATted – a process that will erase all of the information on the hard disk or taken to a data recovery specialist to salvage information off of the hard disk.

Q: How can you check for the Michelangelo virus?

A: Running the DOS CHKDSK command on an infected system will reveal that 653,312 bytes (638Kb) of memory is available instead of 655,360 bytes (640Kb). However, this symptom can apply to other viruses such as the Stoned or can be caused by having a bus card mouse (PS/2-style) installed or using BIOS shadowing on a PC. The most effective way to check for Michelangelo is to use an anti-viral program.

Q: How can I protect my PC from it?

A: The current versions of most anti-viral programs will detect, remove, and protect against the Michelangelo virus. If you are unsure if an anti-viral program will work against it, then contact the supplier. While older packages may not detect the Michelangelo virus, many manufacturers have bulletin boards or CompuServe Forums where updates to detect the virus can be downloaded. If you have a CompuServe account, then you can download public domain and Shareware programs to detect and remove viruses from the Computer Virus Help Forum (GO VIRUSFORUM).

JUST WHAT IS A STEALTH VIRUS?

Well, a stealth virus about to infect a file first takes a "snapshot" of the file's image, infects it and adds the "snapshot" to the file's tail. Having done that the virus makes itself resident by attaching itself to the disk controller interrupts. Thereafter, whenever you issue requests to look at parts of the infected file, the resident program simply returns parts of the snapshot area – so as far as you can tell the file is exactly the same as it always was.

That's why this type of program is called a stealth virus, and the only way to prevent them infecting your PC is to make sure you install your own anti-stealth software (such as Dr. Soloman's VirusGuard, or the Central Point or Norton anti virus toolkits) on a 100% guaranteed clean machine, so that it can keep a look out for any virus attempting to go memory resident.

PC FILE/VIRUSGUARD CLASH WORK-AROUND

There is an incompatibility between PC File 5.01 from Buttonware and the memory resident virus scanner VirusGuard. The cause of this problem is known and there is a work-around, supplied by S&S International – the distributers of VirusGuard.

When PC File opens a database, it looks for a macro file with the same name as the other database files and the extension .KEY. If this file does not exist, it tries to read from a file with the impossible handle of 0FFFFH. Normally DOS returns an error code for this attempt and PC File recovers its equilibrium. However, when VirusGuard is resident it intercepts this call and PC File cannot recover.

The work-around is to ensure that there is a file with the .KEY extension for every database you use with PC File. It does not have to contain anything meaningful – it's just needed to ensure that PC File makes its read attempt using a valid file handle.

When creating a new database, the .KEY file should be constructed in advance from the command line, like this:

```
COPY CON DBASENAM.KEY
```

Then press [Space] followed by [Return], and finally [Ctrl][Z] and the file will be created. Note that in place of DBASENAM you should type the name of the database you will be creating. This problem does not occur with version 6 of PC File, as it has been rectified.

There is another security product from Airtech called PC-Guard which also exhibits this clash, and the same solution will work for this product too.

UPGRADING DISK DRIVES

If you want to upgrade from a 5.25" low-density drive (360k) to a 3.5" low density drive (720k), you may find that once the installation is complete the new drive will read and write 720K disks quite happily but it will only allow you to format them to 360K – and even DRIVPARM doesn't always help.

The answer lies in the blocks of memory held by the BIOS known as Device Parameter Blocks. There is one of these blocks for each drive on the machine and they hold information which DOS uses when it formats a disk (this seems to be the only time this information is used, all other functions read information from the boot sector of a disk).

Fortunately DOS provides a function to change the block for each drive. It is (hold your breath) INT 21, Function 44h, subfunction 0Dh, Minor function 60h.

Below is a DEBUG script that makes use of this function to change the BIOS parameter block for drive 2 (the B drive) so that it is suitable for controlling a 720K 3.5" drive. If you are installing your new drive as A:, simply change the line

```
MOV BL,02
```

to:

```
MOV BL,01
```

The file created by the script, FORM720.COM, will work on DOS versions 3.2 and above. But a word of warning is in order. The BIOS will believe exactly what you tell it. If you say that there is a 720K drive fitted when there isn't it will try to format a 360K disk to 720K, resulting in a lot of loud scraping noises from the drive.

```
NFORM720.COM
RCX
32
A
JMP 11E
DB 0,2,0,0,50,0,0
DB 0,2,2,1,0,2,70
DB 0,A0,5,F9,3,0,9
DB 0,2,0,0,0,0,0
MOV AH,44
MOV AL,0D
MOV BL,02
MOV CH,08
MOV CL,40
MOV DX,103
INT 21
MOV AH,4C
INT 21

W
Q
```

Run Debug and then type all of this in. Where you see the blank line after the second INT 21 simply press [Return]. If you have entered everything correctly the file FORM720.COM will be created which you should call up prior to formatting any disks – or place a call to in your AUTOEXEC.BAT file.

RECOVERING FROM RECOVER

If you accidentally wipe a floppy disk containing important data using the RECOVER command, all is not lost as you should be able to regain access to your data with any good disk sector editor.

To start with, use DISKCOPY to take an image of the problem disk so that you have a copy which is safe to work on. Then, using this new copy, run your disk editor and switch to the root sector of the disk where there should be a display showing various files with the name FILExxxx.REC, where xxxx are numbers in ascending order. These files have been created by RECOVER and hold the contents of all the files and subdirectories that were on the disk prior to the RECOVERy.

Directly following each REC extension you will find the attribute byte which should read either 20H or 00H (hexadecimal) for a normal file. Change this to 10H for each of the files (which makes DOS think each file is really a directory) and exit the disk editor. Now run CHKDSK on the drive with the /F option, like this:

```
CHKDSK A: /F
```

Ignore any comments about "cross linked" files, and if asked "Convert directory to file?" answer "Yes". Your original directory structure should now be restored, along with all the files. Where you had any subdirectories you will find all the files and sub-subdirectories are now also fully restored. All of these will still be referred to by all the FILExxxx.REC files in your root directory, but you can ignore those files with the exception of the following:

If you originally had some files in your root directory then they will not have had their names restored, but they will be the first few FILExxxx.REC files on the disk. To see which file is which, re-enter your disk editor, have a browse through them and when you have worked out what each file used to be, rename them to their original filenames. Now all you need to do is to copy the files you need to either your hard disk or to a new floppy, and all your data should be restored. Don't use either the original RECOVERed disk, or the floppy containing the image you took – these should be reformatted in case they exhibit further problems.

Incidentally, if you change a directory's attribute byte from 10H to 20H you will make the directory inaccessible until you change the byte back to 10H – this is a little-known (but very handy) way to hide sensitive data.

You should note that sometimes changes made to a disk in this manner are not always immediately noticed by DOS, but you can force it to update itself by running CHKDSK on a floppy – making sure you DON'T use the /F option. And if you are at all unsure about this tip, only try it on disks from which you have taken backups.

But why was such a potentially damaging program ever included with MSDOS? Rather than recovering disks it actually seems to make a complete mess of them. Nevertheless some people use this command as a quick, brute force method of wiping a floppy disk, using a batch file such as this:

```
RECOVER A:
DEL A:*.REC
```

But please be extremely careful when trying the above "format" program! Once you've pressed [Return], there's no going back other than by following the above solution – which takes a lot of patience, hard work, judgement – and luck.

USING RESTORE ACROSS DOS VERSIONS

Many people use the BACKUP command, only to find that when they later come to using the companion RESTORE command it simply will not bring back their data.

The answer is usually quite simple in that this normally only happens if you change DOS versions in the meantime, but why on earth it should happen in the first place is a mystery – surely the BACKUP and RESTORE combination is the one area of DOS in which compatibility must be maintained through all versions? However, the problem remains, and so do the complaints. So let's take a look at what can be done if this happens to you.

One solution is to buy version 5.0 (or higher) of MS-DOS, which offers complete backward-compatibility with all previous versions of the BACKUP command down to 3.3, and if you backed-up under DOS 3.2, Microsoft will supply a utility free of charge that enables you to restore the file.

Since version 5, DOS is available as an Upgrade Kit with an installation program intelligent enough to make the upgrade practically painless; it installs the new version onto your hard disk without disturbing your existing programs. A fail-safe system is also included, so that if you are unhappy (or the installation is not successful) you can immediately 'uninstall' the new version and return to your old DOS.

Alternatively, if you can find someone running a matching version of DOS on their machine you could try RESTOREing your files to their hard disk, and then copy them to floppies in the normal way with COPY. Another variation on this problem is software distributed in BACKUP form – a foolish thing to do, it has to be said, but some people don't even realise there are pitfalls to this method.

So if you need to RESTORE files to someone else's machine but you keep getting the "Incorrect DOS version" message, try the following technique:

Always carry a version of your own RESTORE.COM utility around with you on disk. When you encounter this problem on a foreign PC, simply rename the target machine's version of this file as RESTORE.OLD and put your copy on the hard disk in its place. After the RESTORE process is over, delete it and rename their version back to normal.

Finally, if you are a software writer who insists on distributing your files in BACKUP form, put your own RESTORE.COM file on the distribution disk. Make sure that the installation program, whether a batch file or otherwise, calls this version explicitly.

This guards against your installation utility changing to drive C: at some point, where normally the target machine's RESTORE command would get priority.

USING DEVICE NAMES AS FILE NAMES

You should always avoid using device names in any part of a filename. It is a little-known feature of DOS that not only does it allow you to redirect output to any legal device, such as NUL or PRN, but you can also treat any device as a file! For example, try the following:

```
DEL PRN
```

You may be intrigued to find that your computer, rather than collapsing in a fit of giggles, treats this command seriously and responds with:

```
Access denied
```

If you think about it, you've seen this sort of thing before; remember this one, from the DOS manual?

```
COPY CON AUTOEXEC.BAT
```

Yes – it's exactly the same sort of thing. No pipes, filters or other redirection is involved; it simply tells DOS to copy a file called CON to one called AUTOEXEC.BAT, and it's the standard way of configuring your computer when you don't have a text editor (at least it was prior to DOS 5).

DOS obligingly obeys, and the file CON is immediately copied, ultimately creating AUTOEXEC.BAT when [Ctrl][Z] is pressed. Of course CON isn't a file at all, but the console device – however DOS doesn't know this. It is programmed to be flexible with its input and output, as are all good operating systems, and being able to interchange filenames with devices is a necessary part of any OS.

But this flexibility cuts both ways. If you ever use a device name by accident as the filename for a document you are writing, you won't be able to save it. It's not as unlikely as you might think, once you consider how many legal device names there are: NUL, PRN, CON, LPT1, LPT2, COM1, COM2, AUX...

The most likely result of trying to save a document called, for example, AUX, is the following message (depending on your word processor):

```
File exists - Overwrite (Y/N)?
```

This is because most word processors that are about to save a file will ask DOS if such a file already exists – and in this case, it does. DOS, oblivious of the fact that the whole procedure is impossible anyway, looks for a file called AUX. And sure enough, one already exists – as far as DOS is concerned.

So what happens if you reply "Yes" to this question? It's a tempting thing to try, but unfortunately you won't see anything interesting – just the "Access denied" message (but you weren't sure for a while there, were you?).

The lateral thinkers amongst you might already have thought of using ATTRIB to remove any read-only attributes from these "files"! Unfortunately (for them, at any rate), DOS suddenly starts behaving reasonably again, and forgets all about interchangeable file and device names – all you'll get in response to:

```
ATTRIB -r AUX
```

is the rather curt:

```
File not found
```

And using DIR in this manner gets the same treatment. Apparently the programmers at Microsoft have enough forethought when it suits them... More fun and games can be had with serial and parallel ports. For example, typing:

```
TYPE COM1
```

will send your PC off into a black hole. [Ctrl][C] should bring it back, but whatever you do don't try this one:

```
COPY CON NUL
```

or you'll be reaching for the big red button before you can say "endless loop".

There is one useful tip to come out of all this; copying any file to NUL is an instant way to verify its integrity without physically creating another instance of that file. It's a very useful way of testing that files you've just copied to floppy disk were transferred successfully, because you'll receive any of the error messages that would occur during a normal copy.

SIMPLE COPY PROTECTION

These days outright copy-protection has gone out of favour with the software industry as a whole; after may years of complaints from users that the "key" disk no longer works, or that they can't make safety backups of an expensive game or application, companies began to realise that it was in their own interest – as well as everyone else's – to back down over the issue.

The current vogue is to put the protection elsewhere, and this usually means putting it in the manual itself. The first attempts at this method of protection involved printing manuals in strange colours which wouldn't photocopy. Documentation in shades of midnight blue began to appear, and for a while all of the latest games were distributed like this.

But not only did it not prevent the software from being pirated – however annoying the lack of printed instructions might be – users weren't prepared to risk their eyesight peering at microscopic type faces lovingly rendered in black-on-blue. And the advent of new, cheaper colour photocopiers meant that the average pirate could simply take a stroll down the high street to the nearest printing bureau and run off a few copies (if he or she was too lazy to copy the thing by hand in the first place).

The longest-surviving and most popular method for copy protecting software is to have it ask the user to enter certain words from the manual at the start of each session. Again, not foolproof, but it's as good a trick as any. You have to copy the entire manual, not just the operating instructions and game control section, or at some point it's going to ask you for something on a page you haven't got.

Having said all that, there's still nothing to stop anyone from going the full hog and copy-protecting the actual disks – it's a matter of personal choice, and if you have written a program in any language and you want to experiment with ways of protecting it, you may be interested in some of the following simple techniques which are designed to safeguard small-scale programs from casual misuse.

HIDDEN FILES

All of the techniques mentioned here are non-destructive and one hundred percent safe, because they all make use of hidden files to fox inexperienced pirates.

As you probably know, all files can be hidden from casual inspection by setting their "hidden" attribute. This used to be the province of professional programmers only, but the advent of cheap utilities and, more recently DOS 5, put full control of file attributes in users' own laps. The trick is to include a "dummy" file as part of your software, which can be zero bytes long if you like. Make this file hidden, either by using a disk editor like Norton's, or by typing the following command in DOS 5:

```
ATTRIB +h filename
```

Use the name of the file to be hidden in place of the word "filename" above. Now if you try typing DIR, it'll be gone from the directory listing.

The next stage is to include in your program a simple check for that file's existence. If you want, you can even do this in the batch file that launches your program (if it uses one); it might look something like this:

```
@ECHO OFF
IF EXIST filename GOTO ok
ECHO This is an unauthorised copy,
ECHO and will not run.
GOTO end
:ok
BASIC filename
:end
```

Don't forget to replace "filename" with the name of your program. If you have acquired a utility to issue a warm (or even cold) boot, you could insert a call to it in the batch file in place of the "GOTO end" line – that will annoy a few pirates!

There are two reasons this method works so effectively. Firstly it makes no difference to the "IF EXIST" check whether the file in question is hidden or not; if it's there, it will be found. Secondly, COPY ignores all hidden files. And if you want an extra bonus, go for the zero-length option as well; COPY won't touch zero-length files, so if your hidden file is also zero bytes long, you're covered two ways!

So if a light-fingered user has swiped the entire program directory on to floppy disk and given the disks to a friend, said friend will be a file short when copying them onto his or her PC – and the batch file will refuse to run the application.

Now it is relatively easy to spot this technique in a batch file, and therefore very easy to remove the checks. So you might choose instead to place the checking inside your application proper. The only problem is that your particular programming language might not support the ability to verify the existence of hidden files.

But don't worry; there's a way around this one, too. One of the features of DOS is its ability to run hidden files, so if you can split your application into two (or more) separate, self-contained EXE or COM program files you can make one dependent on the other.

For example, you only need a small EXE file who's sole purpose in life is to call the main program. If you make this small file hidden, the whole chain collapses if the programs are copied to another machine.

The only drawback is that you either need to write your programs in a language which can be compiled into EXE files, or write the "stepping block" program as a batch file. This is actually quite workable, and can look like this:

```
@ECHO OFF
BASIC mainprog
```

Replace the word "mainprog" with the filename of your program, save the file to disk with a name like "START.BAT" and change the word "filename" in the first listing to "start" – now you have quite an efficient protection system, for free.

Not that it is assumed that the main application is written in BASIC, but the principle is the same for all applications.

CHAPTER 7

HARDWARE PROBLEMS

In order to understand how your PC works and so make better and more efficient use of it, it is helpful know some technical details. Don't worry if you think that this chapter will "go over your head", because all the information you need has been explained in as simple terms as possible, so you should find the following explanations, tips and advice to be clear, informative and helpful. That said, this chapter covers all aspects of your PC's hardware so it's worth reading all the way through it because you'll probably pick up a few ideas that are likely to help you.

IBM COMPATIBILITY

Everything in your PC rests on everything else, apart from the raw electronics at the lowest level which support the whole weight of the system.

The BIOS sits somewhere in the middle, between DOS and the hardware, and it is the BIOS which is at the heart of so-called "IBM compatibility". The only reason that so many computers built by so many different manufacturers can run each other's software is that each machine contains a copy, or at the very least an emulation, of the original IBM BIOS. But what does it do? Well, at the simplest level it takes commands from DOS, which in turn takes them from applications, and translates them into direct hardware calls to the various devices which together make up the physical computer.

Because IBM produced the original BIOS over ten years ago, computer manufacturers have had a long time in which to study and emulate it. At first IBM tried to resist this perceived attack on its sales by taking various rivals to court. This practice was dropped as IBM finally realised that the competition was in everyone's best interests, as customers weren't going to commit themselves to one hardware standard over several dozen different ones, even if it had IBM stamped on the chassis.

Competition from Apple helped to spur IBM in its decision to let go of its monopoly – if everyone worked together, the competitive angle would change to one of "who makes the best PC?", rather than "which type of computer should I buy?" So today we have several well-established, non-IBM makes of BIOS. The names AMI and Phoenix ring with as much user-confidence as do IBM, Compaq and Olivetti.

Above the BIOS lies DOS, which is cushioned from the differences which still remain between different manufacturers BIOS' by the I/O system – often considered to be a part of the BIOS, but as it is software it is really closer in nature to DOS than to the BIOS. DOS is nothing more than a system for managing files and devices through a standard system of "DOS calls". It's a little bit like the BIOS, because they both translate commands from a standard set into something that a lower-level part of the system will understand.

Above DOS lies the applications which you run on your machine. These include, strangely enough, the DOS command processor, because it is only a program that passes commands through to DOS proper. Applications can make DOS or BIOS calls, or can even ignore them altogether and call the hardware directly.

This used to be a major headache for users, resulting in a growing number of "rogue" programs which became well-known throughout the computing community. Some even gained "cult" status because they ran so fast (they weren't hampered down by the need to pass commands down through a chain of interpreters), but they weren't guaranteed to work across the growing diversity of IBM-compatibles.

These days, most computers are what is known as "hardware compatible" with the original IBM standard, as well as being able to emulate the BIOS almost exactly. This means that it is now a lot safer to run "rogue" programs – indeed, it is fairly established practice to write to the hardware directly, especially in the games industry where speed is of the essence – and now it is computers which are considered to be "rogue", and non IBM-compatible, if they can't run programs which attempt to control the hardware!

PC BUSES – ISA, EISA and MCA EXPLAINED

With the power of modern PCs rocketing ever higher with each new generation of the 80x86 processor, users need to be aware more than ever of the potential advantages and disadvantages of lumping their investments under any particular hardware umbrella.

We're talking about buses here – not the big red things which travel in flocks around the South Circular, but the fast data highways built into your PC through which your data flows on its way between processor, memory and peripherals. There are three types of PC bus currently in use, and most of us never have to worry about what they actually do. But with real multimedia just around the corner (real, interactive audio-visual software as opposed to a few pictures and noises slung together on a CD ROM), requiring data to be thrown around the system at speeds which only five years ago were though to be impossible in a personal computer, the choice of which machine to invest in now extends past the sculptured, high-tech casing to the invisible data highways that lie within.

So what exactly is a bus? The answer is fairly simple; it's a collection of wires down which data travels. The wider the bus, the more bits can travel along it simultaneously, and that brings in another question: How wide should a bus be?

The answer to this one is also fairly clear; a bus needs to be wide enough to accommodate the data that travels around the system. This varies according to the processor in your machine; an eight-bit processor can manage quite happily with an eight-bit bus – essentially a group of eight parallel "wires". A sixteen-bit processor requires a sixteen-bit wide bus, and so on.

And there are two kinds of buses; a processor's data bus is the path along which its internal data moves – this is exactly as wide as the processor's architecture (bit size). Then there's the address bus, so called because it is the bus through which external memory is "addressed" (written to or read from).

But there is a complication, even at this early stage. Some processors can move data around themselves internally (along the data bus) in groups of 32 bits, but can only communicate with the outside world along a sixteen-bit address bus. This is done to reduce the high costs involved in equipping the entire computer to deal with twice as much data at once, and it will obviously slow the processor down as it is forced to split each "word" of data in two, sending the halves separately. But it's often a good compromise because if such a system is designed properly, it can happily use true 32 bit operating systems and software which would normally require a "full" 32-bit system to run on.

The 386-SX is such a chip, and it's because of the cheaper mother boards required to implement the processor – essentially nothing more than revamped 286 boards – that the 386-SX quickly became the entry-level PC. Of course, things have moved on a bit since then and we're now supposed to regard the 486-SX as entry-level kit (which by the way has "full" bus communication, and doesn't cut the exterior bus width in half – just to confuse you).

The original IBM PC was designed to use the 8088, which was an eight-bit processor. It was provided with a 20-bit address bus, which was considered more than adequate at the time – after all, it could address up to a megabyte of memory! The data lines on this bus were still only eight bits wide, though, and as processors became faster the restrictions of such a narrow bus width became apparent.

When the AT standard was introduced, the ISA (Industry Standard Architecture) bus was born. This had a full sixteen data lines and 24 address lines, so it was matched perfectly to the new generation of machines.

Unfortunately, processors are now whizzing data around (or trying to) at up to 32 bits, and the bus is causing a bottleneck in the system. At this point, the bright boys at IBM came up with the MCA (Micro Channel Architecture) bus, which was a full 32 bits wide (although the first version was in fact only sixteen) in every direction, both in terms of data and address lines. There was only one catch; it was totally incompatible with the ISA bus. If you bought an MCA machine, you couldn't plug in any of your expensive ISA-compatible expansion cards into it.

But of course most people saw this as mainly a marketing ploy in not-so-heavy disguise, designed to woo people away from the clone-bashers and back to Big Blue, who of course only had our best interests at heart.

But several companies thought differently, and clubbed together to thrash out a new bus standard which was as fast (or almost as fast) as MCA, but which accepted the old ISA cards. What they came up with was called the EISA (Extended Industry Standard Architecture) bus, and it worked a treat. The MCA bus has now bitten the dust, and lies there as a (very expensive) monument to IBM's last stand against the clones.

EISA machines are still very expensive, and can only be found at the higher end of the market. But don't make the mistake of thinking that because you are planning on buying a juicy 486-based machine, it's going to come equipped with an EISA bus.

ISA technology is still widely used by manufacturers of high-spec machines, so if you are going to need super-fast video, disk or memory at some point in the future – and you have the cash – make sure the guy behind the counter has heard you right; you said EISA, not ISA – didn't you?

PROCESSORS EXPLAINED

The 8088/8086 chip was designed into the original IBM PC. This chip has 20 address lines, and can therefore address 2^{20} (or 1,048,576) bytes (1 Mbyte) of memory. The PC design provided 640 Kbytes of user memory, and reserved 384 Kbytes of memory for screen driver cards, BIOS ROM and so on. The way this chip works is now known as "real mode" which is what DOS and the huge majority of programs need. The chip was used in the original PC, and then the XT.

The 286 (there was never a 288) has 24 address lines, and can address 2^{24} (or 16,777,216) bytes (16 Mbytes). This chip was used in the original AT, and is still available in lower end PC ATs. Unfortunately, the address space above 1 Mbyte can't be accessed in real mode because the segment/offset addressing in real mode can only generate addresses up to FFFFFh (1,048,575 decimal).

The main benefit of the 286 to PC users was the additional speed available, until programs like Windows arrived which could run in what is called "protected mode". This is where a PC's memory can be made up of logically mapped in chunks placed into the memory map wherever convenient. Protected mode can also be used to stop programs from reading from or writing to memory they don't own, providing safer multitasking conditions. However, because of a missing instruction in the 286, changing back from protected mode to real mode could only be done with external hardware (the keyboard controller), and was slow. A few operating systems became available which ran fully in protected mode, but these have proved unpopular due to their inability to run standard PC programs conveniently.

The 386 has up to 32 address lines (depending on the version), and addresses all the omissions of the 286. Like the 286, in real mode, it can't handle more than 1 Mbyte. But it is a fully 32 bit chip with 32 bit registers (which look like 16 bit in real mode or 286 emulation).

Programs like Windows 3 can make full use of these capabilities, and can use an effectively boundless amount of memory (up to 4 Gbytes, which is 4,096 Mbytes). Switching from real mode to protected mode is easy and fast, and for the most advanced programs, complete paging of memory is supported (in 4 Kbyte pages).

The 386 was the first Intel processor able to handle demand-paged multi-tasking operating systems, where memory is only requested by a program when needed. So, theoretically a 500K program could run in less than 16K if you had at least 500K of disk space. The chip brought a significant speed advantage, and on some high-end PCs also used a mainframe trick called "caching", where heavily used data and instructions are held in a special high-speed memory, allowing for very fast access, so speeding things up even more.

The 486 is like a 386 but even more so. The advances in chip design allow this chip to do more per clock tick than the 386, and it also includes the equivalent of a 387 maths co-processor (not on the SX version) which makes programs like Lotus run up to 10 times faster than without. So that a 486 running at the same speed as a 386 will perform far faster. It also has on-chip caching, so the high speed memory is next to the processor, and yet a further speed increase is achieved. In the final analysis a 486 running at 33MHz can be expected to perform around 40 times faster than the original IBM XT on the same programs!

MEMORY MANAGEMENT

The most confusing aspect of memory management is the good old Expanded vs Extended memory quandary. This subject confuses more people than perhaps all other PC-related topics put together. It is worth clarifying the whole issue, once and for all, and hopefully after you've read the following explanation and history of expanded and extended memory, some of the fog will have finally lifted.

To recap on the history of the subject, the need for expanded memory arose from the memory addressing limitations of the 8088 and 8086 processors. Both chips have a 20 bit address bus, giving access to only one Mbyte of memory. Originally, the designers of the IBM PC split this 50-50 between RAM and ROMs, allowing 512 Kbytes for each. This was deemed more than sufficient way back in 1981, but IBM soon relented and allocated a further 128 Kbytes for RAM-based programs. Thus the familiar 640K DOS memory limit was born.

The remaining 384 Kbytes out of the maximum one Mbyte was therefore reserved for the BIOS ROMs, expansion card ROMs and display memory – strictly out-of-bounds for poor old DOS programs. This wasn't too much of a problem initially, until the arrival of first the 286 and then the 386 family of processors. With a maximum address capability of 16 Mbytes and 4 Gbytes respectively, these devices possessed a special processor mode known as Protected Mode which allowed them to make full use of these vast amounts of memory.

Unfortunately, Protected Mode is not compatible with DOS programs, which need to run in what is known as Real Mode – essentially a backwards-compatible mode provided on the 286 and 386 series chips, specifically to allow DOS programs to run unchanged. As a result these processors were positively crippled by the constant need to run in Real Mode – that is, unless you didn't want to run DOS at all, which was hardly likely.

In 1984/5, Lotus Corporation, Intel and later good old Microsoft themselves clubbed together to thrash out a method by which memory above the 640K limit could be used by any processor which needed to run DOS programs. Jointly they created the Lotus/Intel/Microsoft (LIM) Expanded Memory Specification (EMS) version 3.2, with the first application intended to use it being the new, memory-hungry Lotus 1-2-3 release 2 (then still under development).

The idea was to make use of unallocated memory locations in the upper 384K of system memory, which is addressable by any processor from the 8088 upwards. The fact is that the IBM engineers vastly over-estimated the amount of system ROMs and hardware add-ons that would be used in the average machine, assuming that 384K would cover all future needs. It certainly did, and as a result large gaps of valuable processor-addressable memory were going to waste in this area, that would be useable as RAM if it weren't for the fact it was reserved.

The LIM EMS design allowed up to four 16K chunks of expanded memory at any one time to appear inside known unused locations, or holes in this address space. This extra 64K was called a page-frame, and was under program control.

Using an installable device driver known as an EMS or LIM driver, these pages could be rapidly switched in and out of the unused address space, providing virtually unlimited memory for data storage. Furthermore, small programs (less than 64K in size) could actually load and run in expanded memory.

The standard was soon adopted by other software developers, notably Ashton-Tate, who expanded (sorry) the standard to allow page frames of up to one Megabyte in size to be mapped into the standard one Mbyte of conventional memory. This new standard was called EEMS, and was fully compatible with LIM EMS 3.2. Not to be outdone, In 1987 Lotus, Intel and Microsoft once more joined forces and improved further on the EEMS specification to produce EMS 4.0. While remaining fully downward-compatible with EEMS, the most notable improvement was the increase in expanded memory supported – up to a maximum of 32 Mbytes.

The confusion between expanded/extended memory arises from the fact that all extra memory above the conventional 1024K which is fitted to an 80286 or 80386 processor based system is known as extended memory, regardless of how it is configured. This is simply the term for memory which lies within the CPUs address space, but which is above the conventional 1024K limit – it is just raw, unconfigured extra system memory which can only be used directly by 286/386 processors.

Expanded memory, in contrast, is fitted either as expansion boards, or is converted from the system pool of extended memory, and conforms strictly to the LIM EMS standard.

If you have a 286 or 386 based system with extended memory fitted, you will almost undoubtedly be able to convert any portion of it to behave as if it were expanded EMS/EEMS 3.2 or 4.0 compatible memory from your CMOS setup screen. If you do this you will no longer be able to use the memory directly in 286/386 Protected Mode, and will need to have a LIM EMS driver (or a compatible driver such as Quarterdeck's QEMM386 EMS manager) loaded in CONFIG.SYS to use it at all.

The advantage of configuring your extended memory as expanded is that currently there are still too few programs available which really make full use of true extended memory on 286/386 systems, whereas most major programs these days are capable of making use of expanded memory on any processor if an EMS driver is installed.

If in doubt, our advice is to keep your extended memory configured as expanded, unless you plan to use Windows in Protected Mode, or run other Protected Mode programs – you can always change it back again if you need it later.

EXTENDED MEMORY AND DOS 5.0

DOS 5.0 makes use of a number of tricks which use extended memory in order to free up as much lower memory (below 640 Kbytes) and upper memory as possible (from 640 Kbytes to 1 Mbyte) for your programs, device drivers, and TSRs.

The first trick (implemented if you say DOS=HI) is to use a quirk of the 286/386 architecture, which is that in real mode more than 1 Mbyte can be addressed. As you may know, real mode addresses are made with a segment and offset. So that the address with the segment B000h and offset 8000h is actually address B8000 (or the start of CGA text mode RAM). In other words, multiply the segment by 16 and add it to the offset to get the full 20 bit address, like this:

```
Segment             [ ssss ssss ssss ssss ]
Offset              [ oooo oooo oooo oooo ]
Address             [ aaaa aaaa aaaa aaaa aaaa ]
```

In the '88 and '86 chips this was totally true, and the largest possible address is FFFFFh, while higher addresses wrap back through 00000h. In the 286 and higher members of the family, address arithmetic involves more than 20 bits.

The largest segment value possible is FFFFh, and the largest offset is FFFFh, so the highest possible address can be determined like this:

```
Segment             FFFF0
Offset              0FFFF
Address             10FFEF
```

This means that addresses 10000h through 10FFEFh are addressable in real mode, nearly 64 Kbytes over the 1M boundary. Naturally, this was not overlooked, and DOS 5.0 tucks parts of itself that would otherwise be in lower memory up here, so that's 64 Kbytes of your memory gone.

Depending on the switches you give DOS 5.0, it can also map ROM to RAM because ROM memory is slow compared to RAM. It does it in two stages, by copying the ROM to extended memory and then using the 286/386 virtual memory mapping hardware to make this memory look as though it's at the same address as the ROM was.

When DOS runs, it sees the same bytes at the same addresses but – here's the benefit – those bytes can be read two or three times faster. However, there is a price for using extended memory, because the memory manager has to keep track of all extended memory in tables and, if you've got lots of memory, these tables can get fairly large.

In a standard PC, there are 64 Kbytes of BIOS ROM, and between 16 and 64 Kbytes of other ROMs (EGA/VGA BIOS, network drivers and so on). So you will lose between 64 and 128 Kbytes of extended memory.

It all goes to show, there's no such thing as a free lunch. You can get the memory used for ROMs back by giving the memory manager the proper switches, but that will slow things down markedly, and if you use Windows you'll need all the speed you can get. You can get the DOS HI part back, but then about 40 Kbytes of lower memory will be used instead.

WAIT-STATES EXPLAINED

Another source of confusion is the subject of CPU wait-states. Users generally understand that a wait-state is something to do with the CPU having to be slowed down to match the speed of cheap on-board memory chips, but are often puzzled by the ability of most modern PCs to change between zero or one wait-states, often by changing an option in the CMOS setup screen.

Why do PCs allow such frivolous alterations to the heart of their hardware, and how can they be trusted to work reliably when you haven't even changed the RAM to the faster, more expensive type? Indeed, some PCs lock up solid if you try and "turbocharge" them by forcing a zero wait-state.

So at last, here's the definitive guide to wait-states. What they are, why we need them and when it's safe to change them from their factory-set defaults.

Wait-states are so called because some CPUs are so fast that they literally have to wait for data to come from the slower system memory, resulting in performance much below what would have been possible if faster system RAM were fitted. Each wait-state corresponds to the processor stopping for one tick of the system clock while the data arrives from RAM, so obviously the lower the wait-state rating, the faster – in theory – the PC's overall operation will be.

System RAM generally comes in three or four basic "speeds", which represent the access time for a single bit of information. These range from 120ns (nanoseconds), which is the slowest RAM in general use, to 70ns – which is the nippiest you can get without paying daft amounts of cash.

Even systems fitted with fast 70ns RAM may require one or more wait-states if this RAM is fitted on an expansion card. This is because the data has to arrive via the expansion bus, which is the route data must take between the processor and all expansion cards. This is much slower than the internal data bus, which is the direct route between the processor and memory fitted to the mother board.

However, this doesn't apply if you have a super-fast EISA or MCA bus-based system – but that's another story in itself.

Systems advertised as having zero wait-states either have super-fast RAM, and/or a cached CPU. Caches can reduce the number of wait-states because they use fast static RAM (SRAM) chips and, in closed processor program loops (the equivalent of a FOR-NEXT or REPEAT-UNTIL loop), the data required for the next instruction is usually present in the cache after the first pass round the loop. If it is, the instruction is fed to the processor fast enough that no waiting is required.

However, a cached CPU alone is usually not enough to guarantee zero wait-states during operation. Due to the fact that wait-states are not directly measurable in cached CPU designs, manufacturers often quote what are known as "effective" wait-states for such machines. But, as effective wait-states are calculated statistically rather than directly, the result may sometimes be fractional! For example, it is not unusual to see 0.5 wait-states quoted in advertising copy.

In summary, setting your PC to run with zero wait-states will almost certainly cause it to crash, unless it has very fast system RAM and/or a cached CPU – bear in mind that if certain low-spec PCs allow you to change this setting when they're not even equipped to be fitted with faster RAM, the manufacturer is almost certainly cutting costs by fitting the same BIOS used on their more up-market models.

This isn't a problem – the defaults for your machine should always be set correctly before it leaves the factory, and a tried-and-tested BIOS is a good thing to have. But make sure you know exactly what you have under the bonnet before you start fiddling around – otherwise, change wait-states at your peril!

MULTITASKING IN DOS

The difference between multi-tasking and task-switching is often an area of confusion which is further confused by the difference between the Intel range of processors – 8086, 286, 386, 486 and now the Pentium. Which of these can multitask, and which can't? Well, it's certainly possible to multitask on a 286 based PC – with certain restrictions. On an 80806 or 80286 based PC, DOS programs will not run in a DESQview window unless written specifically for DESQview – rather, they take control of the entire screen while running, until shut down or switched out to disk. The situation is similar when using Windows 3, which on the whole runs DOS programs with a lot more trouble and a lot less available memory.

When all your applications are DOS based and you don't want to change them, the choice of operating system is narrowed considerably. In cases like this you might want to use DESQview which, while not an operating system as such (even Windows 3.1 can't claim to be anything other than a huge parasite which sits on top of good old MS-DOS), is a program which offers true multitasking for 386 processors and upwards, pseudo-multitasking for the 286, and excellent task switching for anything lower than that.

Task switching is simply the ability to suspend the current program and switch over to another, saving the current state of things to memory or disk to that it can pick up afterwards from where it left off. A good task-switcher has the feel of multitasking, except that no program except the one currently "switched in" can do any processing. But to stem the tide of protest from irate Windows devotees, let us explain the reason for suggesting DESQview as a candidate for DOS users who want to multitask. There is a simple rule for deciding which system is appropriate to any given task:

Windows and OS/2 are certainly the more visually attractive options, and have by far the best front end. After all, they are true GUIs, which DESQview definitely is not – anyone wishing to show off their VGA displays to the full won't be disappointed with Windows or OS/2.

DESQview, by contrast, is very brutal on the eye. Its front end is entirely text based, and doesn't win any awards for being pretty. However, it seems to have proved by far the more solid of the systems on offer, apart from the occasional irritating Exception 0013 errors which pop up from time to time when there are severe and unresolved hardware conflicts (mind you, Windows is still more likely to throw up the infamous Unrecoverable Application Error).

There is also the consideration of speed. While many stalwart Windows users say they run Windows quite happily on their 80286 and even 8086 based systems, on a cached 25 MHz DELL 386 the mouse pointer seems to spend far too long being an hourglass, which leads to the conclusion that for satisfied 8086 and even 80286 Windows users it really is a case of what you've never seen you don't miss.

The sluggishness of Windows is understandable – there's an incredible amount of work being done behind the scenes in Windows when, for instance, a help window is opened, and no-one would deny that the context-sensitive help is anything short of a dream to use.

But if all you want to do is to multitask standard DOS programs, then you'll find that DESQview is just the ticket. It's as uncomplicated as such things can be under the circumstances, and as its windows run in text mode you won't be kept waiting long for things to happen.

On a 386 system DESQview offers true, no-frills multitasking with little or no fuss, and if you are more interested in getting a background task done while working on something else – in other words, you want hard productivity – than having a pretty display, then give it a try. It's cheap, and you don't have to junk all your hard-earned software.

By the way, there is a Shareware program called Dosamatic which actually offers all of the task switching capabilities of DESQview. It's a little less sophisticated, and has a few bugs, but then what can you expect for free (well, free to evaluate at any rate). It won't let you run more than one program at once, but you can switch tasks at a keystroke. It's currently able to switch DOS programs only, but a windows version may well be on the cards. Contact your preferred Shareware vendor to order a copy.

AMSTRAD MOUSE PROBLEMS

There are some well-known problems associated with the Amstrad mouse, leading to its failure to work properly with some programs. There are some third-party fixes stocked by many PD and Shareware libraries, but if you are having problems the best course of action is to contact Amstrad UK for their official mouse driver upgrade. The address to write to is:

Amstrad PLC, PO Box 462, Brentwood, Essex CM14 4EF

Alternatively, if you subscribe to Compuserve you can find information on the UKCOMP forum. Type GO UKCOMP and then BROWSE the forum libraries.

OPTICAL MOUSE IMPROVER

If you have an optical mouse and have been experiencing problems with it, you may be able to improve its efficiency by simply covering any joins which strong light could get through with dark tape. Read-only tabs are ideal. For example, if you try this out on Logitech mice the difference is instantly obvious.

CAREFUL CACHEING

When using a disk caching utility such as PC Cache, be sure to flush or disable it before editing a recently accessed file using a byte-level editor such as PC Tools or Norton Utilities. Otherwise, even though you will appear to have modified the disk, if you exit your application before saving, your changes will not be saved.

And note that programs which execute a reboot, such as the Public Domain program RECFG.EXE (which allows you to control several sets of AUTOEXEC.BATs and CONFIG.SYS's), will not allow any cached data to be saved first. But then neither do the three-fingered salute ([Ctrl][Alt][Del]) or the BRB (Big Red Button).

More seriously, remember that it is extremely undesirable to use a cacheing program that does not immediately "write through" data. PC-Cache, the program mentioned, has, in common with most such programs, the facility to disable write cacheing, something which is strongly recommended.

The time saved by ignoring this safety feature which most caches offer is minimal compared to the risk of having unsaved data floating around in your PCs memory for several seconds, after you think it has been saved. The moral is to be extra safe, always save everything in sight before exiting any application or rebooting.

DIRTY KEYBOARDS

Dirty keyboards can cause problems which at first sight appear to be hardware-related (which they are, strictly speaking!).

If you ever find that random spaces or other characters appear in your text at irregular intervals while you are typing then your keyboard may simply need a good clean. Strip it down and carefully dust everything in sight, and with a bit of luck everything should work fine when you put it back together – for a few more months, anyway. Some keyboards are more prone to failure than others, and if cleaning doesn't work you may need to replace the keyboard entirely.

XT versus AT KEYBOARDS

Some users find that replacing their keyboard causes more problems than it solves, but this is usually easily cured. If you find that booting up your computer with the new keyboard plugged in causes it to hang, or results in the keyboard not responding, or – more mysteriously – the new keyboard which didn't work is okay if you switch it over after booting with the old one, then you may find the problem is nothing more serious than a switch in the wrong position.

On many keyboards you'll find a switch at the back labelled A and X. The A standing for AT and X for XT. If your keyboard has such a switch, it may be in the wrong position for your type of computer and you should try switching it over. If your keyboard doesn't have a switch, your problem is more serious and you should take the keyboard and/or computer back to your dealer.

INTERLACED versus NON-INTERLACED MONITORS

Many people are confused about interlaced and non-interlaced monitors, and the brief jargon found in the advertisements which abound in the pages of the glossies don't do much to help. The technique of interlacing is where every other line of a picture is transmitted every 25th of a second, while the other half of the picture (the lines in between them) is sent in between the first pictures. So although only 25 different frames are displayed each second, 50 physical frame redraws actually take place, smoothing out the overall flicker to a tolerable level.

But while interlacing can help a TV picture's appearance, if you stare at a normal television out of the corner of your eye you'll notice that there is still a lot of flicker present in the picture. For general purposes 50 Hz interlaced TV pictures are fine, as long as you are a few feet away from the set and are looking directly at the screen. But on the other hand, staring at a computer monitor all day from an average distance of two feet puts a strain on the eyes.

To overcome this and to offer higher resolution, newer monitors and graphics cards now offer a higher frame display rate. So that (just as an example) you might have an actual frame rate of 50 Hz, non-interlaced. Therefore, as all the picture is on screen all of the time, rather than half the picture, half the time, you will have a more stable and easier to watch image.

Incidentally, interlaced graphics screens are usually displayed at a frame rate of 59 to 67 Hz, fully-interlaced – giving better results than a television. While a non-interlaced monitor might typically have a similar frame rate, all the picture is visible on screen all of the time, resulting in a rock-steady image. So, until Liquid Crystal Display monitors become commonplace, if you have the money to buy a non-interlaced monitor and you want the best image you can get, don't settle for interlacing.

ADDING MEMORY

Choosing what type of memory to add to your PC is another source of confusion for most users, novice and experienced alike.

Most people want to increase their RAM to take better advantage of Windows and other programs that need it, but are not sure how to go about it. But before going any further, the first question to consider is do you actually need the memory, and what specific benefits will it give you?

Firstly, if you haven't got an AT class machine (286-based processor or higher), the only memory your computer can make use of is EMS (Expanded Memory). Most major programs will use EMS if it is available, letting you work on bigger spreadsheets or larger documents. Also Windows in Real mode (the only mode on XTs) will use EMS if it is available – but don't expect too much from it.

You can also create RAM disks with EMS, and these can offer huge speed increases if you copy your frequently used programs onto RAM disk in your AUTO-EXEC.BAT file. Don't forget to place the RAM disk in your PATH though. For many programs, you'll need at least 512K for this trick to work, but 384 Kbytes is often sufficient.

For XTs, you can expand 512K machines to 640K by filling the empty chip sockets on the mother board with DRAMs. Consult the PC documentation for the chip type needed. However, buying a new mother board to place in your PC is almost as cheap and can be much more effective if you're technically capable.

To add EMS, about all you can do is buy Expanded Memory boards. They are rather expensive, and no longer widely available, as most machines now use SIMMs (Single In-line Memory Modules). If a bargain comes your way, you may want to consider it though.

With AT Class machines, life is usually much easier. First off, with 286 or higher processors, Extended Memory is possible, because the processor can address more than 1 Mbyte of store. And these processors can do cunning tricks to convert some or all of this memory to EMS. Even better, most AT mother boards have SIMM sockets. You'll find lots of people selling SIMMs in advertisements throughout this magazine – the down side is that they come is several flavours of socket type and speed, so again your system documentation is a must.

Usually, there are sockets able to take 4 Mbytes of SIMMs on mother boards which support them, but high end mother boards can take up to 16 Mbytes. On AT machines with large amounts (4 Mbytes or more) of memory, Windows starts working very nicely. If you're using Quarterdeck's QEMM or similar memory manager, you can also stuff device drivers and TSRs into Upper memory, freeing more of your main memory for applications.

On 386 and higher machines, the benefits are much the same, except as you'd expect things are even faster. Programs are starting to appear which will use XMS (Extended Memory) if it is available – this is like EMS but faster.

There are lots of things you can do with RAM disks, hard disk Cache programs, high loading and so on – but you'll need to experiment a few times to get your CONFIG.SYS file just right.

In summary, the more memory you have the better – provided your machine is capable enough to support it fully. On the whole, XT owners should first expand the basic 512K to the full 640K, and when that no longer suffices (it will only be a matter of time, in today's world of memory-hungry Windows and OS/2) you'll have no option but to change your computer, or at the very least the entire mother board.

KEYBOARD TIPS FOR DISABLED PEOPLE

Many programs for the BBC Micro and Amstrad CPC machines have been designed to be used by disabled people (who often have impaired finger and/or hand control) and here is a short list of some useful programs for PC compatibles:

1-Finger and Staydown, used together with Mindreader (a Shareware program) provide a very useful toolkit for those with limited use of the hands for keyboard input.

The IBM version of Borland's **Superkey** program has a One-finger Mode option especially for people who have to use mouth sticks. It can also change your keyboard layout into DVORAK, or any other layout you choose. Superkey is primarily a keyboard enhancer, allowing you to program key macros. This means that one or two key strokes can be made to replace even lengthy sentences of key strokes.

There is also the **Support Centre for People with Disabilities** who specialise in this area of computing, available on Freephone 0800 269 545. They can also provide the above programs for evaluation.

Another solution to keyboard accessibility lies in the applications we use. The word processor **Protext** makes typing easy because the [Shift], [Alt] and [Ctrl] keys are configurable to be "sticky" – once pressed, the program remembers the fact and applies the shifted operation to the next normal key press. For example, suppose that you have to call a macro to merge a name, address and telephone number; you can press [Shift], followed by [Alt] and then [B] as separate key depressions with the program interpreting them as though they had been pressed simultaneously.

On the subject of word processors, some users find that a **Dexxa mouse**, which has menus for Symphony, Wordstar and Wordperfect, can help. They can use the mouse to call options which would normally require multiple key presses, and if no menu exists for an application, the menu generator allows them to produce one.

And finally a short historical note which may be of interest to disabled computer users who are frustrated by their keyboards.

Many disabled people understandably can't see the point of modern QWERTY keyboards, and wonder how they came into being. Well, we have all heard versions of the same story which tell us that after the invention of the typewriter, typists became so fast that the keys and hammers used to jam together, forcing typewriter designers to place the keys in a strange configuration in the hope that it would slow people down again!

But a designer of ergonomic keyboards for disabled people has a different, more convincing story: It appears that the intention, far from trying to slow typists down, was to help them increase their speed still further.

What the designers did was move the keys with the most commonly used letters away from each other. This meant that if you were to type the word SOME, for example, you would hit the left, right, left and right sides of the keyboard – ensuring that the keys are far enough away from each other that they won't jam.

At the same time, though, trained typists will find that their fingers sit neatly over these four letters and, if the keyboard were laid out alphabetically, there would ultimately be no difference at all in the speed of typing.

So, it seems, this "slowing down the typists" business is really a popular myth.

TIPS FOR MONOCHROME MONITORS

Here are a couple of tips for monochrome monitor users. Firstly, monochrome monitors can display anything that can be displayed on a similar standard colour monitor. An error message saying that it needs a colour monitor can be overridden by just typing:

```
MODE CO80
```

at the DOS prompt.

Secondly, Windows 3.0 gains 3D buttons and scroll bars, and generally looks better if you change the display settings in Windows Setup from MONOCHROME VGA to just VGA.

In Shareware there are two programs to look out for which also solve these problems. They are HGCIBM and LAPVIEW. HGCIBM is actually a CGA emulator for monochrome displays, but it can also be used to improve monochrome displays during normal use. LAPVIEW, although primarily designed for use with laptops, offers many options for emulating different types of displays. As with all Shareware programs, contact your preferred vendor to order a copy.

BOOT PROBLEMS

When you boot your machine, either with the power switch or [Ctrl][Alt][Del], do you ever see reports and error messages which are anything like the following?

```
Error: Faulty ROS ROM checksum
Error: Faulty VDU RAM
Error: Faulty floppy disk controller or disk drive
Error: Faulty memory (parity error)
```

Or do you get a fuzzy coloured screen, flashing coloured blocks, or even a totally blank screen – perhaps accompanied by a total keyboard lock-up as an extra bonus?

If so, you may be experiencing a problem with your NVR (Non Volatile Ram). This is the tiny piece of system memory commonly referred to as the CMOS (Complementary Metal Oxide Silicon) Ram which stores vital parts of your system setup after switch-off.

It's normally battery-backed by long-life (usually lithium) cells, which have an average life of two to five years. When the cells run down, these problems and others can start to occur with increasing regularity – most noticeably in Amstrads – and there are several things you can do to verify that this is indeed the cause of your problems. Try parking your drive, switching off and taking the batteries out – on Amstrad machines these are located under the monitor. Now wait a minute or two before turning on again and you should find the problem has gone, although you may be asked to set the correct time before the machine starts up DOS proper.

If the problems seem to have gone, simply replace the batteries with new ones and remember to change them every year or so. If you still get the errors then you have a genuine hardware fault, so you should talk to your local repair centre.

VIDEO CARDS

The issue of display cards puzzles a lot of users, and it's not surprising given the number of different standards that have emerged over the years. And although things have settled down into the more-or-less standard VGA, the arrival of SuperVGA (or SVGA) has opened up a new can of worms.

The original IBM display card was the MDA – Mono Display Adaptor – which was followed closely by the CGA standard (Colour Graphics Adaptor). This extended the MDA standard by providing low-resolution graphics, as well as colour.

Meanwhile, Hercules released their HMGA card (Hercules Mono Graphics Adaptor) providing quite high-resolution monochrome graphics. For a long time this was accepted as a universal standard, until the first EGA boards started to appear.

With the arrival of the EGA (Enhanced Graphics Adaptor) came the first true high-resolution colour display for the PC, but it was limited because of its digital nature and in 1987 was replaced by the Video Graphics Array, or VGA. The VGA card provided a fixed-frequency analogue high-resolution colour display, offering 256 simultaneous colours out of a palette of 262,144. Unfortunately, the standard wasn't taken up widely until 1989, because of the high cost (in those days) of the hardware – not to mention the lack of any software which could take advantage of the new features.

All of these cards are downwards-compatible with the previous standard, but few machines with a true CGA display are still in existence – some EGA machines are still floating around, but it's fairly safe to assume that most machines (especially those based on the 286 processor and upward) will support the full VGA standard. However, the VGA card comes in several flavours; the highest resolution is generally accepted as being 800x600 in 16 colours (to obtain the full 256 colours the resolution dropped to 320x200).

What confuses people is that some VGA cards support much higher resolutions, and/or colours – but many insist that these really come under the SuperVGA umbrella.

An easy rule of thumb, and one which clears up the confusion of the different VGA and SuperVGA standards, is to look at the memory requirement of the display modes offered by a given card. A card with 256k memory is "true" VGA card. It can support the display resolutions mentioned above, and no more. The next card up uses 512k of video RAM, and now we are really into Super VGA territory. A 512k SuperVGA card offers up to 800x600 in full 256 colours, but can be pushed to a resolution of 1024x768 by dropping to 16 colours.

Now we come on to the "real" SuperVGA cards – the 1024k (or 1MB) Rolls Royce of the PC display adaptors. It too can display graphics at a resolution of 1024x768, but at the full 256 colour level – really stunning pictures can be rendered with a card like this, but – you guessed it – there are a few caveats.

Displays at this resolution and colour bandwidth are very slow to draw – not surprisingly, considering the 1MB of memory needed to be thrown around. And then there is the question of monitors. To make use of the highest display modes, you need a very good quality multi-synch monitor – and they're not cheap.

In general, if your work requires SuperVGA, you'll already have the cash needed to go the whole hog, and your dealer will be able to advise you on the best setup. But for the rest of us, a good compromise is to go for a machine which offers some of the medium SuperVGA modes, possible with a 512k VGA card built in. Many PC clones come in this configuration, with a dual-frequency monitor capable of utilising the higher frequency modes – but these are not full multi-synch devices, and so you can't expect them to work in the highest modes possible.

If your main reason for going SuperVGA is to get the most from Windows, try and get hold of a video accelerator card – these are custom graphics boards which, in conjunction with the appropriate Windows display driver, will overcome the otherwise-appalling sluggishness of the display.

And finally, just a word about the new XGA standard. An ultra-high resolution standard designed to take IBM PCs into the nineties, it was originally designed to work only in 386 or 486 MCA machines – but in an attempt to make the standard universal IBM have licensed the technology to third-party manufacturers who are producing AT-compatible versions. However it is already coming under fierce competition from a new breed of SuperVGA card that offer up to 32,768 colours simultaneously.

CHAPTER 8

PROGRAMMING PROBLEMS SOLVED

While this book is intended as a comprehensive reference covering all aspects of using a PC, there is not the space to include complete tutorials for Basic, C, Pascal or other programming languages. However, if you can already program in one of these languages then you'll find several handy hints, tips and ideas which should help to improve your programs and overcome difficulties you may have run up against.

GW BASIC MOUSE HANDLING

GW BASIC is a versatile, powerful dialect of the language, but it has one major flaw – there is no built-in mouse support.

MOUSEDRV.BAS is a short listing that provides mouse handling in GW BASIC, and demonstrates it by asking you to press the left or right mouse button. To quit from the program press [Ctrl][Break]. Try it.

MOUSEDRV.BAS

```
100 KEY OFF
110 REM
120 DEF SEG=0
130 GMSEG=PEEK(51*4+2)+256*PEEK(51*4+3)
140 GMOUSE=2+PEEK(51*4)+256*PEEK(51*4+1)
150 DEF SEG=GMSEG
160 G1%=3
170 DIM CURSOR%(16)
180 DIM SCR%(8000)
190 DIM FULLSCR%(16002)
200 CALL GMOUSE(G1%,G2%,G3%,G4%)
210 X=G3%
220 Y=G4%
230 IF X<6 THEN X=6
240 IF X>313 THEN X=313
250 IF Y<6 THEN Y=6
```

```
260 IF Y>193 THEN Y=193
270 SCREEN 7
280 CLS
290 LINE (110,90)-(220,110),4,B
300 LOCATE 13,17:PRINT "CLICK HERE"
310 GET (X-3,Y-3)-(X+3,Y+3),CURSOR%
320 CALL GMOUSE(G1%,G2%,G3%,G4%)
330 PUT (X-3,Y-3),CURSOR%,PSET
340 X=G3%
350 Y=G4%
360 IF X<6 THEN X=6
370 IF X>313 THEN X=313
380 IF Y<6 THEN Y=6
390 IF Y>193 THEN Y=193
400 IF X>110 AND Y>90 THEN IF X<222 AND Y<110 THEN GOSUB 470
410 GET (X-3,Y-3)-(X+3,Y+3),CURSOR%
420 LINE (X-3,Y)-(X+3,Y),3
430 LINE (X,Y-3)-(X,Y+3),3
440 LINE (X-3,Y)-(X+3,Y),3
450 LINE (X,Y-3)-(X,Y+3),3
460 GOTO 320
470 LOCATE 13,16
480 IF G2% AND 1 THEN PRINT "LEFT  BUTTON":G2%=0
490 IF G2% AND 2 THEN PRINT "RIGHT BUTTON":G2%=0
500 RETURN
```

GW BASIC BREAK KEY DISABLING

The GW BASIC manual recommends that to disable the [Ctrl][Break] key combination you should enter code such as this:

```
10 KEY 15,CHR$(4)+CHR$(70):ON KEY(15) GOSUB 1000:KEY (15) ON
20 ...
30 ...
..
..
1000 PRINT "SORRY, YOU MAY NOT BREAK OUT":RETURN
```

Although this works fine with "real" IBMs, it doesn't seem to work as well with certain clones if either the Caps Lock or Num Lock key is on.

It's possible to get around this problem by resetting the states of these keys at the start of each program using the line:

```
DEF SEG=0:POKE &H417,0:DEF SEG
```

which turns all lockable keys off. But this still doesn't prevent users from setting either of these keys in the course of running a program. Something else is needed:

BREAK.BAS

```
10 DEF SEG=0:POKE &H417,0:DEF SEG:ON TIMER(1) GOSUB 2000:TIMER ON
20 KEY 15,CHR$(4)+CHR$(70):ON KEY(15) GOSUB 1000:KEY (15) ON
```

```
30 REM
100 REM ** Example program **
110 PRINT "Press Q to quit"
120 a$=INKEY$:IF a$="q" OR a$="Q" then END ELSE GOTO 110
130 REM
1000 PRINT "SORRY, YOU MAY NOT BREAK OUT":RETURN
2000 DEF SEG=0:POKE &H417,0:DEF SEG:RETURN
```

Unfortunately this technique is still not entirely foolproof, because the function can be disabled using a TIMER OFF statement inside the program; for example, when the user is expected to enter a word or character in capitals, in response to an INPUT command.

GW BASIC FRACTAL GENERATOR

Here is a short but fun to use GW BASIC program for creating fractal images. It draws each picture in a very unusual way, by scattering dots seemingly at random across the screen which slowly build up into the finished image.

If you want to experiment with the program, try forcing set values to the variables P, Q, R, S, XDISP, XSIZE, YDISP and YSIZE so that you can see exactly which values have what effect.

FRACTAL.BAS

```
100 KEY OFF
110 ON ERROR GOTO 450
120 SCREEN 0
130 CLS
140 PRINT "Press any key to initialise..."
150 WHILE INKEY$=""
160 DUMMY=RND
170 WEND
180 SCREEN 2
190 CLS
200 X=0
210 Y=0
220 P=RND*2000-1000
230 Q=RND*4-2
240 R=RND*2000-1000
250 S=RND*24-12
260 XSIZE=RND*2
270 YSIZE=RND*2
280 WHILE INKEY$=""
290 IF X<0 THEN XEXP=-1 ELSE XEXP=1
300 XCOORD=Y-(XEXP*(ABS(Q*X-R)))^1/S
310 YCOORD=P-X
320 PSET((XCOORD+400)*XSIZE,(YCOORD+300)*YSIZE)
330 X=XCOORD
340 Y=YCOORD
350 WEND
360 CLS
```

```
370 SCREEN 0
380 PRINT "Exit (Y/N)?"
390 IK$=""
400 WHILE IK$=""
410 IK$=INKEY$
420 WEND
430 IF IK$="y" OR IK$="Y" THEN SYSTEM
440 GOTO 180
450 RESUME 360
```

GW BASIC IMPROVED INPUT COMMAND

GW BASIC's INPUT command is very rudimentary. It is designed as an all-purpose function, but is unsuitable for many purposes. So here's a replacement routine that will do everything INPUT manages, plus a lot more.

To use it in your own programs, simply enter the lines beginning at line 10000 (leaving out the remark lines beginning with a single quote if you prefer) and, when you call it using GOSUB, all you need to do is set MAXLEN to the maximum string length you will allow, locate the cursor where you want input to begin using LOCATE and then call the routine. It will then return any entered string in the variable REPLY$.

As it is written, pressing [Escape] allows the user to quit from an input and empties REPLY$. If you don't want to allow for that key, remove line 10430.

You will notice that all control characters such as [Ctrl][A] that would normally be allowed by INPUT are ignored by this routine as they are not usually needed. If you do want to allow them, remove line 10600.

Lines 10 to 190 illustrate exactly how to use the routine.

```
INPUT.BAS

10 CLS
20 LOCATE 10,10
30 PRINT "Enter name?   ";
40 '
50 '     You need to tell the routine
60 '     the maximum allowed string length
70 '     by setting MAXLEN
80 '
90 MAXLEN=32
100 '
110 '     The call to the routine...
120 '
130 GOSUB 10000
140 '
150 '     Which returns the input in REPLY$
160 '
170 LOCATE 12,10
```

```
180 PRINT "You entered: ";REPLY$
190 END
10000 REPLY$=""
10010 '
10020 '     The above string is initialised,
10030 '     prior to the loop start, following,
10040 '     where the INKEY string IK$ is
10050 '     initialised
10060 '
10070 IK$=""
10080 '
10090 '     Here we emulate the cursor with
10100 '     an underscore character.
10110 '
10120 PRINT "_";
10130 '
10140 '     Then we move backwards a
10150 '     character, ready to print
10160 '     over it.
10170 '
10180 LOCATE CSRLIN,POS(0)-1
10190 '
10200 '     WHILE-WEND loop to read
10210 '     the keyboard.
10220 '
10230 WHILE IK$=""
10240 '
10250 '     Store any character in IK$
10260 '     from the keyboard.
10270 '
10280 IK$=INKEY$
10290 '
10300 '     Loop end.
10310 '
10320 WEND
10330 '
10340 '     Evaluation starts here, so:
10350 '     Is it a carriage return?
10360 '     If so return.
10370 '
10380 IF IK$=CHR$(13) THEN RETURN
10390 '
10400 '     Is it the Escape key?
10410 '     If so, clear REPLY$ and return.
10420 '
10430 IF IK$=CHR$(27) THEN REPLY$="":RETURN
10440 '
10450 '     Is it the Backspace key?
10460 '     If so then, as long as there
10470 '     characters in REPLY$, remove
10480 '     to remove the last one.
10490 '
10500 IF IK$=CHR$(8) AND LEN(REPLY$) THEN GOTO 10780
10510 '
10520 '     Is the string as long as allowed?
10530 '     If so, don't use latest character.
```

```
10540 '
10550 IF LEN(REPLY$)=MAXLEN THEN GOTO 10070
10560 '
10570 '     If IK$ is a control code we don't
10580 '     want it, so ignore it.
10590 '
10600 IF IK$<" " THEN GOTO 10070
10610 '
10620 '     Now we have a character,
10630 '     print it to the screen.
10640 '
10650 PRINT IK$;
10660 '
10670 '     And add it to the end of REPLY$
10680 '
10690 REPLY$=REPLY$+IK$
10700 '
10710 '     go back to the loop's beginning.
10720 '
10730 GOTO 10070
10740 '
10750 '     Remove the right-most charcter from
10760 '     REPLY$
10770 '
10780 REPLY$=LEFT$(REPLY$,LEN(REPLY$)-1)
10790 '
10800 '     Move back a character on screen.
10810 '
10820 LOCATE CSRLIN,POS(0)-1
10830 '
10840 '     Erase the last character and cursor.
10850 '
10860 PRINT "  ";
10870 '
10880 '     Now move to the end of the string.
10890 '
10900 LOCATE CSRLIN,POS(0)-2
10910 '
10920 '     And return to the loop's start.
10930 '
10940 GOTO 10070
```

TURBO C MOUSE HANDLING

This set of functions should provide everything you require for full mouse control in Turbo C.

Call m_init() at the start of a program to determine whether a mouse is available and, if so, initialise it for use.

m_hide() and **m_show()** simply show and hide the mouse pointer, which you should do every time you write to a part of the screen that might overwrite the mouse.

m_pos() returns the current mouse position. If you are in text mode you should divide these coordinates by 8 to get actual screen character x and y coordinates. It also tells you which buttons, if any, are pressed.

m_put() is how you move the mouse cursor by force. Usually you would **m_hide()** it, then **m_put()** it where you want it, and finally **m_show()** it again.

m_hlim() and **m_vlim()** set the horizontal and vertical minimum and maximum pixel (or character) areas the mouse is allowed to move in. This is handy for enclosing the use of the mouse in a particular area of the screen. In text mode remember to multiply the 80x25 coordinates by 8 or the cursor will stay in the top left of the screen.

m_curs() lets you specify whether to use a hardware or software cursor and, if hardware (recommended by the way), what the start and end scan lines of the cursor (in text mode) are to be.

Remember that all these functions should be declared in your header file as void, as those that return values do so via pointers rather than function returns.

MOUSE.C

```
#include <dos.h>

m_init( int *m_stat,      /* Mouse Status. 0=Not Installed */
        int *n_buttons)   /* Number of mouse buttons */
{
    struct REGS r;
    r.x.ax=0;
    int86(0x33,&r,&r);
    *m_stat=r.x.ax;
    *n_buttons=r.x.bx;
}

m_show()                  /* Show the mouse cursor */
{
    struct REGS r;
    r.x.ax=1;
    int86(0x33,&r,&r);
}

m_hide()                  /* Hide the mouse cursor */
{
    struct REGS r;
    r.x.ax=2;
    int86(0x33,&r,&r);
}

m_pos(  int *m_button,    /* Button pressed */
                          /* 1=Left 2=Right 3=Both */
        int *m_x,
        int *m_y)         /* Mouse coordinates */
```

```
{
    struct REGS r;
    r.x.ax=3;
    int86(0x33,&r,&r);
    *m_button=r.x.bx;
    *m_x=r.x.cx;
    *m_y=r.x.dx;
}

m_put ( int m_x,
        int m_y)          /* Place the mouse cursor */
{
    struct REGS r;
    r.x.ax=4;
    r.x.cx=mx;
    r.x.dx=my;
    int86(0x33,&r,&r);
}

m_hlim( int m_min,
        int m_max)        /* Horizontal movement confines */
{
    struct REGS r;
    r.x.ax=7;
    r.x.cx=minpos;
    r.x.dx=maxpos;
    int86(0x33,&r,&r);
}

m_vlim( int m_min,
        int m_max)        /* Vertical movement confines */
{
    struct REGS r;
    r.x.ax=8;
    r.x.cx=minpos;
    r.x.dx=maxpos;
    int86(0x33,&r,&r);
}

m_curs( int m_type,       /* 0=Software, 1=Hardware */
        int m_top,
        int m_bottom)
{
    struct REGS r;
    r.x.ax=10;
    r.x.bx=m_type;
    r.x.cx=m_top;
    r.x.dx=m_bottom;
    int86(0x33,&r,&r);
}
```

TURBO C FILE FINDER

Finding files scattered over a large hard disk is a major problem, and utilities to do this for you are common enough these days; but if you're short of cash (or don't have DOS 5.00, which allows you to use DIR for this purpose), you might like to try this program.

The simplest way to search a disk is by using recursion. This means you write one function to scan a directory and then, for each sub-directory found, the function calls itself again to scan that sub-directory, and so on. Although it can appear complicated, recursion is quite elegant – and once you've got the hang of it you can apply it to all kinds of otherwise insoluble problems.

The listing has just two functions; the obligatory **main()**, and one other called **searchdir()**, which is the recursive "engine" that scans directories for files.

The way it works is that **main()** switches to the root directory and calls **searchdir()**. **searchdir()** then prints out the details of all the files in that directory, goes back to the beginning and looks for all the subdirectories. Each time it finds one it switches to it using **chdir()** and then calls itself again, and the process repeats.

When all subdirectories and files in the first directory below the root have been displayed, **searchdir()** switches back down to the root directory and looks for the next sub-directory. When no more have been found it returns to **main()**, which does a **chdir()** back to the directory you started in, displays the number of matches found and returns to DOS.

You could adapt this code in many ways. For example, changing the "*.*" in line 3 of **main()** to "*.DOC" would make the program look for all files with a .DOC extension. You could also make it display each file's date, time, size and attributes, and possibly even allow the filespec parameter that is passed to **searchdir()** to be taken from the DOS command line.

FINDFILE.C

```
#include "stdio.h"
#include "dir.h"

char old_dir[100],current_dir_name[100];
void searchdir(char *);

main()
{
    getcwd(old_dir,100);
    chdir("\\");
    searchdir("*.*");
    chdir(old_dir);
}
```

```
void searchdir(filespec)
char *filespec;
{
    struct ffblk findblock;

    getcwd(current_dir_name,100);

    if (findfirst(filespec,&findblock,0x2f) == 0)
    {
        do
        {
            printf("%s - ",current_dir_name);
            printf("%s\n",findblock.ff_name);
        } while (findnext(&findblock) != -1);
    }

    if (findfirst("*.*",&findblock,0x33) == 0)
    {
        do
        {
            if (findblock.ff_attrib & 0x10)
            {
                if (*findblock.ff_name != '.')
                {
                    chdir(findblock.ff_name);
                    searchdir(filespec);
                    chdir("..");
                }
            }
        } while (findnext(&findblock) != -1);
    }
}
```

TURBO C DATA COMPRESSION

The simplest form of data compression is known as Run-Length Encoding (RLE). This is where each byte of information is saved as a pair of bytes; the second holds the original data, and the first represents the number of adjacent bytes of this value. As most data files contain blocks of repeated information, their RLE-compressed counterparts are usually much smaller then the originals.

The commonest use of RLE compression is in file archiving, especially high-resolution screen images – although RLE is usually adopted as part of a much more efficient overall compression technique.

If we take the example of an imaginary picture that we want to compress using RLE, let's suppose it's 180 pixels wide and the first line comprises a row like this:

```
17 red - 23 black - 1 blue - 128 green - 11 red
```

Assuming that we are using the following colour numbers:

```
black              = 0
red                = 1
blue               = 2
green              = 3
```

this can be encoded much more efficiently by the following bytes:

```
17,1               - 17  red pixels
23,0               - 23  black pixels
1,2                - 1   blue pixel
128,3              - 128 green pixels
11,1               - 11  red pixels
```

If we are allowing up to 256 colours then each pixel is one byte long. So we will therefore have used just 10 bytes in place of 180, or almost a 95% saving.

There is a drawback to this method though, which is that if every pixel is a different colour from the next one you will get no encoding, in fact you will actually double the size of the data. For example, lets take just five pixels:

```
1 blue - 1 green - 1 black - 1 red - 1 green
```

Applying the same method to that creates the following sequence of bytes:

```
1,2,1,3,1,0,1,1,1,3
```

which is not that acceptable. To overcome this problem and also to achieve an even tighter compression (as well as staying fast to both compress and decompress), I have come up with a variant on the run-length encoding principle which guarantees that, in the worst possible case, a file processed by it could never grow more than 1/8th larger than the original – although it is very unlikely you would get anywhere near even 100%.

The way it works is by taking the eight bits in a byte and making each of them represent whether the following data is repeated or not. To illustrate this, let's take a 180 pixel wide row that looks like this:

```
12 red - 32 green - 50 black - 1 green - 1 blue - 25 black - 30 red - 19 blue
```

Here we have eight colours that can processed using a control byte where we set a bit to one if there is more than one of a colour, otherwise it is set to zero. So in the above case the control byte, going from highest to lowest bit, would be 11100111 in binary, or 231 decimal (E7 hexadecimal).

Now the control byte is prepared we put it to one side and start doing the run length encoding like this. The first colour sequence is 12 red pixels, so we store a 12 and a 1. Next we have 32 green, making 32 and 3, and 50 black, making 50 and 0.

The next colour is the interesting one because there's just one green pixel so, because it's just one, we only store that colour, which is number 3. The same also goes for the single blue pixel. The final three colours are then dealt with in the normal way.

Finally the various pieces of data are stored, with the control byte first, like this:

```
231                    - Control Byte
12,1                   - 12 red
32,3                   - 32 green
50,0                   - 50 black
3                      - 1 green
2                      - 1 blue
25,0                   - 25 black
30,1                   - 30 red
19,2                   - 19 blue
```

This takes up 15 bytes, whereas normal run-length encoding would require 16, making this method at least 7% more efficient. In fact, most data contains a large amount of single, one-byte items, so that it appears to actually be about 25% more efficient on the whole.

Anyway, once these eight sets of colours have been processed, a new control byte is prepared and the process repeats until the end of the data is reached, when two zero bytes are appended to the end of the compressed data as an end of data marker.

The following Turbo C source file illustrates this technique by providing you with two functions. The first, **squash()**, takes the data in the first array passed to it, compresses it and stores it in the second. While **unsquash()** takes the compressed data stored in the second array and decompresses it into the first.

Note that the second array MUST be 1/8th and 2 bytes bigger than the uncompressed data to allow for the (very unlikely) worst case. So if your picture is 16384 bytes long, the second array should be set to hold 18434 bytes. The 2 bytes padded on the end are not a legal coding for this compression method so they signify the end of a squashed file.

This technique is especially good for squashing text mode screens but you must bear in mind that these screens are stored with the attribute bytes in between character bytes, so you must copy every other byte into a contiguous block before passing it to **squash()** to compress either the characters or the attributes. In this case you should find you can compress screen images down to about 30% of their original size.

COMPRESS.C

```c
#include <stdio.h>
#include <mem.h>
#include <stdlib.h>
#include <dos.h>
#include <conio.h>
```

```
int    squash(unsigned char *,unsigned char *);
void   unsquash(unsigned char *,unsigned char *);

main()
{
  unsigned char normal[4000], compressed[4502];

  squash(normal,compressed);    /* Compress it   */
  unsquash(normal,compressed); /* Decompress it */
  return 0;
}

int squash(screen1,screen2)
unsigned char *screen1,*screen2;
{
  int j,k,checkbyte,tbuffptr,runcounter,arraypointer,scn2ptr=0;
  unsigned char screenchar,tbuff[16],array[8]={128,64,32,16,8,4,2,1};

  screenchar=screen1[0];
  memset(tbuff,0,16);
  runcounter=arraypointer=tbuffptr=0;
  checkbyte=255;

  for (j=0 ; j < 4001 ; ++j)
  {
    if (screen1[j] == screenchar && runcounter < 255)
      ++runcounter;
    else if (screen1[j] != screenchar || runcounter == 255)
    {
      if (runcounter == 1)
        checkbyte -= array[arraypointer];
      else
        tbuff[tbuffptr++]=runcounter;
      tbuff[tbuffptr++]=screenchar;
      if (++arraypointer == 8)
      {
        screen2[scn2ptr++]=checkbyte;
        for (k=0 ; k < tbuffptr ; ++k)
        {
          screen2[scn2ptr++]=tbuff[k]; tbuff[k]=0;
        }
        tbuffptr=arraypointer=0; checkbyte=255;
      }
      screenchar=screen1[j]; runcounter=1;
    }
  }

  if (tbuffptr != 0)
  {
    screen2[scn2ptr++]=checkbyte;
    for (k=0 ; k < tbuffptr ; ++k)
    {
      screen2[scn2ptr++]=tbuff[k]; tbuff[k]=0;
    }
  }
}
```

```
  else
  {
    screen2[scn2ptr++]=255; screen2[scn2ptr++]=0;
  }
  return scn2ptr;
}

void unsquash(screen1,screen2)
unsigned char *screen1,*screen2;
{
  int j,k,scn1ptr=0,scn2ptr=0;
  unsigned char t,q,ch,array[8]={128,64,32,16,8,4,2,1};

  while (1)
  {
    ch=screen2[scn2ptr++];
    for (j=0 ; j < 8 ; ++j)
    {
      if (ch & array[j])
      {
        t=screen2[scn2ptr++];
        if (t > 0)
        {
          q=screen2[scn2ptr++];
          for (k=0 ; k < t ; ++k)
            screen1[scn1ptr++]=q;
        }
        else
          goto DONE;
      }
      else
        screen1[scn1ptr++]=screen2[scn2ptr++];
    }
  }
DONE: return;
}
```

TURBO C IN-LINE ASSEMBLER

It's possible to do a great deal of assembly language programming these days without ever purchasing an assembler, and it doesn't have to involve DEBUG either.

Many modern high-level compilers include Assembler directives that allow in-line Assembler (in-line with the rest of the source code, that is). Microsoft C, Turbo C and Turbo Pascal all have this facility, and the following Turbo C example show how easy it is to use it:

```
INLINE.C

int keyhead;     /* Head of keyboard buffer */
int keytail;     /* Tail of keyboard buffer */

void getheadtail(void)
```

```
{
    asm
    {
        xor ax,ax          /* Clear AX reg */
        mov es,ax          /* Address seg 0 */
        cli                /* Interrupts off */
        mov ax,es,41ah     /* Get head pointer */
        mov dx,es,41ch     /* Get tail pointer */
        sti                /* Interrupts on */
        mov keyhead,ax     /* Store head pointer */
        mov keytail,dx     /* Store tail pointer */
    }
}
```

Don't expect this to do anything exciting; it's mainly an illustration of how to write a self-contained function in C which uses assembly language to return values into variables.

In one way, in-line Assembly combines the best of both worlds – you have the convenience of being able to program in your favourite language, but wherever necessary you can insert a small chunk of Assembler into your source. And all this without having to go to the trouble of setting up a separate ASM file.

Even better, in your in-line Assembler code you have immediate access to the variable and data definitions in your C or Pascal code – without all of the attendant jargon that this normally involves. For example, if you use a C global variable "fred", you don't have to insert the line extern_fred in the Assembler code – you just use it.

If in-line Assembler is important to you, make sure that the high-level language compiler you buy understands mnemonic instructions like those above – some only support in-line hex code.

TURBO C SAFE HEAP MANAGER

All C programmers suffer from heap allocation problems, and as a result many avoid **malloc()** like the plague. But it is possible to arrange for all uses of the C heap to be rigorously checked. All you have to do is include a header file which defines macros for the standard heap functions **malloc()**, **calloc()**, **realloc()**, and **free()**. This forces any calls to these routines to be passed through some simple safety checks first.

This is how it works. When you call **malloc()**, you are actually calling a routine called _smalloc() which in turn calls the real **malloc()** asking for slightly more memory. **malloc()** marks the start and end of the block which it places on a linked list of used blocks, and returns a pointer to your bit of the block.

Then, when you free a block later, _sfree() checks that the block pointer is on the list of blocks, and that the start and end markers are still intact before calling the real **free()** to give the block back.

All you have to do is include the line:

```
#include "safeheap.h"
```

in each of your program files. Then if anything goes wrong, a message is printed and **abort**() is called, but you could modify **_h_err**() to be more friendly.

If your program fails, just run it under your debugger and place a breakpoint in **_h_err**() – and when the fault happens again, you've got it nailed. The stack back-trace will show you where the offending call was made.

There are also a couple of useful variables to deal with the other notorious heap problem, 'leakers', which is where your memory quietly vanishes down a black hole until there's none left. It is caused by failing to free blocks obtained from **malloc**(). That makes it sound easy to find but it isn't. You can spend many late nights trying to track them down.

An invaluable aid is knowing the number of blocks currently 'on loan' from **malloc**(), and being able to trace each pointer. The variables are:

```
_H_HDR *_h_strt;
long _h_usd;
int _block_count;
```

_h_strt is the head of the linked list of blocks – just follow the 'nest' chain. **_h_usd** is the total amount of memory currently on loan, and **_block_count** is the number of blocks in use. Printing one or more of these values in carefully chosen places can work wonders for your enlightenment.

The listings are in fully ANSI-compliant C, and will work with any of the popular modern compilers in any memory model. Just make sure you compile them using the same model as the rest of your program.

```
SAFEHEAP.H

#include <stdlib.h> /* for size_t definition, and NULL */

#define malloc   _smalloc
#define calloc   _scalloc
#define realloc  _srealloc
#define free     _sfree

void *_smalloc(size_t size);
void *_scalloc(size_t size, size_t count);
void *_srealloc(void *ptr, size_t size);
void _sfree(void *ptr);

typedef struct _h_hdr
{
    struct _h_hdr *next;
```

```
   size_t size;
   size_t magic;
   char chars[sizeof(int)]; /* variable length */
} _H_HDR;

extern _H_HDR *_h_strt;    /* list of allocated blocks */
extern int _block_count;   /* number of blocks on list */
extern long _h_usd;        /* number of bytes allocated */

#define _H_MRK1 0x71fe
#define _H_MRK2 0xfb


SAFEHEAP.C

#include <stdio.h>
#include <string.h>
#include "safeheap.h"

#undef malloc              /* Here onward is the main part */
#undef calloc
#undef free
#undef realloc

_H_HDR *_h_strt = NULL;  /* list of allocated blocks */
int _block_count = 0;    /* number of blocks on list */
long _h_usd = 0L;        /* number of bytes allocated */

void _h_err(char *messg)
{
   fprintf(stderr, "\n%s, aborting.\n", messg);
   abort();
}

int _is_h_ptr(void *ptr)
{
  _H_HDR *hp, *p;

   if (ptr == NULL)
      return 0; /* NULL is never on the heap! */
   hp=(_H_HDR *)((char *)ptr-sizeof(_H_HDR)+sizeof(int));
   for (p=_h_strt; p; p=p->next)
      if (p == hp) return 1; /* object is on the heap */
   return 0; /* not on heap */
}

void *_srealloc(void *p, size_t size)
{
   char *p1 = NULL;
   _H_HDR *hp;

   if (p)
   {
      if (size)
      {
```

```
            if (!_is_h_ptr(p))
                _h_err("realloc: ptr not from malloc");
            p1=_smalloc(size);
            hp=(_H_HDR *)((char *)p-sizeof(_H_HDR)+sizeof(int));
            if (size > hp->size)
                size=hp->size;
            memcpy(p1, p, size);
        }
        _sfree(p);
    }
    return (void *)p1;
}

void *_scalloc(size_t size, size_t count)
{
    void *p;
    long nsize=(long)size*count;

    if (nsize & 0xffff0000L)
        return NULL; /* too big! */
    if (p = _smalloc(size))
        memset(p, 0, (size_t)nsize); /* zero it */
    return p;
}

void *_smalloc(size_t size)
{
    _H_HDR *hp;

    if ((hp=(_H_HDR *)malloc(size+sizeof(_H_HDR)+4 - sizeof(int))) ==
NULL)
        _h_err("malloc: out of memory");
    hp->next=_h_strt;
    _h_strt=hp;
    hp->size=size;      /* record bytes used */
    hp->magic=_H_MRK1; /* note magic marker */
    hp->chars[size]=_H_MRK2;
    _h_usd+=size;
    _block_count++; /* keep track of allocations */
    return (void *)hp->chars;
}

void _sfree(void *ptr)
{
    _H_HDR *hp, *p, *q;
    size_t size;

    if (ptr == NULL)
        _h_err("free: NULL ptr");
    hp=(_H_HDR *)((char *)ptr-sizeof(_H_HDR)+sizeof(int));
    if (hp->magic != _H_MRK1)
        _h_err("free: block head trashed");
    size = hp->size;
    if (hp->chars[size] != _H_MRK2)
        _h_err("free: block tail trashed");
    for (p=_h_strt, q=NULL; p; q=p, p=p->next)
```

```
{
    if (p == hp)
    {
        if (q)
            q->next=p->next;
        else
            _h_strt=p->next;
        _h_usd-=size;
        _block_count--;
        free((void *)hp);
        return; /* freed OK */
    }
}
_h_err("free: ptr not from malloc");
}
```

TURBO C FLOATING-POINT CALCULATOR

CALC.C is the source code for a simple floating point calculator that you can expand on and use as the basis for your own evaluation functions.

The program uses an algorithm called Operator Precedence, which has been used for many years in compilers for many languages, and in interpreters for languages like BASIC. Operator Precedence in computing is exactly the same as that taught in school for mathematics; given an expression like:

1 + 2 * 3

you know that the multiplication should be performed first. Operator Precedence reduces this idea to a rule that: every operator has an associated precedence (just a number).

When reading an expression, place operators on a stack until you can see the next operator. If the stacked operator has a lower precedence than the current one, push the current one on the stack, and carry on.

Oh yes, the end of the expression is always marked with a "pretend" operator which has a lower precedence than any real operator.

If you don't want to know how the whole system works, all you need to do is copy the code into your own programs and call the function parse(). But if you are interested, here's a line-by-line breakdown of the program:

main(): This is the main program loop: it reads lines from the input as long end-of-file has not occurred, and strips the terminating '\n' from the lines. It then passes the line it read to **parse()**, which evaluates the expression if possible in result and returns 0, or if an error occurs returns 1. The result is then printed. You can call **parse()** from your own programs, or get the expression from other sources than **stdin**.

The **#defines**: These lines define some useful macros – firstly the internal token values used during parsing, followed by some useful tests on operators.

dope[] is the operator precedence table. **parse()** evaluates operators with higher priority first, in "1+2*3", the * operator is performed first. You can add your own operators to this table.

The remaining lines upto **parse()** are prototypes for the internal functions used during parsing, and also declare the variables used in parsing.

The function **parse()** starts by initialising the operator and operand stacks, and setting **inptr** to point to the start of the expression to be parsed. It then sets up an error handler in case the function **error()** is called. If so, **setjmp()** returns 1, and **parse()** also returns 1 to indicate that an error occurred.

expect_operand: Expressions must always start with an operand, or a unary operator like – as in "-1", or a parenthesised sub-expression. If none of these are found, there is an error. In this simple parser only numeric constants are allowed, but you could also have variables, arrays and so-on.

expect_operator: After reading an operand, an operator must follow. The end of the expression is taken to be an operator with a precedence lower than any real operator.

While the operator just read has a lower precedence than any stacked operator, the stacked operators and their operands are popped of the stacks, and evaluated by reduce().

There are only three possibilities: the operator was) and there should be a matching (on top of the stack; it is the special End Of Expression operator, in which case we're done; otherwise the operator is stacked and the next symbol read.

If EOS was read and the only thing on the stacks is a single value, everything is fine. Otherwise, there was an error.

The function **scan()** reads tokens from the input expression. These lines handle single character tokens. Note that white space is simply ignored.

Reading floating point numbers is slightly tricky. This code counts the digits after the decimal point, and then divides the number by 10 that many times. It can't handle exponents.

DO_DOT: If the character is not a digit, . or one of the operators, the user made an error. If you extend this program, this is where you would add tests for variables and so on.

The function **reduce()** pops the operator off the operator stack, and the operands off the operand stack. It then evaluates the operator using the switch at line 205, and pushes the result back on the operand stack at line 214. Note that no test is made for division by zero or other errors.

The function **error()** is only called if the other routines detect a problem. It prints a message, and returns control to **parse()** which in turn returns 1 to indicate that the expression could not be evaluated.

CALC.C

```
#include <stdio.h>
#include <string.h>
#include <setjmp.h>
#include <math.h>

int parse(char *expr, double *resp);

main()
{
    char tmp[80];
    double result;

    for (;;)
    {
        printf("> ");
        if (fgets(tmp, sizeof(tmp), stdin) == NULL)
            return 0;           /* end of file */
        tmp[strlen(tmp) - 1] = '\0';
        if (parse(tmp, &result) == 0)
            printf("= %.9g\n", result);
    }
}

/* From here on is the expression parser. */

#define NUM     1
#define ADD     2       /* + */
#define SUB     3       /* - */
#define MPY     4       /* * */
#define DIV     5       /* / */
#define POW     6       /* ^ */
#define LPAR    7       /* ( */
#define RPAR    8       /* ) */
#define NEG     9       /* unary minus */
#define EOS     10      /* end of string */

#define P(r, b, p)    (0x40 | ((r) < 5) | ((b) < 4) | (p))
#define PREC(op)      (dope[op] & 0xf)
#define IS_BIN(op)    (dope[op] & 0x10)
#define IS_RASS(op)   (dope[op] & 0x20)
#define IS_OP(op)     (dope[op] & 0x40)

char dope[] = {
```

```
    0,              /* not used */
    0,              /* NUM - not operator */
    P(0, 1, 5),     /* ADD */
    P(0, 1, 5),     /* SUB */
    P(0, 1, 6),     /* MPY */
    P(0, 1, 6),     /* DIV */
    P(1, 1, 7),     /* POW */
    P(0, 0, 1),     /* LPAR */
    P(0, 0, 1),     /* RPAR */
    P(0, 0, 8),     /* NEG */
    P(0, 0, 0)      /* EOS - end of input string */
};

int scan(void);
void reduce(void);
void error(char *s);

jmp_buf err;
int token;
double val;
double *opnd_ptr;
char *oprt_ptr;
double opnd[20];
char oprt[30];
char *inptr;

int parse(char *expr, double *resp)
{
    int p, t;

    inptr = expr;
    opnd_ptr = opnd;
    oprt[0] = 0;
    oprt_ptr = oprt + 1;

    if (setjmp(err))
        return 1;                   /* error! */

expect_operand:

    if (scan() == NUM)
        *opnd_ptr++ = val; goto expect_operator;
    else if (token == LPAR)
        *oprt_ptr++ = token; goto expect_operand;
    else if (token == SUB)
        *oprt_ptr++ = NEG; goto expect_operand;
    else
        error("Operand expected");

expect_operator:

    scan();
    if (!IS_OP(token))
        error("Operator expected");
    p = PREC(token);
    while (t = oprt_ptr[-1], p < PREC(t) ||
```

```
        (IS_RASS(token) && p == t))
   {
        if (t == LPAR)
            error("Missing ')'");
        reduce();
   }
   if (token == RPAR)
   {
        if (oprt_ptr[-1] == LPAR)
            oprt_ptr--; goto expect_operator;
        else
            error("Missing '('");
   }
   if (token != EOS)
        *oprt_ptr++ = token; goto expect_operand;
   if (oprt_ptr != oprt + 1)
        error("Syntax error");
   *resp = opnd_ptr[-1];
   return 0;         /* no error */
}

int scan(void)
{
    int c, dexp;

LOOP:

    switch (c = *inptr++)
    {
        case ' ': case '\t':     goto LOOP;
        case '+': token = ADD;   goto END;
        case '-': token = SUB;   goto END;
        case '*': token = MPY;   goto END;
        case '/': token = DIV;   goto END;
        case '^': token = POW;   goto END;
        case '(': token = LPAR;  goto END;
        case ')': token = RPAR;  goto END;
        case '\0': token = EOS;  goto END;
        case '.':  val = 0.0;    goto DO_DOT;

        case '0': case '1': case '2': case '3': case '4':
        case '5': case '6': case '7': case '8': case '9':
            val = (double)(c - '0');
            while ((c = *inptr++) >= '0' && c <= '9')
                val = val * 10 + (double)(c - '0');
            if (c != '.')
                inptr--; token = NUM; goto END;

DO_DOT:         dexp = 0;
            while ((c = *inptr++) >= '0' && c <= '9')
                val = val * 10 + (double)(c - '0'); ++dexp;
            while (dexp--)
                val /= 10.0;
            inptr--; token = NUM; goto END;

        default:
```

```
                        error("illegal character");
    }
END: return token;
}

void reduce(void)
{
    int op;
    double q, r;

    op = *--oprt_ptr;
    r = *--opnd_ptr;

    if (IS_BIN(op))
        q = *--opnd_ptr;
    switch (op)
    {
        case ADD: q += r; break;
        case SUB: q -= r; break;
        case MPY: q *= r; break;
        case DIV: q /= r; break;
        case POW: q = pow(q, r); break;
        case NEG: q = -r; break;
    }
    *opnd_ptr++ = q;
}

void error(char *s)
{
    printf("%s\n", s); longjmp(err, 1);
}
```

TURBO C BREAK HANDLER

This is a [Ctrl][C] and [Ctrl][Break] handler for Turbo C programmers. It can be used to totally disable these key combinations or, by inserting a call to a "tidy up" function, it could be used to exit gracefully in response to either of these key presses.

It works by replacing the standard Interrupt 9 ISR (Interrupt Sub Routine) with a filter to check whether [Ctrl] is being pressed, together with either [C] or [Break]. If so the keyboard is reset and the keystroke discarded. Any other combination is passed directly on to the original handler to be processed as usual.

If your program already uses an Interrupt 9 handler then be careful to avoid any conflicts. Here is the listing:

NEWBREAK.C

```
#include <conio.h>
#include <dos.h>
#include <stdlib.h>

void interrupt new_isr();
void interrupt (*old_isr)();

void main(void)
{
    old_isr=getvect(0x09);
    setvect(0x09,new_isr);

    /* Call the rest of your program */
    /* from here                     */

    setvect(0x09,old_isr);
}

void interrup new_isr(void)
{
    unsigned kbstatus,pb_status;

    kbstatus=peekb(0x040,0x017);

    if
    (
        (
            (kbstatus & 4) == 4) &&
            (inportb(0x60) == 0x2e) ||
            (inportb(0x60) == 0x46)
        )
    )
    {
        pb_status=inportb(0x61);
        outportb(0x61,pb_status | 0x80);
        outportb(0x61,pb_status);
        outportb(0x20,0x20);
    }
    else
        old_isr();
}
```

TURBO C AUTODIALLER

By using the fixed sub-set of commands included in the C source code listing
DIAL.C you will probably be able to get your program to dial out on 95% of
'so-called' Hayes compatible modems.

What you need to do is initialise the modem first for the correct baud rate and COM
port. This is done by calling **setup_port()**. Then you send "ATV1" to the modem to
tell it to return its output in English rather than as error codes and then, for good

measure, tell it to dial blind by sending "ATX3". This is so that the modem won't hang around waiting for a dialling tone, which for some reason certain modems find hard to detect.

Then, depending on whether you wish to use pulse or tone dialling you send "ATDP" or "ATDT", followed by the number to dial and a final semicolon. The semicolon tells the modem not to wait for the call to be answered before accepting the next command.

Finally, if pulse dialling, you ask the user to press a key when connection has been established, at which point you hang up the modem with "ATH". Or, if tone dialling, you don't have to wait for the numbers to click through, so it's safe to issue the "ATH" straight away.

To use this code, insert it in your program, leaving out the function **main**() which is just there for demonstration purposes so that the program can be compiled as a stand-alone utility. Then, when you wish your program to dial out, simply call the function **dial**(), passing it the following four parameters:

A char * string containing with the number to dial

An integer COM port number (1 to 4)

An integer baud rate (300/1200/2400 etc.)

An integer pulse/dial flag (1=pulse/2=tone)

And that's about it. But note that the standard data addresses are assumed. If you want to be thorough you might want options like these to be configurable or passable as parameters, to cater for non-standard setups.

Two points about the code itself. Firstly **inportb** and **outportb** are UNDEFed so that the actual faster C functions rather than Turbo C's slower macros are used. And secondly, no errors are checked for or error codes returned, so you might want to add those features yourself – although you can press a key at any time during the dialling process to abort the dial and return.

```
DIAL.C

/* Compile using:  TCC -w -ms -O -Z -f- DIAL */

#include "stdio.h"
#include "string.h"
#include "conio.h"
#include "bios.h"
#include "dos.h"

#undef inportb
#undef outportb
```

```
char char_waiting(int);
char com_get_char(int);
char com_put_ready(int);

void com_put_char(char, int, int);
void send_modem_string(int, int, char *);
void wait_ok(int,int);
void setup_port(int,int);
void dial (char *, int, int, int);

main(argc,argv)
int argc;
char *argv[];
{
   if (argc > 1)
      dial(argv[1],2,2400,0);
   else
   {
      printf("PC PLUS Autodialler\n\n");
      printf("Type: DIAL nnnnnnnn\n");
   }
   return 0;
}

void dial(number,port_num,baud_rate,pulse_dial)
char *number;
int port_num;
int baud_rate;
int pulse_dial;
{
   int data, stat;
   char dialstring[64];

   switch (port_num)
   {
      case 1: data=0x3f8; break;
      case 2: data=0x2f8; break;
      case 3: data=0x3e8; break;
      case 4: data=0x2e8; break;
   }
   stat=data+5;
   setup_port(data,baud_rate);
   printf("AUTODIALLER: Dialling %s...\n",number);
   send_modem_string(data,stat,"\rATV1\r");
   send_modem_string(data,stat,"ATX3\r");
   strcpy(dialstring,"ATD");
   strcat(dialstring,(pulse_dial) ? "P" : "T");
   strcat(dialstring,number);
   strcat(dialstring,";\r");
   send_modem_string(data,stat,dialstring);
   if (pulse_dial)
   {
      printf("Press any key to hang up modem...\n");
      getch();
   }
```

```c
      send_modem_string(data,stat,"\rATH\r");
      if (bioskey(1))
         getch();
}

void wait_ok(data_addr,status)
int data_addr;
int status;
{
   int ctr=0, done=0;
   char c, test[5];

   strcpy(test,"OK\r\n");
   while (!done && !bioskey(1))
   {
      if (char_waiting(status))
      {
         c=com_get_char(data_addr);
         if (c == test[ctr])
         {
            ++ctr;
            if (ctr == 4)
               done=1;
         }
         else
            ctr=0;
      }
   }
}

char char_waiting(status)
int status;
{
   return (inportb(status) & 1);
}

char com_get_char(data_addr)
int data_addr;
{
   return inportb(data_addr);
}

char com_put_ready(status)
int status;
{
   return (inportb(status) & 0x20);
}

void com_put_char(c,data_addr,status)
char c;
int data_addr, status;
{
   while (!com_put_ready(status) && !bioskey(1))
      ; /* iterate */
   outportb(data_addr,c);
}
```

```
void send_modem_string(data_addr,status,str)
int data_addr, status;
char *str;
{
    int j;

    for (j=0 ; j<strlen(str) ; ++j)
        com_put_char(str[j],data_addr,status);
    wait_ok(data_addr,status);
}

void setup_port(data_addr,baud_rate)
int data_addr;
int baud_rate;
{
    unsigned char val=inportb(data_addr+3);
    int dial_baud=115200L/baud_rate;

    outportb(data_addr+3,val | 0x80);
    outportb(data_addr+0,dial_baud % 0x100);
    outportb(data_addr+1,dial_baud / 0x100);
    outportb(data_addr+3,0x03);
}
```

TURBO C AUTOMATIC KEYSTROKES

Here's a simple C program (which could just as easily have been written in Pascal or any other language), that illustrates how you can save yourself from having to press keys to clear away information screens when you first run a program.

For example, Procomm Plus requires you to press [Space] twice, before you get into the program. Using this technique you simply compile the program, save it in your Procomm Plus directory and then, rather than running Procomm Plus directly from DOS, create a batch file, like this:

```
ECHO OFF
REM PP.BAT
2SPACE
PCPLUS
```

Now, all you have to do to call up the program is type:

```
PP
```

and wait, a few seconds later you'll be in the program and ready to use it.

And you can use this technique for all sorts of things that require automation as it works by pushing characters into the DOS keyboard buffer and then returning. All you need to do to modify it is change the second line of **main()** to something like:

```
char string[]="A SEQUENCE";
```

where "A SEQUENCE" is the sequence of characters to be passed on to the next program to run, or DOS if no program is launched.

KEYPUSH.C

```c
#include <dos.h>
#include <string.h>

main()
{
   union REGS regs;
   char string[]="   ";
   int j;

   for (j=0 ; j<strlen(string) ; ++j)
   {
      regs.h.ah=5;
      regs.h.ch=0x39;
      regs.h.cl=string[j];
      int86(0x16,&regs,&regs);
   }
   return 0;
}
```

This program is most useful for automating the first few parts of a program, because if you try to do the same thing from DOS using the less-than redirection filter (forcing a program to take input from a specified file, rather than the keyboard) like this:

PROTEXT <KEYFILE

then if you get to the end of the file while the program is still running, control IS NOT returned to the keyboard and you have no option other than to reboot. This program gets around this nicely, and returns control to the keyboard immediately the keyboard buffer is empty.

Sequences longer than 16 characters cannot normally be used, as that is the length of the keyboard buffer – unless you have expanded the buffer with another utility.

TURBO C SUPER CHANGE DIRECTORY

Here's a utility which takes you straight to the directory you want just by typing its name. With CDP you can type commands such as:

CDP LETT

And, assuming you have, for example, two directories on your hard disk called:

\HOME\WORDPROC\LETTERS
\BUSINESS\WORDPROC\LETTERS

CDP (short for CDPLUS) will then change to the first directory. But, if you issue the
same command again, it knows it's already in a directory that matches the search
string LETT and will look for another match. In this case it will find the second
directory and switch to it.

CDP.C

```
#include "stdio.h"
#include "dir.h"
#include "dos.h"
#include "string.h"
#include "stdlib.h"

#define TRUE 1
#define FALSE 0

char old_dir[100],dir_name[100],filename[100];
int found_start=FALSE;
void searchdir(char *);
int new_ctrl_break(void);

main(argc,argv)
int argc;
char *argv[];
{
    ctrlbrk(new_ctrl_break);
    getcwd(old_dir,100);
    chdir("\\");

    if (argc > 1)
    {
        if (strlen(old_dir) < 4)
            found_start=TRUE;
        strupr(argv[1]);
        searchdir(argv[1]);
        searchdir(argv[1]);
    }
    else
    {
        printf("CDP - Quick Directory Changer.\n\n");
        printf("     Type: 'CDP dirname'\n");
        printf("Type any part of the directory\n");
        printf("name and I will find it.\n");
    }

    chdir(old_dir);
    return FALSE;
}

void searchdir(filespec)
char *filespec;
{
    struct ffblk findblock;

    if (findfirst("*.*",&findblock,0x33) == 0)
```

```
    {
        do
        {
            if (findblock.ff_attrib & 0x10)
            {
                if (*findblock.ff_name != '.')
                {
                    chdir(findblock.ff_name);
                    getcwd(dir_name,100);

                    if (found_start)
                    {
                        if (strstr(findblock.ff_name,filespec))
                        {
                            printf("Changed to: %s\n",dir_name);
                            exit(0);
                        }
                    }
                    else if (strcmp(dir_name,old_dir) == 0)
                        found_start=TRUE;
                    searchdir(filespec);
                    chdir("..");
                }
            }
        } while (findnext(&findblock) != -1);
    }
}

int new_ctrl_break()
{
    chdir(old_dir);
    return FALSE;
}
```

TURBO C LCD DISPLAY FIXER

Some programs can be a real pain when it comes to displaying colour graphics on a mono display, and this is especially so when LCD laptops are involved. Here's a solution in the form of a powerful TSR (Terminate and Stay Resident) program written in Turbo C which can make sense of even the worst displays.

It sits in memory all the time, manipulating the screen, according to the parameters you pass it. So that you can keep communicating with the TSR, information is passed on via the free area of RAM that is reserved for user applications from 04F8h to 04FAh.

Each time you run the program, the first two bytes are checked to see if they contain the (arbitrarily chosen) values 17h and 23h, if not then a new instance of the program is loaded because, either this is the first instance, or the previous user RAM area was overwritten by another program. Otherwise, the parameters passed to the program are placed in the user RAM for the TSR portion of the program to use, and the program exits.

The program takes three command line options which can be any or all of; a number between 0 and 9, E, M or P. The number is the refresh rate at which the program will adjust the screen, the faster you ask for, the better job it does but, by taking processor time away from the system, your programs will run slower. So this option is configurable so that you can find the best balance. A value of 0 switches the program off, while 1 causes the slowest refresh rate of twice a second, and 9 causes a refresh rate of 18 times a second.

If you select E, and have a Hercules monitor, the program will allow you to run any CGA only, text mode programs by simply copying the CGA screen data across to where a Hercules monitor expects it to be. It does this 10 times a second by default, but the rate can be changed.

With the M option, whether you are using any of a CGA, EGA, VGA or Hercules monitor, all text will be forced to appear in bright white on black (even if you are emulating CGA on a Hercules monitor using the E option). This means CGA laptops (for example) that don't display all 16 foreground colours will, at least try to display all text, even if only in white.

As you may know virtually all CGA cards have at least four **pages** available for display, and only the first one is usually used. The final option, P, forces a CGA system to use the second text page for displays. The computer will continue to write to the first page as normal, but the program will then copy this screen data, manipulate it, and then store it in the second page. This means that the display will flicker less and is easier to see.

When deciding whether to use the **P** option, try it first and then, if there's no improvement or any degradation of performance, ignore it. But it will help to improve the program's effectiveness on quite a few types of CGA card.

You should note, though, that the **P** option will not operate if the **E** option is selected as a Hercules system would then be assumed. So, for example to get a Hercules PC to display a CGA only program in black and white at six times a second, you would type:

```
MONOFIX E M 3
```

On a laptop PC which doesn't emulate all the background and foreground colours, you will probably find that the following setting will best suit your PC:

```
MONOFIX M P
```

Incidentally, any C programmers reading this will find the code useful in its own right as it's a tightly coded TSR, the shell of which – with the minimum of modifications – could be used to create similar small TSRs such as real-time screen clocks.

MONOFIX.C

```c
#include <stdio.h>
#include <dos.h>
#include <mem.h>
#include <ctype.h>

#define TRUE 1
#define FALSE 0
#define TIMER 0x1c
#define INT28 0x28

static void interrupt (*oldtimer)(void);
static void interrupt newtimer(void);

unsigned int offset=0x8000,poll,counter=0;
unsigned int k,n,p,q,r;
unsigned dosseg,dosbusy;
char emulate,monochrome,copypage;

char mask[10][9]=
{
    0,0,0,0,0,0,0,0,0,
    1,0,0,0,0,0,0,0,0,
    1,0,0,1,0,0,0,0,0,
    1,0,0,1,0,0,1,0,0,
    1,1,0,1,0,0,1,0,0,
    1,1,0,1,1,0,1,0,0,
    1,1,0,1,1,0,1,1,0,
    1,1,1,1,0,1,1,1,0,
    1,1,1,1,0,1,1,1,0,
    1,1,1,1,1,1,1,1,1
};

main(argc,argv)
int argc;
char *argv[];
{
    int j;
    unsigned char c;

    printf("MONOFIX: A Mono/CGA toolkit\n\n");
    printf("Options: 0-9 - emulation speed\n");
    printf("         E  : Emulation on\n");
    printf("         M  : Monochrome ON\n");
    printf("         P  : Pagecopy on\n\n");
    _AH=0x34; geninterrupt(0x21);
    dosseg=_ES; dosbusy=_BX;
    disable();
    emulate=monochrome=copypage=FALSE;
    poll=5;
    if (argc > 1)
    {
        for (j=1 ; j<argc ; ++j)
        {
            switch((c=toupper(*argv[j])))
```

```
            {
                case '0': case '1': case '2':
                case '3': case '4': case '5':
                case '6': case '7': case '8':
                case '9': poll=c-'0'; break;

                case 'E': emulate=TRUE; break;
                case 'M': monochrome=TRUE; break;
                case 'P': copypage=TRUE; break;
            }
        }
    }
    enable();
    _AH=0x0f; geninterrupt(0x10);
    disable();
    if (_AL == 7 && !emulate)
        .offset=0;
    pokeb(0,0x4fa,poll);
    pokeb(0,0x4fb,emulate);
    pokeb(0,0x4fc,monochrome);
    pokeb(0,0x4fd,copypage);
    if (peekb(0,0x4f8) == 0x17 && peekb(0,0x4f9) == 0x23)
    {
        enable();
        return FALSE;
    }
    pokeb(0,0x4f8,0x17);
    pokeb(0,0x4f9,0x23);
    enable();
    oldtimer=getvect(TIMER);
    setvect(TIMER,newtimer);
    keep(0,500);
}

static void interrupt newtimer()
{
    if (peekb(dosseg,dosbusy))
        goto LEAVE1;
    disable();
    if (copypage && !emulate)
    {
        _AH=5; _AL=1; geninterrupt(0x10);
        _AH=3; _BH=0; geninterrupt(0x10);
        _AH=2; _BH=1; geninterrupt(0x10);
    }
    if (!poll) poll=peekb(0,0x4fa);
    if (!mask[poll][counter++]) goto LEAVE;
    if (peekb(0,0x4f8) == 0x17 && peekb(0,0x4f9) == 0x23)
    {
        poll=       peekb(0,0x4fa);
        emulate=    peekb(0,0x4fb);
        monochrome=peekb(0,0x4fc);
        copypage=  peekb(0,0x4fd);
    }
    for (k=1 ; k < 4000 ; k+=2)
    {
```

```
    if (monochrome)
        pokeb(0xb000,offset+k,0x0f);
    else
    {
        p=peekb(0xb000,offset+k);
        q=p & 0x0f; r=(p > 4) & 0x0f;
        if ((q > 0) && (q < 8) && (r > 0) && (r < 8))
            pokeb(0xb000,offset+k,p & 0xf0);
    }
}
if (emulate)
    movedata(0xb000,0x8000,0xb000,0,4000);
else if (copypage)
    movedata(0xb000,0x8000,0xb000,0x9000,4000);

LEAVE:

    if (!emulate)
    {
        _AH=5; _AL=0; geninterrupt(0x10);
    }
    enable();
    if (counter > 8)
        counter=0;

LEAVE1:

    oldtimer();
}
```

TURBO PASCAL RANDOM FILE ACCESSING

If you have experienced difficulties using Turbo Pascal's random access file handling commands, the answer probably lies in treating your Turbo Pascal text files as Untyped rather than Text – that is, as a simple block of bytes on the disk – and then opening them as such. You then gain access to the Seek procedure, which allows you to set the file pointer to anywhere inside the open file.

Unfortunately You cannot then use the Read or Write procedures, which would normally allow you to easily manipulate text files as individual lines of text, and at first sight this may seem to be a major drawback. However, the procedures **BlockRead** and **BlockWrite,** the non-Text file versions of the same procedures, provide very fast alternatives.

All you have to do when opening your file with the **Reset** procedure is to specify a **RecSize** – the number of bytes to transfer at a time – and you are away. For example, if you know a file consists of lines exactly 80 characters long, you can safely set **RecSize** to 80 and treat **BlockRead** and **BlockWrite** almost as if they were **Read** and **Write.**

Alternatively, setting the **RecSize** to one – a single byte – allows you to read your files character by character, vet them for control codes and suchlike, and build up internal Pascal character strings from the results as you go.

By the way, this is a good way to write import routines for non-Ascii files, like those created by wordprocessors such as Wordstar or Protext. As a rule of thumb you can throw away any characters with an Ascii value greater than 127 (except for Wordstar, which adds 128 to the Ascii value of the first letter in each word – in this case, just subtract 128 to extract the actual letter).

As an example, here's a program written in Turbo Pascal version 6.0 that will print your AUTOEXEC.BAT file upside down and back-to-front, using random-access file handling:

```
REVERSE.PAS

Program Reverse;

Var
    TextFile:    File;
    Ptr:         Longint;
    Letter:      Char;
    Result:      Word;

Const
    FileName:    String='\autoexec.bat';

Begin
    Assign(TextFile,FileName);
    Reset(TextFile,1);
    For Ptr:=FileSize(TextFile) DownTo 0 Do

    Begin
        Seek(TextFile,Ptr);
        BlockRead(TextFile,Letter,1,Result);
        Write(Letter);
    End;

    Close(TextFile);
End.
```

TURBO PASCAL CURSOR CONTROL

Here's a useful Pascal routine for turning the cursor on and off, which also provides a tall cursor of the sort often used to indicate 'Insert mode' in text editors.

```
CURSOR.PAS

PROCEDURE CursorMode(mode:byte);

begin
{
```

```
    modes as follows 0: cursor off
                     1: Cursor regular
                     2: cursor tall
}

    case (mode) of
      0: inline($B4/$01/$B9/$20/$21/$CD/$10);
      1: inline($B4/$01/$B9/$07/$06/$CD/$10);
      2: inline($B4/$01/$B9/$20/$00/$CD/$10);
    end;
end;
```

NON LANGUAGE-SPECIFIC DATE FORMULAE MANIPULATION

The following BASIC formulae are very useful for manipulating dates, but are particularly good for producing calendars and personal organiser-type diaries.

Leap years are handled correctly and the earliest date is, presumably, when the Gregorian calendar was adopted. So, if the variable YEAR is the year (for example 1992), and MONTH is the month (1 – 12), the number of days to the first of the specified month in that year can be obtained from:

```
NO-OF-DAYS = INT(15.25 * (YEAR + (MONTH < 3))) +
             INT(2.6 * MONTH +1 - (MONTH < 3) * 12)) - 1
```

The following formula calculates the number of days in any particular month, for the specified year:

```
DECADE = VAL(RIGHT$(YEAR,2))
IF DECADE = 0 THEN LEAP = 400 ELSE LEAP = 4
DAYS-IN-MONTH = VAL(MID$("303232332323",MONTH,1)) + (MONTH = 2) *
                (YEAR = INT(YEAR/LEAP) * LEAP) + 28
```

And you can get the actual day number between 0 and 7 (Sunday to Saturday) from:

```
DAY-NO = INT((NO-OF-DAYS / 7 - INT(NO-OF-DAYS / 7) * 7 + .5)
```

These instructions are compatible with GW BASIC but should be easily portable to other languages.

CHAPTER 9

MAKING MONEY

Most programmers have probably wondered whether or not there's any money to be made from their hobby. Indeed magazine cover disk editors receive dozens of program submissions every day, so there are certainly many hopefuls out there. But if you sell a program to a magazine you are only likely to earn anything between £25 and £500 for it, depending on its type. Even though you see magazines offering up to £800 that's actually more like their budget for the entire disk, rather than for each program. Still for simple programs they can be a good source of pocket money.

However, Shareware is really coming into its own in the UK now and it's quite possible for the author of a popular new program to leave his or her day job and start a business within just a year or so – but the program does have to be good and the marketing must be spot on. Alternatively you may want to go down the more conventional 'commercial' route. Either way, here are some thoughts, ideas and suggestions that should stand you in good stead.

MARKETING YOUR PROGRAMS

Shareware is certainly a rapidly growing means of distributing software and some of the best programs can make their authors quite a lot of money, but they will have followed some of the following general marketing guidelines.

Before releasing a program as Shareware you can quite simply copyright it by placing the statement "Copyright (c) 1993 John Smith – All rights reserved" in all your document files and on your programs' opening screens.

To further prove your authorship you could seal a disk containing the software in a mailer with packaging that would show if it were tampered with, and post it to yourself or a solicitor, so that it is post marked. But remember that, although you will be able to prove you wrote it, it could cost you a lot of money to defend yourself or prosecute someone in court.

Secondly, when some authors write Shareware they release their programs too early and let their users perform the bug testing that they should have done themselves. I would suggest that this loses them registrations and that you should never intentionally release a potentially buggy program.

Try to first get your friends, relatives and colleagues to test it out for you. Why not offer them a free registration for doing so? You'll be surprised at some of the suggestions they make, but if you follow their advice, in the end you'll agree that the process has helped to create a better product.

Thirdly, it seems that there's a lot of misunderstanding about Shareware in Britain. Many companies release what they call 'Shareware' versions of their products that have features missing. When they do this it is not Shareware but, if you cannot use it properly, it is purely a demo of the software and is referred to in the business as Crippleware and you should know that the Association of Shareware Professionals (ASP) will not let you join or remain a member if you cripple your programs.

So you might ask yourself, "What incentive is there for someone to register if you've given them a fully working program?". The answer's simple, you have proved to them that you believe in your program enough to allow your users to fully try it out, and that you trust them to register. They also will trust you for doing this and expect you to keep them informed of upgrades.

On the other hand, suppose you write a database program but only allow it to handle 20 records in the 'Shareware' version. How will your users know how fast it will be with 2,000? They have no way of knowing and will probably discard the program and look for another they can test.

Likewise, even if you only disabled printouts. You could say it's virtually a complete program, but then again, your users won't know for sure if your printout facility will work on their printer and, if so, how well.

And if you don't believe it, you should talk to any member of the ASP and they'll tell you that they have proof that uncrippled programs receive up to five times more registrations than otherwise. Many of them started out using crippling techniques, but now they all release complete programs.

It's true, most of your users won't register (at least not straight away) but you should get enough registrations to keep you going, and even normally distributed programs are often quite heavily pirated anyway.

Fourthly, try to get your program into Shareware libraries, by going through your favourite PC magazine and looking for all the Shareware advertisers. Make a note of their details and send each one a copy. You could find that up to 30% of them take your program on. But don't stop there, keep on sending copies out as long as you can afford it, until as many Shareware companies as possible are distributing your program.

One fifth and final point you should bear in mind is to keep your customers happy. Always send them their registration pack by return of post, and make sure you keep developing the program and offer them upgrades from time to time. Many Shareware authors consider upgrades to be their main bread and butter because they are being offered to people who already know and like the program, and have paid money for it.

SOFTWARE PROTECTION

Have you ever considered what is the best and safest way to protect an independently developed piece of software for sending to software houses?

My suggestion is to create an evaluation version of your program which is complete in every respect, with the exception that prominent opening and closing screens say something like: "MEGA SOFTWARE EVALUATION COPY – NOT FOR DISTRIBUTION, (c) J SMITH 1993 – ALL RIGHTS RESERVED".

Then, if you're still concerned, checksum the text in the program and hide the result elsewhere in your source code inside a particularly obscure bit of programming. Then refuse to run the program if the checksum is not correct when the program is invoked from the command line. But I believe it's most unlikely that anyone would try to change your message and rip off your program, particularly as you could prove you wrote it by producing your source code.

As far as marketing goes, your first step should surely be to get as many of your friends and relatives to thoroughly test the program as you can, and listen carefully to their advice and keep working on updates until they run out of suggestions. That way most of the initial pitfalls that could see your program rejected will have been removed, and the program will get a much more favourable response.

Also, if your program needs a manual you should already have written it (even if it will get re-written by a professional if your program is accepted) and, if at all possible, you should enclose a printout of it (even from a standard dot-matrix printer). This is important because evaluators don't want to use trial and error or have to wade through on-disk documentation. If it's on paper they can find out what they need to know much more quickly.

To help you gain an evaluator's initial interest you should also pay a lot of attention to the presentation of your submission. Use a new jiffy bag or suitable protective packaging, make sure the disk is new and the label is clearly written and if you are including a manual put it in a wallet or file of some sort, and make sure everything has your name, address and phone number on it.

If your program is accepted you will probably be offered anything from 10 to 20 percent royalties. If you get 20% that's good. What you might want to do though is insist on an advance on royalties so that a) you have some money if the program doesn't sell as well as expected and b) royalties are often only paid four (or sometimes just two) times a year as it can take time for sales figures to be processed, so you may need some money to keep you going.

EFFECTIVE ADVERTISING

You should bear the following points in mind when producing your advertising copy. But remember, they are by no means intended to be exhaustive, but do illustrate a number of devices you can employ to increase your response figures.

Think hard about your headlines: You must aim to achieve at least two things with your headline. Firstly define your market so that those readers who may be interested in your product are automatically drawn to the advert. For example you may be advertising a utility that speeds up an XYZ2000 microcomputer by 30%, so your headline could read.

TURBOCHARGE YOUR XYZ2000!

Secondly the headline must promise benefits. In fact, the more the better, but one strong benefit will do. In the above example the promised benefit is getting extra speed out of your XYZ2000. Five times as many people read the headlines as read the body copy – do your utmost to pull them in once you've got them that far.

Don't be afraid of writing too much: Once you've grabbed your reader's attention with an eye-catching headline he will be hungry for information. You have promised certain benefits and now's your chance to reveal them.

Choose your words carefully, don't use two words when one will do, but equally make sure you include as many benefits as you can. That's what sells a product – the benefits to the customer. Remember also, the more expensive your program, the harder these words are going to have to work for you, and the more of them you'll need to clinch the sale.

Always caption photographs and drawings: Apart from the headline, the most read part of your advert is going to be the captions. So make sure they're there and fill them with benefits. As they say "a picture paints a thousand words", and if you think about it, it really is true. Open up any magazine at random, and the first two things you'll notice will be the headlines and the pictures, and once you've absorbed them, you'll probably scan the first and last paragraphs and the picture captions. Pictures can carry subtle messages and are easily absorbed. They also serve to arouse a reader's curiosity. Readership of captions is up to five times higher than body copy.

Always tell your readers what you want them to do. If you get readers past your headline they are then most likely to read the first and last paragraphs. Tantalise them with the first one so that they feels compelled to read the next.

In the final paragraph, always tell them what you want them to do, because once you've got the reader there you're close to making a sale. Also bear in mind that coupons definitely increase the response rate of an advert, but don't just bung one on the page, tell the readers to fill it in.

Tell them to order their copies today, or to fill in the coupon for further details. It doesn't matter what you tell them to do – as long as you spur them to action. Tell them at the start, remind them what they could lose if they don't, tell them again later on – in fact tell them as many times as necessary. And don't forget to give your prospects as much room to write in as possible. If you don't think there's enough room on the coupon it would be better for you to lose a bit of copy to make room, rather than to lose a sale because your coupon is too difficult to fill in.

Continue to promise benefits: Having started to promise benefits, you must start backing your claims immediately, so that the reader thinks "Great. What else?". Having done that give them another benefit. And another. Always backing your claims. Ideally you should lead the readers through your copy with benefit, justification, benefit, justification, right to the final paragraph where you tell them to order the program, or send off for further details.

'You' is a powerful word: Always address the reader as you. Never write 'The user' – it's too impersonal. The reader is reading your advert to find out how your product will benefit *him*. Not other people, or any old user. Replace phrases such as '£25 saving' with 'You can save £25!'.

Remember to keep your adverts simple, uncluttered and to the point. If you have a designer working for you don't let him get carried away. He has his job because he's artistic by nature. Art and advertising don't go well together unless it's properly done – and even then the result is usually extremely clear and easy to take in. Strike a balance between pictures, large print and your copy, they all have a part to play, but it's the copy that ultimately sells your product.

WHICH HARDWARE?

Before you start your software empire there are a number of essential items of hardware you are going to need. One or two of them can be left until later, but in the meantime it will be best if you keep your eyes open for any bargains. You can always upgrade your equipment when your cash flow starts growing.

The first essential item you must have is a printer. Handwritten receipts and invoices just won't do. Even with a cheap nine pin dot matrix printer you can achieve quite acceptable results using Near Letter Quality printout, but you will soon find it far too slow.

If you intend to produce manuals of any length, rather than paying through the nose for professional typesetting you would be well advised to have a look at some 24 pin or laser printers (which usually print up to eight pages a minute).

Nowadays you can lease a laser printer for a very low weekly payment. To pay for this you may only have to sell one extra item of software each week. Plus, combined with a decent desk top publishing package you'll also be able to cheaply and quickly produce your own professional looking adverts, safe in the knowledge that no outside hand has introduced any errors into your copy.

If you do buy or lease a laser printer you should make sure that it's HP Laserjet and/or Epson compatible as most software comes with printer drivers for these two. Even better, industry standard Postscript compatibility gives you much more flexibility and excellent printouts, but it does cost more. Even so, nowadays you can now buy software Postscript emulators for a lot less than dedicated printers.

Remember that you are going to lose a lot of sales if you're not on the phone. Not just because customers can't order your goods by credit card, but because many of them like to give a call first to check you have the goods in stock and (perhaps on a more subconscious level) to reassure themselves that you run a reputable business, before they send their hard-earned readies off in the post.

Also, reviewers, magazine editors, retailers and distributors may be put off contacting you if they have to write a letter rather than make a quick call. If you haven't got a phone, get one!

And if you've got a phone, are you in during the day? If not and you don't have an answerphone it's almost as bad as not having a phone at all. If your budget will go to it, try and make sure you get an answerphone with TWO cassettes, the first containing your message and the second for caller's messages.

The one-tape phones are cheap but, because everything has to be recorded on the one cassette, if you are left a number of messages, the time callers have to wait before the machine is ready to record will get longer and longer, and many people won't be bothered to wait and will hang up. Better still than getting an answerphone (except for out of hours callers) give up your day job as soon as you're confident the business will support you.

Before long you'll have to get a Fax machine. Simply because more and more of today's business is being done over these machines. Because it's quicker, more convenient and usually cheaper than the post you will find people want to fax you orders, information, price lists, proofs of advertisements and so on. And you can also send invoices as soon as they are due to help ensure quicker payment.

Another benefit is that a fax message is perceived as more urgent than ordinary mail. Messages sent via one will normally receive greater and faster attention. If you thought a fax would be too expensive to outweigh its benefits you could be pleasantly surprised. There are a number of machines now available incorporating a telephone handset, several memories, last number redial and a document copying facility all at very low prices.

As your customer base grows, you may want to mailshot them when you bring out a new product. This is always a good idea as they are "active" buyers who are already interested in your company's products. You might also wish to have your manuals photocopied, keep copies of your correspondence, enlarge or reduce documents or pictures or perhaps copy a supplement of upgrade details for a product.

Initially, a fax with a document copying facility may suit your needs but, as with all these items, you should keep an eye out for a reasonably priced photocopier, and get one as soon as you can afford it.

Before long you will be mailing a lot of post to your customers. If you arm yourself with a decent set of scales (that can accurately weigh in grams) and a mailing price guide, you can make sure that you never pay more than you have to. A standard set of cooking scales might suffice, but you can also buy highly accurate electronic scales quite cheaply.

By law you must retain all your customer's orders, invoices receipts and so on. When the business is young you may not think there are enough bits of paper to warrant a filing cabinet, and store everything in folders. But pretty soon you'll be snowed under with all manner of documents.

A filing cabinet with four drawers will help you immensely. Keep one for all your orders, split alphabetically so that you can quickly refer to one if you get a query. The second could hold all your enquires, again, alphabetically sorted. The third could be used for all the invoices you receive that haven't yet been paid. And the fourth for all those (thankfully) paid bills. Or use your own system. As long as you have a system and stick to it you'll find it makes life a lot easier.

GETTING FREE PUBLICITY

Let's suppose you've finally got a finished product which you're convinced is going to take the market by storm. You've tested it again and again, trying all possible combinations of options and no further bugs have come to light. Your program is ready to sell.

When you send your program for review always remember to enclose an accompanying letter to introduce the product. Don't assume it will speak for itself. Magazine journalists are busy people and, unless something grabs their attention immediately, your program will be placed in the pending tray, not to re-emerge for possibly many months.

The letter should be type-written or printed out in near letter quality if possible and should pack as much information into as little space as possible. Hand-written letters are out! If you already have your own stationery, so much the better, but the main point is that you get the best features of your program in the first couple of sentences, offering enough of a carrot for the reader to finish your letter.

Always refer to a product as "our latest release", or "we are proud to demonstrate...". Don't use "I" or "my" when you are referring to your company. However, you should use I or me in the following cases: "Please don't hesitate to contact me", or "I look forward to hearing from you".

So, you've sent off the program for review and it's now a week later and you haven't heard anything. What do you do? Cross your fingers and keep on waiting for either a phone call or the review to appear? Certainly not. You call the editor and ask him if he's seen your letter. If he hasn't you tell him about the product and ask if he'd like you to send another copy as the first one may have got lost in the post, which is very unlikely – it's probably in his pending tray, but at least when he receives the second copy he's under more pressure to look at it.

If he has seen the program you ask him what he thinks about it (here's where you DO keep your fingers crossed). With any luck he'll at least say it's interesting. If he doesn't like it, give up on that magazine and try another – you can always come back to this one with your next product.

But let's assume he likes it, even if only moderately. This is where you're in with a good chance of (nearly) free publicity. Remind him you are offering an exclusive on the program and then offer him £1,000 worth of the product to give away in a competition.

But that's not all, as they say "there's more!". If you get him to bite on the competition carrot (and I'd say you've got a pretty good chance), you get two other major benefits. Firstly, it's quite likely that the magazine will devote a full page, often in colour, to the competition – your first advert, free. And secondly, how can he now give the program a bad review?

If he says 'yes' to the competition, tell him you're so pleased that you're prepared to give all the losers a 20% discount voucher off the recommended price so, in terms of discount vouchers that adds even further value to the prizes – and the editor can (if you suggest it) call it the competition nobody loses!

And to send out the vouchers the editor will have to give you the losers' entry coupons. Hey presto, a mailing list of (hopefully) several hundred people, all of whom like the sound of your product so much they want to win it. And if they lose, at 20% off, many of them are likely to send you an order. Remember not to try this trick too often or they'll get wise to it (especially if they've read this! – even so it still has a good chance of working).

You could also try other similar possibilities. For example, some magazines have reader offer pages where they supply product to readers at a discount price. Offer one an exclusive and you could find yourself making a few hundred sales – albeit with a reduced profit margin as the magazine will take a big cut, but with no advertising cost.

CHAPTER 10

PRINTING PROBLEMS

One of the biggest nightmares PC users face is trying to interface equipment together. Although most PCs are called compatible, and they are with each other to a very high degree, peripherals are not, and the most common peripheral is the printer.

Just take a look through the pages of any news stand magazine and you'll see dozens of different types of printer, ranging from 8-pin dot matrix to 24-pin, inkjet, colour ink, colour ribbon, laser, colour laser and many more. Luckily, though, some standards are becoming established and you will often be able to get by if you configure your software to either Epson or Hewlett Packard Laserjet compatible modes. Another standard, IBM, is actually (as near as matters) another clone of the Epson interface.

That said, there are still many weird and wonderful printers and printer interface types so, to help sort out any confusion, this chapter should have enough ideas to solve any but the most stubborn of problems.

CHECKING FOR FINISHED PRINTOUTS

Here's a handy tip for people who use printers which have A4 sheets fed into them via a tray. You can sometimes waste a lot of time printing short letters, trying to work out if the printer has finished its output or not, because the paper will continue moving at the same rate – this is certainly true with HP Deskjets.

You can get around this by creating a batch file called EJECT.BAT, containing just one line:

```
ECHO ?>PRN
```

where the ? represents the form feed character, and is accessible from the keyboard by holding down [Alt] and typing 12. Then when you want to know when printing has finished, type EJECT and the printer will eject the paper as soon as there's nothing left in its buffer.

LINING UP PRINTER LABELS

When lining up computer labels on a printer it's common to end up wasting quite a few (or even several sheets) trying to get the printout to appear in the right place.

A simple solution to this wastage is to turn the labels around and print on the shiny grease-proof backing. Hold them up to the light to check the alignment, and when everything's correct remember the start position for the print, turn the labels round again and you should get perfect results on the first print.

PROTEXT LINE DRAWING ON DMP3000 PRINTERS

The following tip may be useful to Protext users who use DMP3000 printers, or indeed any other printer which insists on printing in bi-directional mode, which results in vertical lines looking anything but.

If you need to use the line drawing facility, which is excellent for drawing boxes around tables, then uni-directional printing (where the carriage only prints while moving from left to right) is essential to get the verticals lined up neatly. The relevant control code is not mentioned in the DMP3000 manual, but you can customise the printer drive as follows:

Load up the EPSON.PPD file (making a copy first, just in case) and look for this sequence:

```
cc 'u'=27,"-",1  ; 27,"-",0
```

and insert this new line underneath it:

```
cc 'v'=27,"U",1  ; 27,"U",0
```

Once you've saved the file, if you need to revert back to uni-directional printing just type [Ctrl][X] followed by [V] at the beginning of the relevant section, and another [Ctrl][X] and [V] at the end to turn it off.

By the way, control codes are a lot easier to set up in Protext if the "Control codes displayed" option is toggled to ON.

COLOUR SEPARATIONS

Most professional art packages these days are able to make use of a colour printer, but oddly enough some still can't produce the colour separations which are so important when the finished artwork is going to be processed at a print bureau.

A simple method for getting around this shortcoming, for those who cannot afford a package with this facility, is to do the following:

Firstly, create your design in full colour and save it. Then delete all but one of the colours, change the remaining colour to black and save the result using a different filename. Now pull in the full-colour original and do the same thing for a different colour – again, saving the result under a different filename.

Repeat the process for each colour in the design – making sure you limit yourself in the original to only the number of colours you can afford – and you should end up with a set of image files in black, one for each colour of the original design.

Take the printouts to your printer, who will be then able to produce the finished leaflet, newsletter or poster with results no different than those obtained from a package which supports colour separation.

Colour printing is always an expensive business, and for this reason is sadly ignored by many home DTP publishers. But this tip can help save you considerable cash by knocking out one of the chargeable stages in producing full-colour artwork.

PRINTSCREEN FIX

If your PRINTSCREENs come out with strange Greek characters in place of what should have been vertical and horizontal lines, then your printer is probably working in Epson mode.

To correct this, check that the DIP switch settings (see the tip Printer DIP Switches in this chapter) are set to IBM Characters. Either character set will do, but you will probably prefer using Character Set 2 if you want your pound signs to be printed correctly.

MISSING POUND SIGNS

Probably the most frequent printer problem (maybe the most frequent problem of all time) is the famous Mystery of the Missing Pound Sign. Experienced readers may well be fed up hearing about this old chestnut by now, but it is still sufficiently misunderstood to earn its inclusion here. Basically, the typical query runs along the lines of "When I print my document, the pound sign comes out as a hash (#)" or "I can't even get a pound to appear on-screen".

The history of this whole subject goes back to the early sixties, when the ASCII character set was designed. Originally a seven-bit code, no characters with a code above 127 existed and no provision was made for the inclusion of the pound sign – it was very hit-and-miss in the early days of personal computers as to whether the manufacturer of your kit had taken this into account.

Thankfully Epson, who were busy setting printer standards worldwide, had thoughtfully added a DIP switch which allowed you to swap between character sets, most importantly between the newly-designed "international" version of ASCII, fully eight-bits and now sporting a pound sign.

The only problem was the code required to get the pound printed was 35, a value which normally represented the hash symbol "#". So as well as losing the ability to print hashes, you had to type hashes to produce pounds. Very sensible.

IBM, meanwhile, had designed their own international character sets, including the pound symbol as ASCII code 156. At last. Except for one thing – printers, adopting the Epson standard en-masse, ignored character 156 completely.

By now, MS-DOS could be configured with KEYB UK (KEYBUK for MS-DOS 3.2) to produce code 156 "£" when [Shift][3] was pressed, instead of 36 "$". It was unfortunate that printers didn't still didn't know what to do with this character . . .

So IBM produced the IBM Graphics Printer, which supported the new code – furthermore, Epson copied the idea and added the IBM character set to its own printers, again configurable from DIP switches. The upshot of all this is that to ensure you get good, honest pound signs from your computer and printer, you need to make sure of the following:

1. If you have DOS 3.2, put the line KEYBUK in your AUTOEXEC.BAT file, making sure the file KEYBUK.EXE is present in the root directory of your hard or floppy disk.

If you have DOS 3.3 or higher, use the command KEYB UK,437 and make sure the file KEYB.EXE is in the root (alternatively, specify where it is to be found with KEYB UK,437,C:\DOS).

2. Make sure the line COUNTRY=044,437 is in your CONFIG.SYS file (again, specify its directory if it isn't).

3. Make sure your printer DIP switches are set to "IBM Character Set 2", if your printer supports IBM mode.

4. Try setting your printer DIP switches to UK character set, although this isn't guaranteed to work.

If all else fails, run the DOS utility GRAPHTABL first – it can "force" programs which run in graphics mode to support the pound symbol.

PRINTER DIP SWITCHES

The good old Missing Pound dilemma, among other printing mysteries, is a good reason to check out your printer's DIP switches if you haven't already done so. These can yield surprisingly useful results when fiddled about with carefully, depending on the printer. For example, if your PRINTSCREENs come out with strange Greek symbols where there should have been straight lines, your printer is probably not in IBM mode. Just turn it off, flip a couple of switches, turn it on again and Presto!

The exact arrangements of DIP switches vary from printer to printer, not to mention between manufacturers as well. But there will generally be certain functions you can expect to find included as DIP switch settings, and here are some of the commonest:

International Character Set:

This is usually a set of three switches on a block of eight, although sometimes they are separate. Set these to the UK to ensure pound signs are printed instead of hashes.

IBM/Epson character set:

This switch determines whether your printer works in Epson mode, where characters above 127 represent Epson type face styles such as italics, or whether it will accept the full eight-bit IBM character set.

Draft/NLQ:

Set your printer to your preferred style; draft mode is crude but fast, NLQ is a must for any business of official correspondence.

Zero Character:

This is a useful switch; If you are printing program listings, you will probably prefer your zeros to look like zeros, with the conventional diagonal slash through the middle. For letter writing, you will probably want the more usual O shapes.

Page Length:

Very important; although page length (as well as all other page formatting commands) is set to your preferences by most software packages, when you print "raw" from DOS the printer will revert to its defaults. As you will probably have settled on a particular type of paper, it makes good sense to tell your printer about it. A4 paper needs this switch set to 12 inches, while the usual listing paper – which is always just that bit too fat to fit in a decent A4 folder – requires the 11 inch setting.

USING THE IBM CHARACTER SET IN PRINTOUTS

To make sure you get the best results from your printer, you need to know about the characters it prints. The IBM Character Set is the setting you will probably be using the most, even if your printer is Epson-compatible. This is because you need to be sure that what you see on screen is what you'll get on paper.

All PCs use the IBM character set, and if you want to use these same characters in your printouts without having to resort to the limited effects of PRINTSCREEN, then take a look at the following table:

DEC	HEX	CHR	DEC	HEX	CHR
0-31	0-1F	(Control codes	74	4A	J
32	20	(Space)	75	4B	K
33	21	!	76	4C	L
34	22	"	77	4D	M
35	23	#	78	4E	N
36	24	$	79	4F	O
37	25	%	80	50	P
38	26	&	81	51	Q
39	27	'	82	52	R
40	28	(	83	53	S
41	29	)	84	54	T
42	2A	*	85	55	U
43	2B	+	86	56	V
44	2C	,	87	57	W
45	2D	-	88	58	X
46	2E	.	89	59	Y
47	2F	/	90	5A	Z
48	30	0	91	5B	[
49	31	1	92	5C	\
50	32	2	93	5D	]
51	33	3	94	5E	^
52	34	4	95	5F	_
53	35	5	96	60	'
54	36	6	97	61	a
55	37	7	98	62	b
56	38	8	99	63	c
57	39	9	100	64	d
58	3A	:	101	65	e
59	3B	;	102	66	f
60	3C	<	103	67	g
61	3D	=	104	68	h
62	3E	>	105	69	i
63	3F	?	106	6A	j
64	40	@	107	6B	k
65	41	A	108	6C	l
66	42	B	109	6D	m
67	43	C	110	6E	n
68	44	D	111	6F	o
69	45	E	112	70	p
70	46	F	113	71	q
71	47	G	114	72	r
72	48	H	115	73	s
73	49	I	116	74	t

DEC	HEX	CHR	DEC	HEX	CHR
117	75	u	161	A1	í
118	76	v	162	A2	ó
119	77	w	163	A3	ú
120	78	x	164	A4	ñ
121	79	y	165	A5	Ñ
122	7A	z	166	A6	ª
123	7B	{	167	A7	º
124	7C	|	168	A8	¿
125	7D	}	169	A9	⌐
126	7E	~	170	AA	¬
127	7F	(Del)	171	AB	½
128	80	Ç	172	AC	¼
129	81	ü	173	AD	¡
130	82	é	174	AE	«
131	83	â	175	AF	»
132	84	ä	176	B0	▓
133	85	à	177	B1	▓
134	86	å	178	B2	▓
135	87	ç	179	B3	│
136	88	ê	180	B4	┤
137	89	ë	181	B5	╡
138	8A	è	182	B6	╢
139	8B	ï	183	B7	╖
140	8C	î	184	B8	╕
141	8D	ì	185	B9	╣
142	8E	Ä	186	BA	║
143	8F	Å	187	BB	╗
144	90	É	188	BC	╝
145	91	æ	189	BD	╜
146	92	Æ	190	BE	╛
147	93	ô	191	BF	┐
148	94	ö	192	C0	└
149	95	ò	193	C1	┴
150	96	û	194	C2	┬
151	97	ù	195	C3	├
152	98	ÿ	196	C4	─
153	99	Ö	197	C5	┼
154	9A	Ü	198	C6	╞
155	9B	¢	199	C7	╟
156	9C	£	200	C8	╚
157	9D	¥	201	C9	╔
158	9E	?	202	CA	╩
159	9F	ƒ	203	CB	╦
160	A0	á	204	CC	╠

DEC	HEX	CHR	DEC	HEX	CHR
205	CD	=	248	F8	°
206	CE	╬	249	F9	.
207	CF	╧	250	FA	·
208	D0	╨	251	FB	√
209	D1	╤	252	FC	ⁿ
210	D2	╥	253	FD	²
211	D3	╙	254	FE	■
212	D4	╘	255	FF	(Blank)
213	D5	╒			
214	D6	╓			
215	D7	╫			
216	D8	╪			
217	D9	┘			
218	DA	┌			
219	DB	█			
220	DC	▄			
221	DD	▌			
222	DE	▐			
223	DF	▀			
224	E0	α			
225	E1	β			
226	E2	Γ			
227	E3	π			
228	E4	Σ			
229	E5	σ			
230	E6	μ			
231	E7	τ			
232	E8	Φ			
233	E9	θ			
234	EA	Ω			
235	EB	δ			
236	EC	∞			
237	ED	φ			
238	EE	ε			
239	EF	∩			
240	F0	≡			
241	F1	±			
242	F2	≥			
243	F3	≤			
244	F4	⌠			
245	F5	⌡			
246	F6	÷			
247	F7	≈			

All of these characters are usable – every one. To obtain any character you see in this table, hold down your [Alt] key and type the DECIMAL value shown in the left hand column before releasing [Alt]. Note that you can't do this from within some word processors, but this is quite rare and you'll often find that such software provides its own facility for entering these characters.

When you've designed your page or document, send it to the printer in the usual way – and if your printer is set to the IBM character set, rather than Epson or some other mode, everything will print out as expected.

EPSON CONTROL CODES

These days, most printers understand more than one of the established standards for dealing with things like font selection, paper size, line spacing and so on. One of the most enduring of these standards is one designed by Epson in the early eighties, and it is still being built on today.

Known variously as Epson Escape Codes, Epson Mode, Epson Compatibility and by many other names, the Epson standard was quickly adopted by printer manufacturers throughout the world. Like IBM, Intel and Microsoft, Epson were the standard-setters of printer compatibility. Any printer which could handle Epson codes was guaranteed sales, and Epson-compatible printers flourished everywhere. As a result, your printer is almost guaranteed to have this compatibility built in, regardless of make. Some manufacturers do this in different ways; for instance modern laser printers take smart cards which change their identity in an instant.

If you can get your printer to emulate an Epson, you can take control of a large, extremely powerful set of commands for doing just about anything you could wish. And what's more, any program you write which takes advantage of these codes is guaranteed a huge platform of compatible printers to work with.

The Epson standard is fairly straightforward, although it can seem complex at times. This is only natural; it has evolved over a period of one-and-a-half decades, and whilst you won't get TrueType fonts out of an Epson, you will get almost total control over everything else: Graphics routines that work the way you want, with sensible scaling factors; controlled page layout; special effects by direct control of the print head – anything that the printer can do is within your control.

Controlling a printer is the same regardless of make or model; you fire a sequence of codes at it and, if it understands them, it will carry out the instructions. Epson codes are instantly recognisable by their "Escape" sequence format; this simply means that the Escape code, ASCII 27, usually marks the beginning of all Epson code sequences.

The Epson Escape Codes naturally fall into groups of commands with similar purposes; the table below gives a listing, by group, of the standard set of Epson commands, together with a brief introduction to each.

Where you see the word ESC, substitute the number 27. Where you see letters, such as C (as in ESC C n), substitute that letter's ASCII code. And the number n is any valid parameter for a given command. So the first entry "ESC C n", where you want n to be 11, the complete sequence of bytes to send to the printer would be 27 67 11.

Where you see a word like "SO" or "DC4", refer to the table of ASCII Control Codes below; each ASCII code below 32 has an actual name, dating back to the days of computer terminals, and when you see one just look it up in the chart and substitute its ASCII value.

THE EPSON CONTROL CODES

PAGE FORMAT COMMANDS

ESC C n	Set Form Length in Lines. The form length is not the same as page length. Allowable values for n are 1 to 127.
ESC C 00 n	Set Form Length in Inches. Allowable values for n are from 1 to 22 inches, in integers only. 0 is ignored.
ESC Q n	Set Right Margin. Sets the right margin to column n, which must be to the right of the left margin.
ESC l n	Set Left Margin. Sets the left margin to column n, which must be to the left of the right margin.
ESC N n	Set Perforation Skip. Sets the distance between the last print line on the current page and the first print line on the next, so that fanfold perforations can be skipped.
ESC O	Cancel Perforation Skip. Cancels ESC N setting.

CHARACTER WIDTHS AND PRINT ATTRIBUTES

ESC M	Select Elite Mode. Selects 12-point character font. Will take precedence over Condensed and Proportional modes.
ESC P	Cancel Elite Mode.
ESC SO	Set Double-Width Single-Line Printing. Double-width printing will cease at the next carriage return.
DC4	Cancel Double-Width Single-Line Printing.
ESC W n	Set/Cancel Double-Width Printing. Set n to 1 or 0 respectively. Double-width printing will remain active until cancelled with ESC W 0.
ESC SI	Set Condensed Mode.
DC2	Cancel Condensed Mode.
ESC E	Set Emphasized Mode.
ESC F	Cancel Emphasized Mode.

ESC 4	Set Italics Mode.
ESC 5	Cancel Italics Mode.
ESC – n	Start/End Underlining. The "-" is the minus sign, (ASCII 45).
ESC S n	Start Superscript or Subscript. Set n to 0 or 1 to select Superscript or Subscript respectively.
ESC T	Cancel Superscript or Subscript.
ESC P n	Set/Cancel Proportional Mode. Set n to 1 or 0 respectively. If Elite mode is currently active, Proportional mode will not take effect until Elite mode is cancelled.

PAPER FEED COMMANDS

ESC 0	Set 1/8 inch Line Spacing.
ESC 1	Set 7/72 inch Line Spacing.
ESC 2	Set 1/6 inch Line Feed.
ESC 3 n	Set n/216 inch Line Feed Pitch.
ESC A n	Set n/72 inch Line Feed Pitch.
LF	Line Feed.
ESC J n	Make n/216 inch Line Feed. Use this command to issue an immediate n/216-inch line feed, without altering the current line feed pitch.
ESC j n	Make n/216 inch Reverse Line Feed. This is only supported on some printers, and is useful for double-pass print effects.

TAB CONTROL

HT	Horizontal Tab. If any tab stops are set, this command moves the carriage to the next stop – by default, tab stops are placed at every eighth column.
ESC D n1 n2 ... 00	Set/Clear Horizontal Tabs. Set tabs at the positions n1, n2 ... nk. Clears all stops if no parameters are used. Always end the sequence with a zero.
VT	Vertical Tab. Moves the print head to the left margin of the line containing the first vertical tab following the current print head position.
ESC B n1 N2 ... 00	Set Vertical Tab. Sets vertical tabs at lines specified by n1, n2 etc. Clears all stops if no parameters are used. Always end the sequence with a zero.

THE ASCII CONTROL CODES

From time to time you will come across some strange-sounding code words associated with printer control. Words like DC1 and SO are bandied about in printer manuals with the obvious assumption that they are part of everyday computer-speak. It might come as a surprise to computer manufacturers that most professional programmers know only a handful of these codes and their purpose, and even fewer understand their origins and meanings.

Most computer users come to understand that there is a part of the ASCII character set reserved for control purposes only, which are not printable in the normal course of events. These are the ASCII codes from zero to thirty-one, the so-called ASCII Control Codes.

What still confuses many users is the fact that in nearly all tables of the ASCII character set, there are shapes, or symbols printed beside these numbers – and yet these codes can't be printed. What exactly are these codes, anyway?

When the ASCII (American Standard Code for Information Interchange) character set was designed in the sixties, a lot of careful thought went into its layout; upper and lower-case characters were spaced apart at a fixed distance of 32, allowing easy conversion between the two cases. The printable codes began at 32 with the space character, and the first 32 codes were reserved for control purposes.

Most of these control codes are no longer in common use; they were designed mainly for communication between long-distance computer terminals, their mainframe hosts, and printers. Only the most important of these – CR, LF, BS, HT and so on – are still in common use and have a function on modern computers. The rest retain some function in modem communications but are now largely unknown, their original purpose forgotten by all but the most ardent of hacks.

Below is a table detailing each of these 32 codes, together with their name – or mnemonic – and a brief description of their original purpose. Where a code retains a present-day function in connection with printers, or even computers, this is mentioned.

The "printable" symbols which have entered the IBM version of the ASCII table at these positions are omitted, as they have little or no bearing on printers and can only appear on computer screens when software chooses to display them.

The ASCII Control Codes

DEC	HEX	NAME	MEANING
00	00	NUL	Null – No action, cancel or End of Sequence
01	01	SOH	Start of heading
02	02	STX	Start of text
03	03	ETX	End of text
04	04	EOT	End of transmission
04	05	ENQ	Enquire
06	06	ACK	Acknowledge
07	07	BEL	Bell – Sound the bell on printer or computer
08	08	BS	Backspace – Printer or computer
09	09	HT	Horizontal tab – Printer or computer
10	0A	LF	Line feed – Printer or computer
11	0B	VT	Vertical tab – Printer or computer
12	0C	FF	Form feed – Also CLS code on computer
13	0D	CR	Carriage return – Printer or computer
14	0E	SO	Shift out
15	0F	SI	Shift in
16	10	DLE	Data link escape
17	11	DC1	Device control 1, or XON
18	12	DC2	Device control 2
19	13	DC3	Device control 3, or XOFF
20	14	DC4	Device control 4
21	15	NAK	Negative acknowledge
22	16	SYN	Synchronous mark
23	17	ETB	End of transmission block
24	18	CAN	Cancel
25	19	EM	End of medium
26	1A	SS	End of file – Also EOF marker in text files
27	1B	ESC	Escape – Also generated by Escape key.
28	1C	FS	File separator
29	1D	GS	Group separator
30	1E	RS	Record separator
31	1F	US	Unit separator

EMULATING IBM LINE CHARACTERS

If you have an Epson compatible printer which can't print out the IBM line characters, you will probably have encountered many documents that emerge from your printer with strange characters or italic Ms instead, making them look very messy.

But there is a solution if you have a word processor capable of allowing you to redefine characters as they are sent to the printer. Protext is a particularly good example of a program that does this well so the following examples are built around it.

Remember that if you don't have Protext but your wordprocessor allows it, as long as you enter exactly the same sequences of bytes for each of the characters in the relevant portion of your word processor, you should find you can achieve exactly the same results. To try out these examples you should switch to your Protext directory and load in the file FX80.PPD. If it's not in the directory then you should find a copy on one of your distribution disks.

FX80.PPD is a text file which contains all the instructions necessary to control an Epson FX80/RX80 and may other Epson compatible printers. Once it's loaded, the first five lines or so tell you all the printers it will work with, so you can check that yours is one of them before continuing.

When you've done that, rename the program to FX80PLUS.PPD by typing "N FX80PLUS.PPD" from Protext's command mode. This makes sure you don't lose your original copy. Next scroll down through the file until you find several lines of character redefinitions, with the first one beginning **"rc 179=..."**. These lines make up a set of just the single line IBM characters and will not fit with the new definitions. So, when you find them delete all 11 lines, as you will be redefining all these characters to make them fit with the various combinations of single and double line characters.

Having done that, type in all the 40 replacement lines listed below and save the new driver by pressing [S] followed by [Return] twice from command mode. To now use the new printer driver simply type "PRINTER FX80PLUS" from command mode and it will be set to go.

Now you are ready to load in and print out any documents with line characters or you can create your own by pressing [Ctrl][F7] to enable line printing. Once activated, hold down the [Alt] key and press any of the cursor keys to draw a line in that direction. Protext is quite clever about this and notes when lines cross over and meet, and joins them up accordingly. To toggle between single and double line mode press [Shift][Ctrl][F7].

The way it all works is really quite simple. FX80PLUS.PPD is processed by Protext when you issue the PRINTER command and any lines beginning with **rc** notify Protext that when the character specified is to be sent to the printer, that the following sequence of characters should be sent in its place.

Here are the replacement character redefinitions:

```
rc 179=27,"K",6,0,0,0,0,255,0,0,8,27,"J",12,27,"K",6,0,0,0,0,15,0,0,27,"j",12
rc 180=27,"K",6,0,8,8,8,255,0,0,8,27,"J",12,27,"K",6,0,0,0,0,15,0,0,27,"j",12
rc 181=27,"K",6,0,40,40,40,255,0,0,8,27,"J",12,27,"K",6,0,0,0,0,15,0,0,27,"j",12
rc 182=27,"K",6,0,8,255,0,255,0,0,8,27,"J",12,27,"K",6,0,0,15,0,15,0,0,27,"j",12
rc 183=27,"K",6,0,8,15,8,15,0,0,8,27,"J",12,27,"K",6,0,0,15,0,15,0,0,27,"j",12
rc 184=27,"K",6,0,40,40,40,63,0,0,8,27,"J",12,27,"K",6,0,0,0,0,15,0,0,27,"j",12
rc 185=27,"K",6,0,40,239,0,255,0,0,8,27,"J",12,27,"K",6,0,0,15,0,15,0,0,27,"j",12
rc 186=27,"K",6,0,0,255,0,255,0,0,8,27,"J",12,27,"K",6,0,0,15,0,15,0,0,27,"j",12
rc 187=27,"K",6,0,40,47,32,63,0,0,8,27,"J",12,27,"K",6,0,0,15,0,15,0,0,27,"j",12
rc 188=27,"K",6,0,40,232,8,248,0,0
rc 189=27,"K",6,0,8,248,8,248,0,0

rc 190=27,"K",6,0,40,40,40,248,0,0
rc 191=27,"K",6,0,8,8,8,15,0,0,8,27,"J",12,27,"K",6,0,0,0,0,15,0,0,27,"j",12
rc 192=27,"K",6,0,0,0,0,248,8,8
rc 193=27,"K",6,0,8,8,8,248,8,8
rc 194=27,"K",6,0,8,8,8,15,8,8,8,27,"J",12,27,"K",6,0,0,0,0,15,0,0,27,"j",12
rc 195=27,"K",6,0,0,0,0,255,8,8,8,27,"J",12,27,"K",6,0,0,0,0,15,0,0,27,"j",12
rc 196=27,"K",6,0,8,8,8,8,8,8
rc 197=27,"K",6,0,8,8,8,255,8,8,8,27,"J",12,27,"K",6,0,0,0,0,15,0,0,27,"j",12
rc 198=27,"K",6,0,0,0,0,255,40,40,8,27,"J",12,27,"K",6,0,0,0,0,15,0,0,27,"j",12
rc 199=27,"K",6,0,0,255,0,255,8,8,8,27,"J",12,27,"K",6,0,0,15,0,15,0,0,27,"j",12

rc 200=27,"K",6,0,0,248,8,232,40,40
rc 201=27,"K",6,0,0,63,32,47,40,40,8,27,"J",12,27,"K",6,0,0,15,0,15,0,0,27,"j",12
rc 202=27,"K",6,0,40,232,8,232,40,40
rc 203=27,"K",6,0,40,47,32,47,40,40,8,27,"J",12,27,"K",6,0,0,15,0,15,0,0,27,"j",12
rc 204=27,"K",6,0,0,255,0,239,40,40,8,27,"J",12,27,"K",6,0,0,15,0,15,0,0,27,"j",12
rc 205=27,"K",6,0,40,40,40,40,40,40
rc 206=27,"K",6,0,40,239,0,239,40,40,8,27,"J",12,27,"K",6,0,0,15,0,15,0,0,27,"j",12
rc 207=27,"K",6,0,40,40,40,232,40,40
rc 208=27,"K",6,0,8,248,8,248,8,8
rc 209=27,"K",6,0,40,40,40,47,40,40,8,27,"J",12,27,"K",6,0,0,0,0,15,0,0,27,"j",12

rc 210=27,"K",6,0,8,15,8,15,8,8,8,27,"J",12,27,"K",6,0,0,15,0,15,0,0,27,"j",12
rc 211=27,"K",6,0,0,248,8,248,8,8
rc 212=27,"K",6,0,0,0,0,248,40,40
rc 213=27,"K",6,0,0,0,0,63,40,40,8,27,"J",12,27,"K",6,0,0,0,0,15,0,0,27,"j",12
rc 214=27,"K",6,0,0,15,8,15,8,8,8,27,"J",12,27,"K",6,0,0,15,0,15,0,0,27,"j",12
rc 215=27,"K",6,0,8,255,8,255,8,8,8,27,"J",12,27,"K",6,0,0,15,0,15,0,0,27,"j",12
rc 216=27,"K",6,0,40,40,40,255,40,40,8,27,"J",12,27,"K",6,0,0,0,0,15,0,0,27,"j",12
rc 217=27,"K",6,0,8,8,8,248,0,0
rc 218=27,"K",6,0,0,0,0,15,8,8,8,27,"J",12,27,"K",6,0,0,0,0,15,0,0,27,"j",12
```

DEFINING A 6 X 8 CHARACTER

		C	O	L	U	M	N	S
		1	2	3	4	5	6
	128		★		★		
P	64		★		★		
I	32	★	★		★	★	★
X	16						
E	8	★	★		★	★	★
L	4		★		★		
S	2		★		★		
	1		★		★		

To define a character simply decide which dots (or pixels) are to go where in the 6 x 8 grid and then add up each column, from left to right, to obtain six numbers, like this:

Column 1: 8 + 32 = 40

Column 2: 1 + 2 + 4 + 8 + 32 + 64 + 128 = 239

Column 3: 0 = 0

Column 4: 1 + 2 + 4 + 8 + 32 + 64 + 128 = 239

Column 5: 8 + 32 = 40

Column 6: 8 + 32 = 40

So the sequence of characters to be sent to the printer will be: 40, 239, 0, 239, 40, 40.

CHAPTER 11

COMMUNICATIONS

Perhaps the fastest growing area of modern technology is telecommunications. Already the fax machine is considered an indispensable office tool, and you can even buy cards you plug into your PC that emulate fax machines, allowing you to send crystal clear faxes straight from your PC, without using a fax machine to first 'scan' in the text.

Many of these cards will also sit quietly in the background saving any incoming faxes to your hard disk, while you get on with other things. You can then browse through all received faxes and save paper (and time) by only printing out those faxes you need to. But more than that, the modem is revolutionising electronic communications (many modems also act as fax machines too). The current 'standard' high speed modems can transmit data at 14,400 bits per second and if you allow for data compression of four to one the effective throughput can be up to 57,600 bits per second or as much as a megabyte in two and a half minutes maximum.

And if that sounds fast the new ISDN phone lines will soon offer speeds many times faster than that. This means that more and more computers are linking up worldwide, often using huge bulletin boards like CompuServe (which has over a million members) as stepping stones to other services. Even today, if you need a program in a hurry, the chances are that you'll be able to log onto a bulletin board and download a suitable item of software in under an hour. But, as with all new technologies, there are many potential pitfalls, particularly in the area of compatibility. Therefore this chapter contains a collection of hints, tips, ideas and on-line services you can call that should help you get the best out of your modem.

BULLETIN BOARDS

If you have recently acquired a modem you may be wondering which bulletin boards you can call up with it. Well, there are literally hundreds of them in the UK and the following list is just a selection of the many available. Please bear in mind that bulletin boards can come and go and that people may move during the lifetime of this book, so some of the numbers may be out of date. If in doubt, ring from a voice phone first to avoid annoying people with modem whistles.

AREA	NAME	NUMBER
EAST	ARMADILLO	0362 695 314
EAST	ATHENA	0732 461 158
EAST	BABBS TOWER	0394 276 306
EAST	BOB'S BIZARRE	0394 279 644
EAST	DARK TOWER	0473 221 139
EAST	EUREKA	0603 250 689
EAST	FELIXSTOWE OPUS	0394 673 655
EAST	FREELANCE	0480 406 261
EAST	MIRACOM SUPPORT	0473 231 571
EAST	PETE'S PLACE	0206 862 354
EAST	RAINBOW BBS	0732 870 248
EAST	TRANS ALANTIC RES.	0375 25375
EIRE	DUBLIN FIDO	0001 854 522
LONDON	ALICE'S RESTAURANT	071 602 9714
LONDON	ALTERNATIVE VIEWDATA	081 761 8220
LONDON	ARKHAM OPUS	081 952 5128
LONDON	ARRAKEEN	071 738 7304
LONDON	BANAT UK 2	081 783 1151
LONDON	BODY MATTERS	071 603 7581
LONDON	BROWN BAG	071 404 0897
LONDON	CABB	081 773 0408
LONDON	CLUB 1512	081 204 8755
LONDON	CROWN GREEN	071 245 1512
LONDON	CRYSTAL TOWER	081 886 2813
LONDON	DATA NETWORK	081 478 5464
LONDON	DATAFLEX INFO	081 543 7020
LONDON	DATAFLEX INFO	071 978 8540
LONDON	DATASEL	081 680 5330
LONDON	DATASEL	081 681 8081
LONDON	DIRECT LINE 1	081 841 1847
LONDON	DIRECT LINE 2	081 842 2030
LONDON	EMERALD TOWER	071 405 8983
LONDON	FINGERFONE	071 253 3064
LONDON	FINGERFONE	071 490 1545
LONDON	FLIGHT PATH	081 759 1957
LONDON	JOLLY ROGER	081 742 1640
LONDON	KEYDATA	081 676 0072
LONDON	LONDON BB	081 455 6607
LONDON	LONDON CONNEXION	081 657 3240
LONDON	LONDON MAIL CENTRE	081 534 1200
LONDON	LONDON METROPOLIS	081 519 1055
LONDON	LONDON SURBURBAN	081 423 3575
LONDON	MARCTEL	081 346 7150
LONDON	MBBS MITCHAM	081 648 0018
LONDON	MICRO LIVE BB	081 567 6500
LONDON	MICRO UPDATE	081 877 1529
LONDON	MICRO VIEW	081 509 0729
LONDON	MICROMOLA	081 316 7402
LONDON	MUSICTEL 1	081 455 0843
LONDON	MUSICTEL 500	081 458 9704
LONDON	ODDBALL	081 679 2583
LONDON	ORGANIC GARDEN	081 464 3305

LONDON	OSI LIVES!	081 429 3047
LONDON	OUT OF THE BLUE	081 660 6807
LONDON	PARADIGM OPUS	071 251 8255
LONDON	PC ACCESS	081 853 3965
LONDON	PC SERVE SHOP	081 864 2633
LONDON	PC SUPPORT HQ	071 823 3296
LONDON	POLY OPUS	071 580 1690
LONDON	ROS LONDON	081 801 0708
LONDON	SHADY HOLLOW	081 884 1187
LONDON	SIRIUS/WBBS	081 542 3772
LONDON	SKULL'S TOWER	081 943 1194
LONDON	SPHINX'S LAIR	071 930 3903
LONDON	ST LONDON BBS	081 443 2432
LONDON	SW10 WAREHOUSE	071 351 7262
LONDON	TBBS ROVOREED	081 542 4977
LONDON	TERMINAL NET	081 423 5262
LONDON	THE CO OP BOARD	081 316 6488
LONDON	THE EMBASSY	081 366 1778
LONDON	THE GRAPEVINE	081 440 2849
LONDON	THE PYRAMID	071 239 0871
LONDON	THE VILLAGE	081 464 2516
LONDON	THE ZONE	081 683 4507
LONDON	THIRD WAVE 2	071 585 3163
LONDON	TIME HORIZONS	081 769 4841
LONDON	TWILIGHT ZONE	081 788 0884
LONDON	UKAS BBS	081 469 2244
LONDON	UNDERGROUND	081 427 8856
LONDON	UNDERGROUND	081 863 0198
LONDON	WOOD GREEN	081 889 5624
MIDLANDS	ATS BBS	021 456 2401
MIDLANDS	ATS BBS	021 456 2402
MIDLANDS	C 4 C	0926 428 294
MIDLANDS	CBABBS	021 430 3761
MIDLANDS	CENTRAL BBS	021 711 1451
MIDLANDS	CHASE NET BBS	0922 642 206
MIDLANDS	CHRONO'S LAIR	021 744 5561
MIDLANDS	CORBY TOWN OPUS	0536 205 113
MIDLANDS	CORRUPT COMPUTING	0203 76831
MIDLANDS	DIGITAL MATRIX	021 705 5187
MIDLANDS	LEICESTER CENTRAL	0533 700 914
MIDLANDS	M.W.C.F.E.	0926 421 844
MIDLANDS	MABBS	021 444 8972
MIDLANDS	MURDOCH'S HANGOUT	021 711 2620
MIDLANDS	NICC LEICS	0509 826 339
MIDLANDS	OLDBURY MAILBOX	021 541 1625
MIDLANDS	PLUG 'OLE	021 472 0256
MIDLANDS	POACHER OPUS	0476 62450
MIDLANDS	POWER TOWER	0533 880 114
MIDLANDS	PROJECT BBS	0384 401 770
MIDLANDS	SANDIE'S BEACH	0905 774 477
MIDLANDS	SHERWOOD FOREST	0602 397 113
MIDLANDS	SOFTMATIC INNOV.	0733 322 540
MIDLANDS	STARGATE OPUS	0476 74616

MIDLANDS	SUNBURN INC.	021 449 5269
MIDLANDS	THE ARK	021 353 5486
MIDLANDS	THE ROCK	0203 473 558
MIDLANDS	THE WHAT'S HIS NAME	0536 725 180
MIDLANDS	TUG II	0905 775 191
MIDLANDS	WELLAND VALLEY	0858 66594
MIDLANDS	WOLVES BBS	0902 745 337
NORTH-EAST	ARGUS PROJECT	091 490 0327
NORTH-EAST	BELLE VUE	0274 498 221
NORTH-EAST	BRADFORD BB	0274 480 452
NORTH-EAST	CONSETT WILDCAT	0207 506 179
NORTH-EAST	DAVE'S OPUS	0943 830 820
NORTH-EAST	EBBS 1	0274 541 156
NORTH-EAST	LASER TBBS	0532 438 430
NORTH-EAST	LEMS	0532 600 749
NORTH-EAST	LOG ON IN TYNEDALE	0434 606 639
NORTH-EAST	LOG ON THE TYNE	091 477 3339
NORTH-EAST	MARANATHA 1	0274 735 962
NORTH-EAST	MBBS LEACONFIELD	0964 557 045
NORTH-EAST	MERLIN BBS	0274 573 481
NORTH-EAST	MICROLOG	0422 71921
NORTH-EAST	MUSICTEL 2	0482 655 798
NORTH-EAST	NORTH YORKS OPUS	0423 868 065
NORTH-EAST	ODDYSSEY	0482 870 919
NORTH-EAST	OPTIX	0482 872 294
NORTH-EAST	SHARROW BB	0765 707 887
NORTH-EAST	SUMMER WINE	0484 653 234
NORTH-EAST	TASUG OPUS	0904 760 129
NORTH-EAST	THE BAR	0904 642 560
NORTH-EAST	THE PHANTOM	0226 732 140
NORTH-EAST	THE PUBLISHING SHOP	091 261 5228
NORTH-EAST	TYPESETTERS WORKSHOP	0274 370 381
NORTH-WEST	ARENA	0625 539 063
NORTH-WEST	ASPECTS	061 792 0260
NORTH-WEST	BREAKTHROUGH	051 734 5817
NORTH-WEST	DIGGERTEL 1 & 2	0925 411 265
NORTH-WEST	JAHBULON BBS	0254 59352
NORTH-WEST	LIVERPOOL MAILBOX	051 428 8924
NORTH-WEST	MATRIX	051 737 1882
NORTH-WEST	MEKTRONICS	061 773 7739
NORTH-WEST	MERKINSTEAD	061 434 7059
NORTH-WEST	OBBS 1	061 427 1596
NORTH-WEST	ROAD RUNNER	061 483 4105
NORTH-WEST	STUN USER NETWORK	061 429 9803
NORTH-WEST	THE CO OP BOARD	061 832 1961
NORTH-WEST	THE GAS LAMP	0706 358 331
NORTH-WEST	THE HOBBIT'S ARMPIT	0772 735 122
NORTH-WEST	THE JUNCTION	0270 580 099
NORTH-WEST	THE MANCUNIAN	061 227 9095
NORTH-WEST	UK HEALTHLINK	0942 722 984
SCOTLAND	ABERDEEN SBBS	0224 781 919
SCOTLAND	EMU OPUS	041 762 2338
SCOTLAND	JOCKS AWAY!	031 225 5368

SCOTLAND	LAMBDA BOARD	031 556 6316 ✓
SCOTLAND	MAGPIE	041 941 1333 ✗
SCOTLAND	SCOT AIR	041 884 7170
SCOTLAND	SCOTTISH OPUS	041 880 7863
SCOTLAND	SCOTTISH WILDCAT	0357 22582 ✗
SCOTLAND	SOUTH SIDE W/CAT	041 649 9043 ✗
SOUTH-EAST	AIRTEL	0342 717 800
SOUTH-EAST	ALT.REALITY	0959 76695
SOUTH-EAST	ASD OPUS	0923 247 637
SOUTH-EAST	AUDIO OUTPUT	0932 244 906
SOUTH-EAST	BANAT UK	0865 882 872
SOUTH-EAST	BAS OPUS	0256 728 331
SOUTH-EAST	BBS 09 III	0705 736 025
SOUTH-EAST	BITMAPP BROS	0245 413 728
SOUTH-EAST	BIXBOX	0634 200 931
SOUTH-EAST	BOOG BB	0252 626 233
SOUTH-EAST	BROWN BAG	0279 74855
SOUTH-EAST	CASTLE BBS	0276 691 872
SOUTH-EAST	CATS BOARD	0628 824 852
SOUTH-EAST	CSLBB	0273 571 457
SOUTH-EAST	DCE BOARD	0296 88165
SOUTH-EAST	DENTAL MICROBOARD	0227 276 162
SOUTH-EAST	DIAMOND OPUS	0791 86504
SOUTH-EAST	DR.SOLOMON'S BOARD	0494 724 946
SOUTH-EAST	DYADIAN BB	0494 778 425
SOUTH-EAST	E SOFT C	0767 50511
SOUTH-EAST	EYE 2	0276 66212
SOUTH-EAST	FLIGHTSTAR	0590 71555
SOUTH-EAST	FOLKSTONE BB	0303 42690
SOUTH-EAST	FOX'S DEN	0689 27085
SOUTH-EAST	FRIX	0734 420 229
SOUTH-EAST	G.A.B.B.S.	0705 524 805
SOUTH-EAST	HEAVEN	0580 83227
SOUTH-EAST	ICHTHUS	0734 484 847
SOUTH-EAST	ID2	0903 700 771
SOUTH-EAST	INDEX LINKED BBS	0227 770 403
SOUTH-EAST	JUST THE PLACE	0705 258 694
SOUTH-EAST	KOMPUTER KNOWLEDGE	0844 274 056
SOUTH-EAST	KOMPUTER KNOWLEDGE	0844 44430
SOUTH-EAST	LAMBETH CONFERENCE	0227 762 635
SOUTH-EAST	LAMPLIGHT QBBS	0705 811 531
SOUTH-EAST	LIMELIGHT	0580 212 043
SOUTH-EAST	LUTON HATS 'N CATS	0582 457 336
SOUTH-EAST	MEDWAY BBS	0634 280 031
SOUTH-EAST	MEDWAY BBS	0634 280 032
SOUTH-EAST	MIRRORWORLD	0883 844 044
SOUTH-EAST	MIRRORWORLD	0883 844 164
SOUTH-EAST	MONUSCI	0293 545 665
SOUTH-EAST	MOUNTAIN MUG	0276 31173
SOUTH-EAST	MOUNTAIN MUG	0276 35546
SOUTH-EAST	MUSICTEL PLUS	0843 590 000
SOUTH-EAST	MUSICWORLD	0784 252 278
SOUTH-EAST	PC SERVE HQ	0494 728 094

SOUTH-EAST	PD SIG FIDO	0892 661 149
SOUTH-EAST	REFLEX	0703 685 527
SOUTH-EAST	SBBS THE FIRM	0273 513 872
SOUTH-EAST	SCARY MONSTER	0734 320 297
SOUTH-EAST	SENTINEL	0628 781 429
SOUTH-EAST	SHADES	0342 810 905
SOUTH-EAST	SHADOW BBS	0705 511 501
SOUTH-EAST	SKYLINE 1	0234 741 691
SOUTH-EAST	SOFTNET B	0895 420 164
SOUTH-EAST	SPIDERS WEB	0329 45824
SOUTH-EAST	STAINES BB	0784 65794
SOUTH-EAST	THE CO OP BOARD	0202 532 701
SOUTH-EAST	THE CO OP BOARD	0705 754 851
SOUTH-EAST	THE HAM BOARD	0767 51846
SOUTH-EAST	THE HAVEN	0932 345 735
SOUTH-EAST	THE IVORY TOWER	0245 415 321
SOUTH-EAST	WAZZY'S OPUS	0223 213 784
SOUTH-EAST	WORDMONGERS	0296 437 262
SOUTH-WEST	AIX 386	0905 52536
SOUTH-WEST	BRAINDEAD	0823 254 352
SOUTH-WEST	BUBBLE BBS	0793 851 454
SOUTH-WEST	C SIDE BBS	0242 222 981
SOUTH-WEST	DATASOFT OPUS	0460 54615
SOUTH-WEST	EDDIE'S BBS	0635 71324
SOUTH-WEST	FIDO UK 1	0734 713 909
SOUTH-WEST	FIREFOX	0793 831 121
SOUTH-WEST	HAWK'S CASTLE	0344 411 621
SOUTH-WEST	JERSEY OPUS	0534 39389
SOUTH-WEST	KERNOW OPUS	0209 821 670
SOUTH-WEST	LAZER TOWER	0272 783 733
SOUTH-WEST	LIGHTFINGERS	0202 485 723
SOUTH-WEST	MICRODEAL	0726 65422
SOUTH-WEST	MIRROR II	0272 583 816
SOUTH-WEST	PSYCHOBABBLE	0534 52086
SOUTH-WEST	ROS SW	0392 53116
SOUTH-WEST	STABB	0793 855 176
SOUTH-WEST	SWINDON BBS	0793 616 683
SOUTH-WEST	SYSTEM G	0635 36688
SOUTH-WEST	THE MANOR	0980 863 031
SOUTH-WEST	TRINITY 1	0392 410 210
SOUTH-WEST	TRINITY 2	0367 22764
SOUTH-WEST	VIDEOTEX	0481 711 760
SOUTH-WEST	WHITE LIGHTNING	0635 37529
SOUTH-WEST	WINCHESTER REMOTE	0962 69322
SOUTH-WEST	WORLD OF CRYTON	0458 47608
WALES	ALTERNATE REALITY	0352 85528
WALES	ARC	0970 624 575
WALES	LIQUORICE ALLSORTS	0633 244 345
WALES	MGBBS	0443 733 343
WALES	PLUS & MINUS	0559 322 766
WALES	SUNSHINE BBS	0834 4562
WALES	WGBBS	0792 203 953

MAKING THE MOST OF MERCURY

As you may know, when you dial a telephone number via Mercury you also have to include your access code. If you are using a comms package or a program with an autodial facility for use with a modem, you may find that you have to re enter your access code in front of every number in your database - that's if there's room.

The solution, for Hayes compatible modems, is to put the Mercury access code in the modem's non volatile memory N1, as follows:

```
AT &Z1=131,999999999999
```

Where the 9s represent the access number, and your dialling string, which is buried in your comms package, appears:

```
ATDT
```

The phone number entry is then reduced to something like this:

```
N1 081 234 5678
```

This means that you don't have to use Mercury unless you choose to by putting N1 in front. If you are not yet on a digital exchange you would have to set the N1 to be:

```
131,T999999999999
```

And the dialling command would be:

```
ATDPN1 081 234 5678
```

This ensures that 131 and any local numbers go out in loop disconnect, but tone dialling is resumed once connection is made to a digital network.

THE HAYES COMMAND SET

There will be cases when you have to modify the initialisation and other parameters in your communications program. To the uninitiated this can be a daunting task, but it's actually not that difficult to follow once you understand which commands are available and what they do.

Using these details, incorporating the following list in your initialisation string would set your modem's speaker to low volume and the tone dial speed to 50:

```
AT L1 S11=50
```

After the S11=50 you could leave a space and continue to add further parameters. Here is a list of the most commonly used (and so the most compatible) commands:

A/	Re executes last command if modem has not made connection

A	Modem goes off hook in answer mode

B	set CCITT v.22 operation for 1200 bps/CCIT v.21 for 300 bps
B1	set BELL 212A operation for 1200 bps/BELL 103A for 300bps

D	Dial number following the D

E	Modem does not echo commands back to the terminal
E1	Modem echos commands back to the terminal

H	Modem goes on hook (hangs up)
H1	Enables switch hook and auxiliary relay

I	Displays the product identification code
I1	Performs checksums on firmware ROM and displays the value
I2	Performs checksums on firmware ROM and returns error or OK

L1	Speaker volume low
L2	Speaker volume medium
L3	Speaker volume high

M	Speaker always off
M1	Speaker on until carrier detected
M2	Speaker always on
M3	Speaker on until carrier detected except when dialling

O	Return to on line
O1	Return to on line with retrain

Q	Modem returns result codes
Q1	Modem does not display result codes

S0=n	Set number of rings before auto answering to n. Set to 0 to disable auto answer
S1=n	Set number of rings the modem detects before it answers a call to n
S2=n	Set the Escape character to n (default: 43)
S3=n	Set the Carriage Return character to n (default: 13)
S4=n	Set the Line Feed character to n (default: 10)
S5=n	Set the backspace character to n (default: 8)
S6=n	Set wait time before dialling to n. The minimum is 2 (default 2)
S7=n	Set length of time to wait for a carrier after dialling to n
S8=n	Set the pause time for the pause character (,) to n
S9=n	Set length of time a carrier must be present before being recognised to n
S10=n	Set length of time before hanging up the line after losing a carrier to n
S11=n	Set speed of tone dial to n milliseconds per digit. 50 is the fastest, 255 the slowest

Sr?   Display contents of S register

V   Short numeric result codes
V1   Full verbal result codes

X   "CONNECT" result codes enabled
X1   "CONNECT nnnn" result codes enabled, blind dial, busy signal not detected
X2   Wait for dial tone before dialling, all "CONNECT nnnn" result codes enabled, busy signal not detected
X3   Blind dials all "CONNECT nnnn" result codes enabled, modem sends "BUSY" if busy signal detected
X4   Wait for dial tone before dialling, all "CONNECT nnnn" result codes enabled, modem sends "BUSY" if busy signal detected

Y   Long space disconnect disabled
Y1   Long space disconnect enabled

Z0   Load stored profile configuration 0
Z0   Load stored profile configuration 1

&P   Pulse dial make/break ratio 39/61 (USA/Canada)
&P1   Pulse dial make/break ratio 33/67 (UK/Hong Kong)

&R   CTS (Clear To Send) follows RTS (Request To Send)
&R1   Ignores RTS, CTS is always ON

&S   DSR (Data Set Ready) always on
&S1   DSR is compatible with EIA RS 232C

&Z0=n   Store phone number n in non volatile RAM location 0
&Z1=n   Store phone number n in non volatile RAM location 1
&Z2=n   Store phone number n in non volatile RAM location 2
&Z3=n   Store phone number n in non volatile RAM location 3

THE 'V DOT' TERMS EXPLAINED

Here's a quick breakdown of what the V.nn terms actually mean that you often see when modems are discussed (bps = bits per second):

V.17   Extended Group 3 Fax 12000 and 14400 bps
V.21   300 bps
V.22   1200 bps
V.22bis   2400 bps
V.23   1200/75 bps
V.27ter   Group 3 Fax 2400 and 4800 bps
V.29   Group 3 Fax 9600 and 7200 bps
V.32   Full duplex 9600 bps plus 2400 and 4800 bps if required

V.32bis As V.32 plus 14400, 12000 and 7200 bps speeds
V.42 Same as MNP (a misnomer really)
V.42bis Similar to MNP 5 Compression

As you will have noticed V.42 is NOT an even faster protocol, rather it signifies whether a modem has MNP support. It's hard to see why these V numbers were chosen but you should note that when you see V.42 or V.42bis, don't think you've seen a really cheap and fast modem. In fact you can get a standard 2400 bps modem with V.42 support. Useful but certainly not as good as having a V.32 modem.

Talking about MNP, here are the MNP 'classes'. Remember that only MNP 5 offers data compression:

MNP 1 Half duplex error control - rarely used
MNP 2 Full duplex error control
MNP 3 As MNP 2 plus packetizing of data
MNP 4 As MNP 3 plus improvements to reduce overheads
MNP 5 Compression under MNP up to four times modem speed

When two modems negotiate, the answering modem will first negotiate the highest possible common speed, then V.42 (assuming it has V.42), or go to MNP. Then, if the answering modem has V.42bis compression it will ask the other modem if it is capable of it and, if so, will enable compression.

You should note that although the CompuServe V.32 nodes do have compression they are locked at 9600 bps, so compression offers no benefits as both ends must have port speeds greater than 9600 bps for compression to occur.

A new modem standard, called V.fast is currently being worked on. If all goes to plan, it will have appeared before the end of 1993. A V.fast modem should reach a raw speed of between 19,200 and 24,000 bps over normal telephone lines and will probably be known as V.34 when it's released.

But in a year or two we may not even need modems any more as a new service ISDN (Integrated Services Digital Network) should take over. It is estmated that by the end of 1994 about half the telephone connections in the US will have access to it, and the UK won't be far behind.

With ISDN, you won't need a modem as no MOdulation or DEModulation (hence the name MODEM) will be necessary. All you will need is an ISDN adapter and a new ISDN line to be installed to your home or office. Each line carries three digital channels. There are two "B" channels that carry various data at 64,000 bps and a "D" channel at 16,000 bps that can carry control signals or serve as a third data channel.

So, if a single ISDN channel can transfer uncompressed data bi-directionally at 64,000 bps, if you combine that with data compression we should soon be able to transfer data at up to about six megabytes a minute, per channel!

OTHER COMMS TERMS

BAUD - Term for modulation used for older, low-speed modems. Each bit of data being transferred generated a tone or baud. Newer technology combines multiple bits in one baud so 'baud' is no longer an accurate term.

BPS - Bits Per Second. Measures rates of modem data transfer up to today's theoretical maximum of 57,600 BPS (based on a maximum of four to one compression on a transfer speed of 14,400 BPS).

CCITT - Consultative Committee for International Telephony and Telegraphy. Based in Geneva, Switzerland, the committee sets general standards for modulation, data compression and error control.

MNP - Microcom Networking Protocol. Older proprietary standards of error control and data compression. Comprises several levels, including MNP 2-4, which define error control, and MNP 5 which defines data compression.

LAP-M - Link Access Procedure-Modem. A CCITT standard for modulation and error control.

ELIMINATING LINE NOISE

One of the more common introduction points of line noise is in the telephone grid system itself. There are a number of ways it can occur as signals can be routed through a number of exchanges before they make it to the other end, and some of these exchanges are not yet digital. Also physical connections at one of these junctions may not be 100% intact.

If the problem can be solved by hanging up and calling back, then it's likely that you were previously connected through an intermittent or dirty connection. There's not much you can do about this other than report the problem to British Telecom.

There are many more possible sources of interference closer to you - in your house in fact. Here you can do something about it. Many homes have televisions, radios, microwave ovens, videos and PCs and all of these radiate radio waves that could possibly get into your phone lines and cause noise.

Electric motors and mechanical dimmer controls can also introduce noise into the electrical wiring in your house and cause problems. If your line noise problem doesn't go away after repeated hanging up and calling back, then you may be suffering from one of these household problems.

You can take steps to eliminate the noise by turning off everything except the fridge (and even that for a moment if the problem continues). If the noise goes away start turning things back on one at a time, checking the computer each time until the noise starts up again. Remember that it could be that it's not just a single piece of equipment causing the problem but several working collectively. So this process of elimination may take a while.

Don't forget you should also check your computer/modem wiring and you can use noise suppressors on your power connections to both the PC and the modem. If it's external, use a shielded cable to connect your modem to the PC - ribbon cables should be avoided as, being unshielded, they can often cause problems.

As a final thought, if you live in a built up area then interference from CB radios or taxis could be the problem. Extra shielding around your PC or aluminium foil around the inside of the case could solve the problem, but make sure you only ever open your PC with the power off, and that no foil is loose (or could become loose) and create a short circuit.

MAJOR MODEM MANUFACTURERS

Here is a list of some of the major modem manufacturers' bulletin board systems. They are all in the US, but may have useful fixes and other tips on line if you are really stuck and can't get help from a UK supplier. All numbers are as you should dial them from the UK. To log on from another country replace the preceding 0101 with your international access code followed by a 1 and then the rest of the number.

ATI Technologies	0101 416 756 4591
Cardinal	0101 717 293 3074
Compucom	0101 415 499 7711
Hayes	0101 800 874 2937
Intel	0101 503 645 6275
Microcom	0101 617 551 1655
MultiTech	0101 612 785 9875
Practical Peripherals	0101 805 496 4445
Prometheus	0101 503 691 5199
Supra	0101 503 967 2444
U.S. Robotics	0101 708 982 5092
Zoom	0101 617 451 5284

And here is a list of some of the bulletin boards of major communications software houses in the US:

Crosstalk for Windows (DCA)	0101 404 740 8428
HyperAccess 5 (Hilgraeve Inc.)	0101 313 243 5915
MicroPhone II (Software Ventures)	0101 415 849 1912
Procomm Plus (Datastorm Technologies, Inc.)	0101 314 875 0523
Qmodem (The Forbin Project, Inc.)	0101 319 233 6157
Telix (Exis Inc.)	0101 416 439 9399

You may also be able to obtain support from many of these companies if you are a CompuServe member. Use the 'Find' facility to see which companies are currently supporting their products there.

CALL WAITING PROBLEMS

If you have subscribed to BT's Call Waiting service when you are on the phone and another call comes in you hear a signal informing you of it, and you can then put the current call on hold or finish it before answering the new one.

But if you happen to be on-line when a call comes in your communication link can be completely interrupted by the signal. This can be particularly annoying if it happens right at the end of a very long program download so that you have to re-log on and start over again.

In the US and some other countries around the world you can get around this problem by temporarily disabling call waiting by dialling *70 before the number you are calling. Unfortunately though, BT have not as yet implemented this standard.

However, help is still at hand because you can turn off your Call Waiting service completely by dialling #34#. Once done you will not hear a signal when another call is made to you, and the caller will simply hear the busy signal, rather than "We are trying to connect your call".

You can then get on-line without any worry of interference (other than line noise). When you have finished and wish to return to voice communication all you need to do is dial *34# to switch Call Waiting back on again.

USING EMOTICONS

Emoticons are groups of three characters or so which you usually read by tilting your head ninety degrees to the left. When you do this you'll see that the characters make up simple icons.

These emoticons (emotive icons) as they are known, are an essential part of electronic messaging because it can be quite hard to convey the spirit and meaning that your voice does over the phone. So when you are joking, rather than risking offending anyone, you can use an emoticon to clarify exactly what you mean.

Here are a few useful (and a couple of tongue in cheek) emoticons which will stand you in good stead (there are many, many more than this and it's also good fun to make up your own):

:-)	Humour
;-)	Sardonic incredulity
:-*	Oooops (covering mouth with hand)
:-{	Count Dracula
:-x	Kiss kiss
:-(	Unhappy
(:-)	Messages dealing with bicycle helmets
<:-)	For dumb questions
I-(	Late night messages
2BI^2B	Message about Shakespeare
{	Alfred Hitchcock

Before off-line readers (programs that log on, grab your messages and log off again quickly) came along, sending electronic mail could become expensive, so a number of abbreviations were invented, letting you convey whole phrases or sentences with just a few characters. But this has become such a habit now that most people tend to continue using these abbreviations anyway, so it's as well to know some of the more common ones. Here are a few:

BTW	By The Way
IANL	I Am Not (a) Lawyer (but)
IMHO	In My Humble Opinion
OIC	Oh, I See!
OTOH	On The Other Hand
PITA	Pain In The ''Acronym''
ROFL	Rolling On (the) Floor Laughing
RTFM	Read The ''Flipping'' Manual
SUFID	Screwing Up Face In Disgust

As with emoticons there are dozens more abbreviations and you can have a lot of fun making them up and seeing if the recipients of your messages can work out what you mean.

Following are some of the biggest and busiest commercial bulletin board services in the UK:

1: COMMERCIAL SERVICES

COMPUSERVE

CompuServe is a global electronic communications centre. Its computers are based in the US but local access points to them are provided to countries all over the world. In fact, there are nearly a million members of the service worldwide. It has facilities for messaging, database searching, uploading and downloading software, performing company searches, checking stock prices and more than there's room to cover here.

Anyone interested in Shareware will find CompuServe a perfect source for all their needs. Whether you are looking for a certain type of program (there are over 35,000 on CompuServe), have written one and wish to make it available, or need advice or technical help, all of this is available with CompuServe, 24 hours a day. Here are some of the first CompuServe forums you may wish to visit:

GRAPHICS FORUMS
As well as general forums including examples of graphics there are a few forums dedicated solely to the subject. You can get to the Graphics Forums menu by typing GO GRAPHICS, then select the Forum you want with the mouse and, if it's the first time you have entered it, select JOIN to become a member.

MIDI/MUSIC FORUM (GO MIDI)
As well as CompuServe's powerful graphics capabilities the world of sound and music is available to you in the Midi/Music forum. Although you cannot play music while on-line there is a vast library of music ranging from classical to rock and roll, Country to nursery rhymes. And if you're new to computer based music making, the experts on this forum will help guide you through all the jargon.

UK SHAREWARE (GO UKSHARE)
The UK Shareware forum is the place to find out about all the latest Shareware releases in Britain. These include right-up-to-date versions of software, in most cases ready for you to download and try out straight away. Shareware Marketing, Nildram Software, STAR, The Thompson Partnership and others are all represented here.

UK COMPUTING & UK FORUM (GO UKCOMP or GO UKFORUM)
The UK Computing and the UK Forum are active services with hundreds of messages on all manner of topics being posted every day. You can discuss anything from British television and Pubs to the EEC. A number of Americans and Europeans also

visit the forum so you can often get a world-wide perspective on the news. Not forgetting that there's masses of information about computing in the UK too.

UK NEWSPAPER LIBRARY (GO UKPAPERS)
The UK Newspaper Library contains articles from the leading British newspapers including the Daily Telegraph, The Financial Times, The Guardian, The Times, The Independent, Today and The Observer. Articles are extracted from current issues of the newspapers, as well as from several years back. You can retrieve full-text articles by searching for a name, word or phrase.

UK NEWS/SPORTS (GO UKNEWS or GO UKSPORTS)
The UK Sports service provides access to full-text articles from the Reuters news wires about sports in Britain, covering the latest UK results and major sports news.

UK COMPANY LIBRARY (GO UKLIB)
The UK Company Library contains directory, credit and financial information on more than 1.2 million British companies. Information is available from leading business databases such as D&B-European Dun's Market Identifiers, Extel Cards, ICC British Company Directory, ICC British Company Financial Datasheets, InfoCheck, Key British Enterprises and Kompass UK. You can retrieve information by entering the company name, industry codes or specific geographic location.

OTHER FORUMS (GO NASA, GO CB, GO WEATHER)
There are literally hundreds of forums on CompuServe - so many, in fact, that there are books you can buy, running into hundreds of pages, to cover them all. There are over 350 leading PC software and hardware companies including Microsoft, Novell, Borland, Wordperfect and many others providing support through forums, But half the fun of the service is searching for new forums, or browsing through the vast amounts of data and newspaper cuttings using the search facilities.

For details call free (voice): 0800 289 458

2: CIX - THE COMPULINK INFORMATION EXCHANGE
Based in Surbiton, CIX offers facilities for hundreds of users to interact at a time. At the heart of it is a sophisticated mailing system which is used by many UK magazines and other companies for receiving copy and data from contributors or employees. As well as sending text messages you can also mail 8-bit files such as programs, compressed files and graphic images and you also get up to 1Mb of temporary storage area on the system which is very handy as a holding area if you send or receive a lot of files.

After the messaging most members probably use CIX most for its conferences. Each conference is a sub-service of CIX offering many sub topics and often with software libraries. (This bit will be of most interest to Shareware users as CIX is literally brimming at the edges with Shareware).

Unlike other similar services, conferences can be created by anybody who wishes to run one and the Sysops (System Operators) are called moderators.

Most conferences are open so you can join them straight away. Others, though, are declared as private and are often used for beta testing new software and so on. If you want to join one of these you have to e-mail the moderator to ask permission. If granted he will 'join' you up. Joining a conference is very simple: all you have to do is type JOIN CONFNAME where CONFNAME is the conference to join. If you want to know which conferences are available take a look at the list in this article or type SHOW ALL to see the complete list while on-line.

Once in a conference you can read messages FORwards, BACKwards and by REFerence by typing the first few letters of each command. Generally reference is probably the best as you get to see messages and their answers all together, rather than just seeing them in the order in which they were sent.

To reply to a message simply type REP and press return. When you have composed your message enter a full stop and press return, then type ADD to add it.

As mentioned, many conferences contain libraries of files. In those that do type FLIST to see a list describing all the files available. To download a file type FDL FILENAME (FDL standing for File Down Load) and then prepare to receive using the Xmodem protocol. You can also upload a file by typing FUL FILENAME.

Incidentally, FDL and FUL can be used to up and download files to your personal holding area, just be sure to type MAIL first to enter it. While on the subject of mail. To send private mail to another member type TO MEMBERNAME then enter your text and type a full stop followed by SEND to send it. If you wish to send a binary (8-bit) file, make sure it's in your personal holding area and type BINMAIL MEMBERNAME FILENAME and it will be sent.

Here's just a small sample of the conferences on CIX:

CIX: NEWSBYTES

nb_business	Newsbytes - Business
nb_comms	Newsbytes - Communications.
nb_general	Newsbytes - General news
nb_government	Newsbytes - Government.
nb_ibm	Newsbytes - IBM

COMPUTING: ONLINE

being_online	Social, legal, ethical & political issues
cixplusplus	Discussions on how to develop conference systems
qbbs.st	QuickBBS-ST conference
searchlight	The Searchlight BBS conference
viewdata	For TeleText/Prestel/Gnome at Home and all

wildcat   Wildcat Bulletin Boards

COMPUTING: BUSINESS APPLICATIONS

accountancy   Accountancy and Software
pegasus   Pegasus Accounts, Payroll, file-firmats, ad nauseum...
project   Discussion of Project Management techniques/tools
sage   Conference for Sage accounts payroll and network users
spreadsheets   Numbers made easy...
symphony   Forum for Symphony or 123 users

COMPUTING: GRAPHICS

adobe   Unofficial conf for users of Adobe graphics s/w
corel   Corel Draw
deluxepaintpc   For users of the Deluxe Paint PC (& Enhanced) packages
digital_video   All about digital video: DVI, CD-I etc...
drawapplause   Draw Applause
ea_conf   Electronic Arts conference for help and advice
gif   To hold GIF files for download
graphics   Discussion of computer graphics programming
images   Graphic images of all kinds.
raytrace   All aspects of raytracing
tiff   Tagged Image File Format
virtual_realit   The place to discuss Virtual Reality

COMPUTING: INFORMATION

autoroute   Help and overlay files for autoroute
cd-rom   CD-ROM on-line databases
hypertext   Discussion of HyperText and HyperText based software
multimedia   All about multimedia

COMPUTING: VIRUSES, PIRACY, HACKING AND PHREAKING

a_v_toolkit   Dr Solomon's Anti-Virus Toolkit Support Conference
hackers   A board for hackers
virus   Virus'/Trojans/Nasties
vis   VIS Anti-Virus Utilities

MAGAZINE CONFERENCES

buyer   Computer Buyer magazine conference
byte   BYTE magazine conference - Journal, BIX, Listings.
compshop   Computer Shopper Magazine conference.
freebies   For obtaining free trade magazines,and other freebies.
macuser   For Mac enthusiasts and readers of Macuser magazine.
pcmag   For the readers and potential readers of PC Magazine
pcplus   PC PLUS Magazine.
pcuser   You've read the mag now see the conference.

pcw	Personal Computer World.
sharemag	To support The Shareware Magazine
windowsmag	Windows Magazine conference
windows_user	For readers of Windows User magazine

OFF-LINE READERS

matrix	Matrix Off-Line cix reader - for beta-testers
olr	General discussion conference for all off line readers
telepathy	TelePathy - the CIX off-line reader conference
wigwam	Telepathy for Windows.

MEDIA: NEWSPAPERS, RADIO, TV, MAGAZINES

audio	Technical forum for HIFI, stereo, studio work etc.
bbc.radio	For listeners to BBC Radio
broadcast	Reception of broadcast radio/tv, from whatever source.
bskyb	News views and moans about British Sky Broadcasting
private_eye	Lord Gnome's Mighty Organ
satel_tv	To discuss all issues relating to Satellite TV

For details call (voice): 081 390 8446

3: ALMAC

Almac BBS is a major on-line service based in Scotland but serving the European market. It differs from most other systems by only charging a simple annual subscription with no on-line time charges. It offers three Gigabytes of files available to subscribers in 96 file areas covering areas such as graphics, technical, pictures, utilities, music, flight simulator, games, basic, c, pascal, unix, and many others.

Almac is a member of the ILink network and provides mail feeds to over 30 other on-line services throughout Europe and South Africa. It is a friendly and informative public message network where you can obtain assistance on a number of topics ranging from computer hardware and software to areas such as travel, gardening, home topics, DOS tips, Windows and travel to name but a few.

Almac is also a full domain site on the Usenet which is a major unix mail network which runs over the Internet. This service connects callers to people all over the world. Some 15 million people world wide have an "address" on the Internet and all can be accessed by callers to Almac.

Through this service callers can connect to other callers on services such as Compuserve, CIX, MCI Mail, Applelink and BT Gold. Many Shareware authors have Internet addresses and so are easily contactable through Almac as the mail is transferred several times a day.

Almac carries 1500 Usenet news groups with mail coming in daily. There is something for everyone on the Usenet and this service connects just about every major university around the world together with research companies, corporates and hobbyists. Together this group provides loads of information on computer related matters.

Fidonet is another mail network also carried by Almac. It is generally considered to be the largest DOS-based public network in the world and through Almac you can send netmail to anyone in the world with access to a Fidonet system. There is a lot of UK content as Fido is, perhaps, the UK's biggest e-mail network.

Almac make it easy to find out information on the service by publishing lots of information in a series of Bulletins. Should you have any queries on the service type [B] to bring up the Bulletin menu. There are some 50 bulletins giving you details on the service and background details on the system as well as hints and tips to make your connection to Almac easier and more effective.

A number of companies such as Tulip, Dataflex and Hewlett Packard, are now also providing customer support through Almac, with more coming on-line each month.

Almac BBS is a friendly service with a lot of great characters already on line. In some ways it's like a family with lots of regulars always willing to help out new callers to the system. There is a New User conference (Number 31) where you can leave messages and either the SysOps or the regulars will be around to help you out.

For details call (voice): 0324 666 336

INDEX

% parameters, 52
286 chip, 130
386 chip, 130
386MAX, 101

A

Adlib synthesizer, 104
advertising, 188
ALMAC, 229
Amstrad mouse, 138
ANSI.SYS, 31, 79
APPEND, 33
ASCII control codes, 205
Assembler, 160
ASSIGN, 2
ATTRIB, 2, 22, 34, 55, 125, 126
autodialling, 171
Automenu, 115

B

BACKUP, 3, 13, 22, 123
BASIC, 147
BIOS, 128
blinking, 26
boot,
    multiple, 73
    problems, 144
    sector, 116
borders, colours of, 27
break handler, 170
break key, disabling, 148
BREAK, 3, 69
BUFFERS, 69
bulletin boards, 211
bus architecture, 129

C

calculator, floating point, 165
CALL, 34, 59
Caps Lock key, 30
CHCP, 3
CHDIR (CD), 4
CHKDSK, 4, 62
CHOICE, 35
CIX bulletin board, 226
CLS, 51
CMOS, 135
code pages, 84
colour separations, 195
colours, background, 26
COM file, 23
COM ports, 97, 124
COMMAND, 4, 35, 59
COMMAND.COM, 115
comms errors, 97
communications, 211
COMP, 4
Compaq, 88
Compuserve, 138
CompuServe, 220, 225
COMSPEC, 115
CON, 124
CONFIG.SYS, 58, 68
configuring, 68
copy protection, 125
COPY, 5, 61, 64, 83, 113
COUNTRY, 69, 73, 82
CTTY, 5
cursor control, 183
Cyclic Redundancy Check (CRC), 113

D

data compression, 156
data security, 115
date, 22
DATE, 5, 61, 82
DBLSPACE, 35
DEBUG, 23
DEFRAG, 36
DEL, 6, 56
DELOLDOS, 37
DELTREE, 37
DeskJet printer, 102
device drivers, 70
device names, 124
DEVICE, 70
DEVICEHIGH, 84
dip switches, 197
DIR, 6, 20, 21, 37
disabled people, provision for, 142
disk, system, 77
DISKCOMP, 6
DISKCOPY, 6, 38, 83
disks, high density, 114
DO, 57
DOS, 1
DOSKEY, 38
DOSSHELL, 39
DR-DOS, 103
DRAMS, 141
DRIVER.SYS, 83
DRIVPARM, 70, 83

E

ECHO, 51, 55
EDIT, 39
EEMS, 134
EISA bus, 98, 131
EMM386, 40, 84, 101
'emoticons', 223
EMS, 96
EMS, LIM, 133
environment, 78
EPS, 106
Epson control codes, 202
error levels, 52
escape characters, 80
ESDI, 101
Excel, 94
EXE2BIN, 7
EXIST, 54
EXIT, 7
EXPAND, 40
external commands, 2

F

FASTHELP, 41
FASTOPEN, 7, 41
FC, 8
FCBS, 71
FDISK, 8, 116
file control blocks, 71
FILES, 71
files,
    attributes of, 22
    batch, 50
    copying, 83
    deleting, 59
    finding, 62, 155
    hidden, 126
    protecting, 64
    random access, 182
    temporary, 17
    verification, 113
FIND, 8, 41
FOR, 57
FORMAT, 9, 42, 62, 114
fractals, 149

G

Gang Screens, 110,112
GRAFTABL, 9
GRAPHICS, 9
GW BASIC, 147

H

hardware, problems with, 128
Hayes command set, 217
heap manager, 161
HELP, 42
high memory, 84
HIMEM.SYS, 83

I

IBM character set, 198
icons (Windows), 90
IDE controller, 101
IF, 53
input, 150
internal commands, 1
Interrupts, 106
ISA bus, 130
ISDN, 211

J

JOIN, 10, 19

K

KEYB, 10
KEYB UK, 197
KEYBUK, 82, 197

L

LABEL, 10
labels, printing, 195
LASTDRIVE, 58, 72
line drawing, 195
line noise, 221
LOADFIX, 43
LOADHIGH, 42, 84
LPT device, 124

M

marketing, 185
MCA bus, 131
MD, 11
MEM, 43
MEMMAKER, 44
memory,
    adding, 140
    expanded, 132
    extended, 83, 83, 132
    high, 84
    management of, 132
    optimising, 96
Menugen, 115
Mercury, 217
MFM controller, 101
Micro Channel architecture, 98
MKDIR, 11
MNP, 220
MODE, 11
mode, display, 31
modems, 220
monitors, 140
monitors, nonochrome, 143
MORE, 11, 17, 18
mouse, 139, 147
    configuring, 90
    with Turbo C, 152
MOVE, 44, 61
MS-DOS, 1
MSD, 45
multitasking, 137

N

NLSFUNC, 11
NOEMS, 84
NOT, 53

NUL, 124
Num Lock key, 29

P

passwords, 115
PATH, 12
PAUSE, 54
PC File, 120
PostScript, 106
pound sign, 196
POWER, 45
Print Screen, 28
print screen, problems with, 196
printers, 92
    problems with, 194
printing, background, 96
PRN, 124
PROMPT, 12, 79
protected mode, 133
Protext, 195
PS/1, 89
PS/2, 91
publicity, 191

Q

QBASIC, 46
QEMM386, 101

R

ram drive, 76, 70
RAMDRIVE.SYS, 91
RD, 13
real mode, 133
reboot, 76
RECOVER, 12, 62, 121
REM, 51
REN(AME), 13, 20
REPLACE, 13
RESTORE, 13, 22, 123
RLL controller, 101
RMDIR, 13

S

SCSI controller, 93, 101, 104
SELECT, 14
SETVER, 46
SHARE, 14
SHELL, 72, 76
SIMMS, 141
SMARTDRIVE, 100
SMARTDRV, 47
SMARTDRV.EXE, 93

software, protection of, 187
SORT, 14, 14, 18, 21
Stacker, 102, 107
STACKS, 72
subdirectories, 54
subroutines, 60
SUBST, 14, 19, 58
SVGA, 144
SYS, 15
SYSEDIT.EXE, 93
SYSTEM, 15

T
TIME, 15, 61
time, 22
TREE, 15, 55
TRUENAME, 19
TrueType fonts, 102
TSR programs, 78
Turbo C, 152
TYPE, 15, 17, 18, 57, 63, 64

U
UMB, 84
UNDELETE, 47
UNFORMAT, 48
UNIX, 109
upper memory blocks, 84

V
V dot terms, 219
VER, 16
VERIFY, 16, 113
VGA, 144
video cards, 144
virus, stealth, 119
viruses, 116
VOL(UME), 16
volume labels, 65
VSAFE, 49

W
wait states, 135
Windows 3.1, 92
Windows NT, 108
Windows, 88
Windows, file manager, 91

X
XCOPY, 16, 22, 83
XMS, 141

Words for the wise - from
Sigma Press

Sigma publish what is probably the widest range of computer books from any independent UK publisher. And that's not just for the PC, but for many other popular micros – Atari, Amiga and Archimedes – and for software packages that are widely-used in the UK and Europe, including Timeworks, Deskpress, Sage, Money Manager and many more. We also publish a whole range of professional-level books for topics as far apart as IBM mainframes, UNIX, computer translation, manufacturing technology and networking.

A complete catalogue is available, but here are some of the highlights:

Amstrad PCW
The Complete Guide to LocoScript and Amstrad PCW Computers – Hughes – £12.95
LocoScripting People – Clayton and Clayton – £12.95
The PCW LOGO Manual – Robert Grant – £12.95
Picture Processing on the Amstrad PCW – Gilmore – £12.95
See also Programming section for *Mini Office*

Archimedes
A Beginner's Guide to WIMP Programming – Fox – £12.95
See also: *Desktop Publishing on the Archimedes* and *Archimedes Game Maker's Manual*

Artificial Intelligence
Build Your Own Expert System – Naylor – £11.95
Computational Linguistics – McEnery – £14.95
Introducing Neural Networks – Carling – £14.95

Beginners' Guides
Computing under Protest! – Croucher – £12.95
Alone with a PC – Bradley – £12.95
The New User's Mac Book – Wilson – £12.95
PC Computing for Absolute Beginners – Edwards – £12.95

DTP and Graphics
Designworks Companion – Whale – £14.95
Ventura to Quark XPress for the PC – Wilmore – £19.95
Timeworks Publisher Companion – Morrissey – £12.95
Timeworks for Windows Companion – Sinclair – £14.95
PagePlus Publisher Companion – Sinclair – £12.95
Express Publisher DTP Companion – Sinclair – £14.95
Amiga Real-Time 3D Graphics – Tyler – £14.95
Atari Real-Time 3D Graphics – Tyler – £12.95

European and US Software Packages
Mastering Money Manager PC – Sinclair – £12.95
Using Sage Sterling in Business – Woodford – £12.95
Mastering Masterfile PC – Sinclair – £12.95
All-in-One Business Computing (Mini Office Professional) – Hughes – £12.95

Game Making and Playing
PC Games Bible – Matthews and Rigby – £12.95
Archimedes Game Maker's Manual – Blunt – £14.95
Atari Game Maker's Manual – Hill – £14.95
Amiga Game Maker's Manual – Hill – £16.95
Adventure Gamer's Manual – Redrup – £12.95

General

Music and New Technology – Georghiades and Jacobs – £12.95
Getting the Best from your Amstrad Notepad – Wilson – £12.95
Computers and Chaos (Atari and Amiga editions) – Bessant – £12.95
Computers in Genealogy – Isaac – £12.95
Multimedia, CD-ROM and Compact Disc – Botto – £14.95
Advanced Manufacturing Technology – Zairi – £14.95

Networks

$25 Network User Guide – Sinclair – £12.95
Integrated Digital Networks – Lawton – £24.95
Novell Netware Companion – Croucher – £16.95

PC Operating Systems and Architecture

Working with Windows 3.1 – Sinclair – £16.95
Servicing and Supporting IBM PCs and Compatibles – Moss – £16.95
The DR DOS Book – Croucher – £16.95
MS-DOS Revealed – Last – £12.95
PC Architecture and Assembly Language – Kauler – £16.95
Programmer's Technical Reference – Williams – £19.95
MS-DOS File and Program Control – Sinclair – £12.95
Mastering DesqView – Sinclair – £12.95

Programming

C Applications Library – Pugh – £16.95
Starting MS-DOS Assembler – Sinclair – £12.95
Understanding Occam and the transputer – Ellison – £12.95
Programming in ANSI Standard C – Horsington – £14.95
Programming in Microsoft Visual Basic – Penfold – £16.95
For **LOGO**, *see Amstrad PCW*

UNIX and mainframes

UNIX – The Book – Banahan and Rutter – £11.95
UNIX – The Complete Guide – Manger – £19.95
RPG on the IBM AS/400 – Tomlinson – £24.95

HOW TO ORDER

Prices correct for 1993.
Order these books from your usual bookshop, or direct from:

SIGMA PRESS,
1 SOUTH OAK LANE,
WILMSLOW, CHESHIRE, SK9 6AR

PHONE: 0625 – 531035; FAX: 0625 – 536800

PLEASE ADD £1 TOWARDS POST AND PACKING FOR ONE BOOK.
POSTAGE IS FREE FOR TWO OR MORE BOOKS.

CHEQUES SHOULD BE MADE PAYABLE TO **SIGMA PRESS.**

ACCESS AND VISA WELCOME – 24 HOUR ANSWERPHONE SERVICE.

VISA